The Greatest Dog Stories Ever Told

Books edited by Patricia M. Sherwood

The Quotable Dog Lover

An Honest Angler

The
Greatest
Dog Stories
Ever Told

Great Writers from Ray Bradbury to Mark Twain
Celebrate Man's Best Friend

EDITED AND WITH AN INTRODUCTION BY
PATRICIA M. SHERWOOD

The Lyons Press
Guilford, Connecticut
An imprint of the Globe Pequot Press

Introductions and Foreword copyright © 2001, 2004, 2009 by Patricia M. Sherwood

The Lyons Press is an imprint of The Globe Pequot Press.

Text design: Compset, Inc.

Library of Congress Cataloging-in-Publication Data is available on file.

ISBN 978-1-59921-793-2

Printed in the United States of America

10 9 8 7 6 5 4 3 2 1

This one is for the coming generation: my grandchildren, who show every sign of being besotted animal lovers, as is only proper.

So to
Daniel and Nicholas and Thomas and Clara,
this book is dedicated with love from Madame.

Contents

Foreword

The Gift which I am sending you is called a dog, and is in fact the most precious and valuable possession of mankind.

—Theodorus Gaza
Laudation Canis: An Address to Mohammed II

Everyone likes to talk about his dog. Whatever the animal's apparent lack of charm, brains, or looks, you'll still hear all about it if you sit still long enough.

There are 68 million "owned" dogs in the United States—and that figure probably doesn't include the dogs who are not registered, licensed, or otherwise accounted for in the files and records of bureaucracy.

Those 68 million dogs live in some 40 million households, which works out to an average of 1.7 dogs per household. (That number, of course, is wildly wrong—not only because of the seven-tenths thing, but because there are people like me. At one time in my life I had in my household 11 Irish wolfhound puppies, 3 grown hounds, a couple of Shetland sheepdogs, a collie, and a whippet.)

Assuming at least two people per household, that's 80 million people only too eager to tell you how special *their* pet is. They will listen, with boredom thinly disguised, while you talk about your dog; what they really want is for you to listen while they talk about theirs. "My dog," they start off pridefully, "*my* dog . . ."

In clement weather my border collie rides around with me in my car, accompanying me to work, to school, and on my errands. I was in the laundromat the other day when a little old lady cornered me; she'd spotted Fire in my car and wished to tell me how she couldn't take her dog anywhere because he'd tear up the car if she got out and left him. She was obviously quite proud of his bad behavior—it made him an individual, set apart from other, less interesting, dogs.

A reviewer at the *Spectator* in 1955 said of James Thurber: "The more they bite him, scorn him, embarrass him in front of people, turn sick in his car and prefer to be fed by anyone else, the more he appears to dote on them." Clearly, Thurber is not alone.

All in all, however, the mutual devotion between dog and owner is very touching. I had an elderly woman come up to me while I was walking Fire to tell me about her Chihuahua—in detail. She concluded by saying, "He's very good company. I love him." It seems that those of us who are, as the French say, "of a certain age" find especially deep and meaningful relationships with our dogs. The dog of our youth is not the dog of our silvering years—our need is much greater now.

Not long ago I appeared on the local radio station to boost my last book.* Without exception, the entire staff sought me out to tell me that they owned dogs, what kind of dogs they owned, and how they felt about those dogs. The host hadn't had a dog since his childhood—nonetheless he identified strongly with *his* breed and had a number of anecdotes to share . . . all dating back 40 years or more.

The newscaster had a beagle. "The most loyal dog in the world," he said. The receptionist had a pair of miniature schnauzers. "Not very well behaved," she admitted, half embarrassed, half proud, "but we love them."

Wherever I go, the minute it becomes known I have a special interest in dogs, I hear about the quirks and foibles and splendid characters of people's companions and friends, their dogs.

John and Jane Doe are not alone in their desire to brag about their dogs. Better-known people—people with talent and imagination and the skill to transport us to other places and other feelings—those people too want to talk about their dogs. Even when what they write is intended to be read as fiction, I firmly believe there is a real dog underneath—one whom the author knew well.

T. H. White, whose own familial relationships were somewhat awry, wrote a poem on the death of his dear companion, Brownie:

> My coward who leaned on my care
> In vain, my child and wife.
> My mother with the golden pelt,
> Myself with melting eye.

The Quotable Dog Lover (The Lyons Press, 2000)

Clearly, Brownie filled a void not warmed by closer human ties.

Willie Morris titled his autobiography after his dog, calling it *My Dog Skip.* Mutt, Farley Mowat's *Dog Who Wouldn't Be,* touched not only Mowat's life with wonder and amusement, but that of much of Saskatoon as well. It seems that the dogs of these authors' childhoods became local characters, known for their odd and eccentric ways, and providing endless amusement to the populace.

And then there are the dogs who work. *Winterdance,* Gary Paulsen's tale of running sled dogs, tells us how deeply affected he is by his dogs, and in so doing, affects us as well. R. B. Robertson is only an observer of the finely tuned working sheepdog, but his admiring description of rounding up a reluctant ram in "That'll Do!" puts us right there on the hill.

Some authors are as proud of their bad dogs as was my friendly lady in the laundromat. James Thurber owned a dog who, as he proudly proclaims, "bit people." And E. B. White confesses that training a dog is beyond him—at least training Fred, the dachshund, is.

There are dogs here who hunt, and dogs who talk back, and dogs who live the high life in Provence . . . dogs who write poetry, dogs who paint pictures, dogs who star in the movies.

Rudyard Kipling wrote about devotion, Thomas Mann about companionship, John Graves about loss. And Lord Dunsany wrote about a gent who, under the influence, reverted to his former life as a dog himself.

They all wish to tell us about their dogs, and they've done it in wondrous ways.

Permissions Acknowledgments

A Faded Photograph

From *My Dog Skip*

BY WILLIE MORRIS

*M*Y DOG SKIP, from which this chapter is taken, is one of the most charming autobiographies ever written. In it, Willie Morris tells us of his life in Yazoo City, Mississippi, in the golden years before the Second World War. It is idyllic, funny, sweet. And whether he was playing football or raising a kitten, his constant companion was . . . his dog Skip.

Eventually, Morris left the slow meander of southern life to become the editor of one of America's leading literary magazines, *Harper's Magazine,* and a prominent writer and essayist.

This selection was made for the very good reason that I love it. I love the description of Skip's football prowess, I love the exceptional conversations Skip has with his family, and, most of all, I love the picture of Skip driving down the road in the old green DeSoto, amazing the church-going folk.

★ ★ ★ ★ ★

I CAME ACROSS A photograph of him not long ago, his black face with the long snout sniffing at something in the air, his tail straight and pointing, his eyes flashing in some momentary excitement. Looking at a faded photograph taken more than forty years before, even as a grown man, I would admit I still missed him.

It was 1943. I was nine years old and in the third grade when I saw him for the very first time. I had known we were getting him. My father had ordered him from a dog breeder he had heard about in Springfield, Missouri. Daddy had picked him up at the Illinois Central train depot, and when I came home that day from school he had just put the wire portable kennel on our back porch. I opened the door to the box and looked inside. I saw a little puppy drinking water from a container attached to the bottom. He glanced up at me.

"Come here, boy," I said.

He walked on unsteady legs toward me. I was sitting on the floor of the porch when he came out. He jumped into my lap and began nuzzling my hand with his nose. When I leaned toward him, he gave me a moist lick on my chin. Then he hugged me.

I led him into the house and gave him some puppy food in a dish. Then I followed him as he gingerly explored every room in the house. That night he jumped into my bed and stared at me, as if he were looking me over. Then, perhaps because he missed his mother in Missouri, he went to sleep in my arms. I was an only child, and he now was an only dog.

This was the first of our many days and years together. We named him Skipper for the lively way he walked, but he was always just Skip to me.

We had had a whole string of dogs before. When I was a very little boy we had big bird dogs, and then two purebred English smooth-haired fox terriers like this one, and I got to know all about dogs, a most precocious expert—their funny or crazy moods, how they looked when they were hungry or sick, when they were ready to bite and when their growling meant nothing, what they might be trying to say when they moaned and made strange human noises deep in their throats.

None of those other dogs ever came up to this one. You could talk to him as well as you could to many human beings, and *much* better than you could to some. He would sit down and look you straight in the eye, a long, mesmerizing gaze, and when he understood what you were saying he would turn his head sideways, back and forth, oscillating his whole body like the pendulum on a clock. Before going to sleep at night, with him sitting next to my face on the bed as he always did in such hours, I would say, "First thing tomorrow I want you to get your leash and then come get me up, because we're gonna get in the car and go out to the woods and get some *squirrels*," and the next morning sure enough he would get his leash, wake up both my father and me, walk nervously around the house with the leash in his mouth while we ate breakfast, and then lead us out to the car. Or I could say, "How about a little *swim*?" and his face would light up and he would push open the back door with his paws and escort me the quarter of a mile down the back alleyway to the swimming hole under the cypress near the bayou. Or, "Bubba's comin' over here today, and we're gonna play some *football*," and he would listen closely to this, and go out and wait around in front of the house and pick up Bubba's scent a block down the street and come tell me he was on his way. Or, "Skip, how about some *catch*?" and he would get up and walk into the front room, open a door in the antique cabinet with his improbable nose, and bring me his tennis ball.

I watched him grow up from the puppy who came to us from Missouri to the sleek, dexterous, affectionate creature who could do all these things, and more. He knew my father by the name of Big Boss. My mother was Bossie, and I was Little Boss or, interchangeably, Willie. (I called *him*, depending on the mood, Skip, Old Skip, and Boy. I have learned that when you love somebody, you will address him or her by different names.) Sometimes my father would hide in a closet and I would ask, "Skip, where's Big Boss?" and he would search the whole house, looking on every bed and under every chair and table until he arrived at the right closet, and began scratching it with his paws.

The town where Old Skip and I grew up together was an unhurried and isolated place then. About ten thousand people lived there, of all races and origins, and it sat there crazily, half on steep hills and half on the flat Delta. Some of the streets were not paved, and the main street, stretching its several blocks from the Dixie Theater down to the bend in the river, was narrow and plain, but down along the quiet, shady streets, with their magnolia and pecan and elm and locust trees, were the stately old houses that had been built long before the Civil War, slightly dark and decaying until the descendants became prosperous enough to have them "restored," which usually meant one coat of white enamel.

All this was before the big supermarkets and shopping centers and affluent subdivisions with no sidewalks and the monster highways and the inno-

cence lost. It was even before there was television, and people would not close
their doors and shut their curtains to watch the quiz games or the comedy
hours or the talk shows where everybody talks at once. We would sit out on
our front porches in the hot, serene nights and say hello to everyone who
walked by. If the fire truck came past, we all got in our cars to follow it, and
Skip was always the first to want to go. The houses were set out in a line under
the soft green trees, their leaves rustling gently with the breeze. From the river
sometimes came the melancholy echo of a boat's horn.

I knew the place then better than I did my own heart—every bend in
every road, every house and every field, the exact spot where the robin went
for her first crocus. It was not in my soul then, only in my pores, as familiar to
me as rain or grass or sunlight. The town was poor one year and rich the next;
everything in it pertained to cotton, and hence to usury and mortgage, deben-
ture and labor. We lived and died by nature and followed the whims of the
timeless clouds. Our people played seven-card stud against God.

It was a sly and silent town then, and Skip and my friends and I ab-
sorbed its every rhythm and heartbeat and the slightest sounds from far away. I
loved those funny silences. The whole town was also abundant with alleys behind the paved thoroughfares inherited from an earlier day, little vagrant path-
ways running with scant design or reason behind the houses and stores and
barns and chicken yards and gardens. You could get away with anything in
those alleys. How Skip adored the freedom of them!

It was a lazy town, all stretched out on its hills and its flat streets, and
over the years Skip also grew to know almost every house, tree, street, and alley.
Occasionally he wandered around the town by himself, and everybody of any
consequence knew who he was. Unbelievable as this may seem, Skip had the
most curious and spooky way of sensing—don't ask me how—where I might
be at any given moment, what a later day called ESP.

Our neighborhood was on one of the broad thoroughfares. In our side
yard was a row of immense pecan trees shaped at the top like witches' caps, and
in the back a huge field, vined and bosky. On the front lawn was a full, towering oak, one of Skip's favorite trees in the entire town.

Every time I shouted *"Squirrel!"* Skip would charge on the oak tree
and try to climb it, sometimes getting as high as five or six feet with his spectacular leaps. This would stop traffic on the street in front of the house. People
in cars would see him trying to shinny up the tree and would pull up to the
curb and watch. They would signal to other passersby and point toward Skip,
and these people would pull over too. They would gaze up into the tree to see

what he was looking for, and, after a respectable pause, ask me, "What's he got up there?" and I would say, "Somethin' small and mean." They seldom recognized that Skip was just practicing.

This exercise was nothing to compare with football games, however. I cut the lace on a football and taught Old Skip how to carry it in his mouth, and how to hold it so he could avoid fumbles when he was tackled. I instructed him how to move on a quarterback's signals, to take a snap from center on the first bounce, and to follow me down the field. Ten or twelve of my comrades and I would organize a game of tackle in my front yard. Our side would go into a huddle, Skip included, and we would put our arms around one another's shoulders the way they did in real huddles at Ole Miss or Tennessee, and the dog would stand up on his hind legs and, with me kneeling, drape a leg around *my* shoulder. Then I would say, "Skip, pattern thirty-nine, off on three"; we would break out of the huddle with Skip dropping into the tailback position as I had taught him. Muttonhead or Peewee or Henjie or Bubba or Big Boy or Ralph would snap the ball on a hop to Skip, who would get it by the lace and follow me downfield, dodging would-be tacklers with no effort at all, weaving behind his blockers, spinning loose when he was cornered, sometimes balancing just inside the sidelines until he made it into the end zone. We would slap him on the back and say, nonchalantly, "Good run, boy," or when we had an audience: "Did you see my block back there?" Occasionally he would get tackled, but he seldom lost his grip on the ball, and he would always get up from the bottom of the pile and head straight for the huddle. He was an ideal safety man when the other side punted, and would get a grip on the second or third hop and gallop the length of the field for a touchdown. After considerable practice, I succeeded in teaching him the "Statue of Liberty" play, always shouting *"Statue of Liberty"* to him and our teammates before the play unfolded. I would take the snap from center and fade back in a low crouch, less a crouch than a forty-five-degree list, holding the ball behind my shoulder as if I were about to pass, all the while making sure the loosened lace was at a convenient angle. Skip, stationed at the left-end position, would circle around behind me, taking the lace of the pigskin between his teeth, then moving with deft assurance toward the right side of the line of scrimmage, where I was leading interference, whereupon he would follow his usual phalanx of blockers to the enemy's end zone for another spectacular score. *"Look at that dog playin' football!"* someone passing by would shout, and before the game was over we would have an incredulous crowd watching from cars or sitting on the sidelines, just as they did when he was after squirrels. The older men especially enjoyed this stunning spectacle. Walking down the sidewalk in front of the house, they would stop and let go with great whoops of astonishment: "Man, that's *some* dog. Can he catch a pass?"

For simple gratification, however, I believe Skip enjoyed our most imaginative intrigue above any other, and there are people still living in the town who will testify to it.

In that place and time, we began driving our parents' cars when we were thirteen years old; this was common practice then, and the town was so small that the policemen knew who you were, and your family, although they of course expected you to be careful. When I started driving our old four-door green DeSoto, I always took Skip on my trips around town. He rode with his snout extended far out the window, and if he caught the scent of one of the boys we knew, he would bark and point toward him, and we would stop and give that person a free ride. Skip would shake hands with our mutual friend, and lick him on the face and sit on the front seat between us. Cruising through the fringes of town, I would spot a group of old men standing around up the road. I would get Skip to prop himself against the steering wheel, his black head peering out of the windshield, while I crouched out of sight under the dashboard. Slowing the car to ten or fifteen, I would guide the steering wheel with my right hand while Skip, with his paws, kept it steady. As we drove by the Blue Front Café, I could hear one of the men shout: *"Look at the ol' dog drivin' a car!"*

Later we would ride out into the countryside, past the cotton fields and pecan groves and winding little creeks on the dark flat land toward some somnolent hamlet consisting of three or four unpainted stores, a minuscule wooden post office with its porch stacked with firewood in the wintertime, and a little graveyard nearby. Here the old men in overalls would be sitting on the gallery of the general store with patent-medicine posters on its sides, whittling wood or dipping snuff or swatting flies. When we slowly came past with Skip behind the steering wheel I heard one of them yell, *"A dog! A dog drivin'!"* and when I glanced slightly above the dashboard I sighted him falling out of his chair over the side of the porch into a privet hedge. One afternoon not long after that Henjie and Skip and I were out and about in the same country vicinity when far up the gravel road we saw a substantial congregation of humanity emerging from a backwoods church after a revival meeting. A number of the people, in fact, were still shouting and wailing as they approached their dusty parked cars and pickup trucks. I stopped the car and placed Skip at his familiar spot behind the steering wheel; then we slowly continued up the road. As we passed the church, in the midst of the avid cacophony a woman exclaimed: *"Is that a dog drivin' that car?"* The ensuing silence as we progressed on by was most horrendously swift and pervasive, and that sudden bucolic hush and quell remained unforgettable for me, as if the very spectacle of Old Skip driving that green DeSoto were inscrutable, celestial, and preordained.

Old Dog

From *On the Edge of the Wild*

BY STEPHEN BODIO

S TEPHEN BODIO FIRST CAME to my attention through his magazine arti-cles, and then his book *On the Edge of the Wild,* from which this selec-tion is taken. His works show respect for the wild, pleasure in nature, and an unexpected and delightful sense of humor.

Clearly he is a thoughtful outdoorsman, a keen observer, a sensitive naturalist, a dedicated hunter, and an extremely talented writer. On everything from training and hunting with a gyrfalcon to fishing for catfish, Bodio brings a fresh and fascinating point of view to his material.

"Old Dog" is a switch—no teary eulogy, this. Instead, Bodio is both admiring of and empathetic to Bart's wholehearted pleasure in the hunt.

★　★　★　★　★

NO, THIS ISN'T GOING to be one of those sentimental "I-knew-an-old-dog-who-died" stories. For one thing, Bart, black-and-white springer, is very much alive. If I take down the dog barrier in the door to my library, he'll be here in an instant, flipping my hand up with his nose, pawing me incessantly. He means two things by this: Pay attention to me! (Not to those young dogs.) And: Let's go. Birds. Hunting.

The thing is, he's old. *Very* old, by some standards. He'll be fourteen in February. His long life has spanned human and animal disasters and triumphs, the publishing of my first book, widowhood, divorce, a new marriage. One of his puppyhood's companions, my old "staghound" Riley, son of a coursing greyhound sire and a Scottish deerhound dam, died of old age five years ago. In his prime he was the scourge of jackrabbits and coyotes, running them down by sheer speed and energy, but he died in his sleep at nine, his great heart and legs broken down by his size and the strains of his profession. That whole canine generation is gone—rattlers, debilitating diseases, disappearance, even once the bullets of some subhuman jerk without a trace of a good dog's nobility. The big back country of southwestern New Mexico can be hard on dogs and people.

Bart has hunted quail here, always; pheasants and blue grouse (he didn't like their habit of treeing) in Montana; ducks everywhere, and, for one season's exile, woodcocks in Maine. He had to live in a kennel there and hated it, though he loved the smelly little woodsnipes once he realized they were dog-legal game.

But when we went out after grouse after a September snowstorm in Montana, I thought he had reached the end of his hunter's road. The cover, willow and aspen, ran up a narrow drainage, from cropland to dark timber, on the west side of a mountain range near Bozeman. Although you could often raise four or five flushes there the woods remained silent as the last flakes sifted down. Bart started valiantly, snorting and dislodging snow from low-hanging branches. Five minutes uphill he began trudging, and his tail began to hang low. In ten minutes he lay down to bite snowballs from between his toes. If fifteen, for almost the first time in his life, he was walking behind me, letting me break trail. When I realized that was what he wanted, I let him.

He surged in front only once, when a yearling black bear feeding on rotting apples galumphed away like a cross between a black Lab and a beach ball. Bart swerved around me to give chase, as he had in the past for—once each—a coyote and a mountain lion. He's nearly deaf now, and it took more than a couple of bellows to call him back. When he returned he got in line behind me again, stopping periodically to chew the ice on his feet. I figured that the aging process, which we first acknowledged when he collapsed on the third day of a mid-winter pheasant hunt east of Grassrange, was complete, and he would now spend his shortening days sleeping on my bed or in front of the stove.

Right after that hunt Lib and I married and moved to my old house in Magdalena, where Bart had been born under the desk that held my late partner, Betsy's, word processor. The old dog seemed to respond to the New Mexico sun. Though it's often cold at sixty-five hundred feet he stopped begging to come in. He spent hours basking, lying in the soft dry dirt in front of the hawk's perch. He stopped growling at the dachshund pup, and—not entirely intelligently—began challenging Bo, the two-year-old Aussie with the glaring blue-marble left eye.

Still, the quail habitat around Magdalena seemed too rugged for an old dog's legs, ranging as it does from six to eight thousand feet, all rocky and vertical and covered with cholla and goat's head seeds and lechiguilla beneath its grass and oaks and piñons. The move and its attendant complications had caught us without a successor for Bart; besides, there are hawks to train, a yard to be refenced, kennels and lofts and mews to build. I decided to teach Bo to be an interim bird dog. He was intelligent and knew "fetch"; his father, Jedediah, flushed quarry for his owner's hawk; he was curious about the sound of the gun and not a bit gun shy. Besides, our mountain hunting is of a rough-and-ready kind; in the same cover we can flush Gambel's quail, occasional scalies, and Mearns' in good years. Nor do we scorn cottontail or hares. Past teams have included such combinations as two springers and a saluki, or a springer, a shooter, and a hawk.

For practice, we took the old dog and the young one to the abandoned dirt-track airfield just north of town, where the quail were never shot and so multiplied even in dry years. In fifteen minutes we were into a big early-season flock; thirty, perhaps even forty birds. Bo leaped about, ecstatic, giving chase like a sighthound. He had never been praised for chasing anything before. Bart didn't even spare the energy for disgust. He was doing what he was born to do, flagged half tail whirling like a propeller, nose low, snorting like a pig. As Bo raced up and down the track like a mad thing Bart crossed and recrossed in the rabbit brush, nosing out single after double after single. He was wide awake and alive, though he kept giving us puzzled looks. Why weren't we *shooting*?

Bart is hunting again. I could end this, neatly and conventionally, by telling you the detailed story of his and Bo's first gun hunt in New Mexico. Of how they nosed out a fat young cottontail in the junipers, and how I snap-shot instinctively with the French gun. Of how I was sure that I had connected and so sent Bo, the nearer dog, to fetch. Of how he didn't come back. Of how Libby finally went in to find Bo standing in puzzlement and, to be fair, fascination over a dead bunny on the clean sand. And of how Bart, grumbling under his breath, shouldered aside the strong young macho and picked up the rabbit to deliver it to my hand, his slightly foggy eyes rolling in his head like marbles, the way they always do.

But that's not an end, not the point. Bart is hunting again, two times, three times a week. At almost fourteen, he still has the fire. His nose—his "turbo sniffer," as Libby calls it—still drinks in the scent despite the lost cells of the aging process and two rattler bites. Bo is back guarding the yard and helping friends round up cattle.

It's late afternoon, and I'm tired and sweated out. My slightly arthritic right knee aches, and I'm passing the light double gun from hand to hand. I want to lean on a tree and rest.

But look at that old dog! He's been hunting for five hours now, going from morning's frost to dry heat, snuffling through rocky arroyos, up and down and up again, from six thousand feet up to sixty-five, down to fifty-five, and back up again. We've moved one covey of Gambel's, a four-point buck, a black-tailed jackrabbit, and an eagle. Sure, he's rested a few times in the shade (he often digs a little and lies on his belly in the cool disturbed earth), and he's soaked himself to the skin in a cattle tank, swimming as he drinks. Still, his tail, docked at two-thirds length rather than a show dog's stub, waves high, flagging his progress through the thorny scrub.

We're nearly to the truck. I'm inclined to call it a day. I tell myself that I don't want to wear Bart out. He's been slowing down a bit for the last half hour, returning from his forays to walk at heel for a few paces, something he could never bring himself to do when he was young. My focus has been drifting, too; I'm daydreaming, and if a quail was to get up, I'd probably fumble the gun and miss it. And why hunt if you're not intense; why hunt at all?

We both see the truck at the same time. Bart stands in the path for a moment, staring, then wags his tail and leaps off the path into the brush-choked arroyo on my left. His turbo sniffer activates, his tail begins to vibrate. He noses under a cholla, emerges, picks a goat's head from his foot, and goes on, directly away from the truck.

See? He's still hunting. I unscrew the cap of my canteen, take a long swallow and a deep breath, and mount my gun more firmly. There are birds out there, tantalizing smells, adventures over the next hill. "Find the birds, Bart. *Find* 'em."

On a Spaniel Called Beau
Killing a Young Bird

BY WILLIAM COWPER

I HAVE THIS WONDERFUL mental picture of William Cowper faced with a deadline. He's got poems to write, due next week—and not an idea in his head. So, like all writers, he makes work. It's important to get everything just so: clean off the desk, sharpen the quill, refill the inkwell, line up the edges of the paper, look out the window.

And as the anxiety level rises, he finally puts pen to paper, probably mostly just to get something, anything, written down. Thus this bit of foolishness addressed to the household pet—and the dog's response.

Cowper did, in fact, write quite a lot of poetry too, and about dogs . . . including this little gem.

★ ★ ★ ★ ★

A SPANIEL, BEAU, that fares like you,
Well-fed, and at his ease,
Should wiser be, than to pursue
Each trifle that he sees.

But you have kill'd a tiny bird,
Which flew not till to-day,
Against my orders, whom you heard
Forbidding you the prey.

Nor did you kill, that you might eat,
And ease a doggish pain,
For him, though chas'd with furious heat,
You left where he was slain.

Nor was he of the thievish sort,
Or one whom blood allures,
But innocent was all his sport,
Whom you have torn for yours.

My dog! what remedy remains,
Since, teach you all I can,
I see you, after all my pains,
So much resemble man!

BEAU'S REPLY
Sir! when I flew to seize the bird,
In spite of your command,
A louder voice than yours I heard
And harder to withstand:

You cried—Forbear!—but in my breast
A mightier cried—Proceed!
'Twas nature, Sir, whose strong behest
Impell'd me in the deed.

Yet much as nature I respect,
I ventur'd once to break

(As you perhaps may recollect)
Her precept, for your sake;

And when your linnet, on a day,
Passing his prison-door,
Had flutter'd all his strength away,
And panting press'd the floor,

Well knowing him a sacred thing,
Not destin'd to my tooth,
I only kiss'd his ruffled wing,
And lick'd the feathers smooth.

Let my obedience then excuse
My disobedience now,
Nor some reproof yourself refuse
From your aggriev'd Bow-wow!

If killing birds be such a crime,
(Which I can hardly see)
What think you, Sir, of killing Time
With verse address'd to me?

Moses

BY WALTER D. EDMONDS

A PROLIFIC WRITER, Walter D. Edmonds wrote over twenty adult novels, something like seventeen juvenile novels, a play, and numerous articles for magazines including the Saturday Evening Post, the Atlantic Monthly, and Harper's Magazine. Probably his best-known book was Drums Along the Mohawk, but he won a Newberry Medal, a Boys' Clubs of America award, and a National Book award for others.

This selection is a charming tale of Heaven and dogs—a perfectly natural combination.

★　★　★　★　★

IT WAS A LONG CLIMB. The scent was cold, too; so faint that when he found it behind the barn he could hardly trust himself. He had just come back from Filmer's with a piece of meat, and he had sat down behind the barn and cracked it down; and a minute later he found that scent reaching off, faint as it was, right from the end of his nose as he lay.

He had had the devil of a time working it out at first, but up here it was simple enough except for the faintness of it. There didn't appear to be any way to stray off this path; there wasn't any brush, there wasn't any water. Only he had to make sure of it, when even for him it nearly faded out, with so many other stronger tracks overlaying it. His tail drooped, and he stumbled a couple of times, driving his nose into the dust. He looked gaunt when he reached the spot where the man had lain down to sleep.

The scent lay heavier there. He shuffled round over it, sifting the dust with an audible clapping of his nostrils to work out the pattern the man had made. It was hard to do, for the dust didn't take scent decently. It wasn't like any dust he had ever come across, either, being glittery, like mica, and silvery in his nose. But he could tell after a minute how the man had lain, on his back, with his hands under his head, and probably his hat over his eyes to shield them from the glare which was pretty dazzling bright up this high, with no trees handy.

His tail began to cut air. He felt better, and all of a sudden he lifted up his freckled nose and let out a couple of short yowps and then a good chest-swelled belling. Then he struck out up the steep going once more. His front legs may have elbowed a little, but his hind legs were full of spring, and his tail kept swinging.

That was how the old man by the town entrance saw him, way down below.

The old man had his chair in the shadow of the wall with a black and yellow parasol tied to the back of it as an extra insurance against the sun. He was reading the Arrivals in the newspaper, the only column that ever interested him; but he looked up sharply when he heard the two yowps and the deep chest notes that, from where he sat, had a mysterious floating quality. It was a little disturbing; but when he saw a dog was the cause he reached out with his foot and shoved the gate hard, so that it swung shut and latched with a sound like a gong. Only one dog had ever come here, and that sound had been enough to discourage him; he had hung round for a while, though, just on the edge, and made the old man nervous. He said to himself that he wasn't going to watch this one, anyway, and folded the paper in halves the way the subway commuter had showed him and went on with the Arrivals.

After a while, though, he heard the dog's panting coming close and the muffled padding of his feet on the marble gate stone. He shook the paper a little, licked his thumb, and turned over half a sheet and read on through the Arrivals into the report of the Committee on Admissions. But then, because he was a curious old man, and kindhearted, noticing that the panting had stopped—and because he had never been quite up to keeping his resolves, except once—he looked out of the gate again.

The dog was sitting on the edge of the gate stone, upright, with his front feet close under him. He was a rusty-muzzled, blue-tick foxhound, with brown ears, and eyes outlined in black like an Egyptian's. He had his nose inside the bars and was working it at the old man.

"Go away," said the old man. "Go home."

At the sound of his voice the hound wrinkled his nose soberly and his tail whipped a couple of times on the gate stone, raising a little star dust.

"Go home," repeated the old man, remembering the dog that had hung around before.

He rattled the paper at him, but it didn't do any good. The dog just looked solemnly pleased at the attention, and a little hopeful, and allowed himself to pant a bit.

"This one's gong to be worse than the other," the old man thought, groaning to himself as he got up. He didn't know much about dogs anyway. Back in Galilee there hadn't been dogs that looked like this one—just pariahs and shepherds and the occasional Persian greyhound of a rich man's son.

He slapped his paper along the bars; it made the dog suck in his tongue and move back obligingly. Peter unhooked his shepherd's staff from the middle crossbar, to use in case the dog tried to slip in past him, and let himself out. He could tell by the feeling of his bare ankles that there was a wind making up in the outer heavens and he wanted to get rid of the poor creature before it began really blowing round the walls. The dog backed off from him and sat down almost on the edge, still friendly, but wary of the shepherd's staff.

"Why can't the poor dumb animal read?" thought Peter, turning to look at the sign he had hung on the gatepost.

The sign read:—

TAKE NOTICE

NO

DOGS

SORCERERS

WHOREMONGERS

MURDERERS

IDOLATERS

LIARS

WILL BE

ADMITTED

When he put it up, he had thought it might save him a lot of trouble; but it certainly wasn't going to help in the case of this dog. He expected he would have to ask the Committee on Admissions to take the matter up; and he started to feel annoyed with them for not having got this animal on the list themselves. It was going to mean a lot of correspondence and probably the Committee would send a memorandum to the Central Office suggesting his retirement again, and Peter liked his place at the gate. It was quiet there, and it was pleasant for an old man to look through the bars and down the path, to re-assure the frightened people, and, when there was nothing else to do, to hear the winds of outer heaven blowing by.

"Go away. Go Home. Depart," he said, waving his staff; but the dog only backed down on to the path and lay on his wishbone with his nose between his paws.

II

Peter went inside and sat down and tried to figure the business out. There were two things he could do. He could notify the Committee of the dog's arrival, or he could give the information to the editor. The Committee would sit up and take notice for once if they found the editor had got ahead of them. It would please the editor, for there were few scoops in Heaven. And then, as luck would have it, the editor himself came down to the gate.

The editor wasn't Horace Greeley or anybody like that, with a reputation in the newspaper world. He had been editor of a little country weekly that nobody in New York, or London, or Paris had ever heard of. But he was good and bursting with ideas all the time. He was now.

"Say, Saint Peter," he said, "I've just had a swell idea about the Arrivals column. Instead of printing all the 'arrivals' on one side and then the 'expected guests' on the other, why not just have one column and put the names of the successful candidates in upper-case type? See?" He shoved a wet impression under Peter's nose and rubbed the back of his head nervously with his ink stained hand. "Simple, neat, dignified."

Peter looked at the galley and saw how simple it would be for him, too. He wouldn't have to read the names in lower case at all. It would make him feel a lot better not to know. Just check the uppercase names as they came to the gate.

He looked up at the flushed face of the editor and his white beard parted over his smile. He liked young, enthusiastic men, remembering how hard, once, they had been to find.

"It looks fine to me, Don," he said. "But the Committee won't like losing all that space in the paper, will they?"

"Probably not," the editor said ruefully. "But I thought you could pull a few wires with the Central Office for me."

Peter sighed.

"I'll try," he said. "But people don't pay attention to an old man, much, Don. Especially one who's been in service."

The editor flushed and muttered something about bums.

Peter said gently, "It doesn't bother me, Don. I'm not ashamed of the service I was in." He looked down to his sandals. He wondered whether there was any of the dust of that Roman road left on them after so long a time. Every man has his one great moment. He'd had two. He was glad he hadn't let the second one go. "I'll see what I can do, Don."

It was a still corner, by the gate; and, with both of them silently staring off up the avenue under the green trees to where the butterflies were fluttering in the shrubbery of the public gardens, the dog decided to take a chance and sneak up again.

He moved one foot at a time, the way he had learned to do behind the counter in the Hawkinsville store, when he went prospecting towards the candy counter. These men didn't hear him any more than the checker players in the store did, and he had time to sniff over the gatepost thoroughly. It puzzled him; and as the men didn't take any notice, he gumshoed over to the other post and went over that, too.

It was queer. He couldn't smell dog on either of them and they were the best-looking posts he had ever come across. It worried him some. His tail drooped and he came back to the gate stone and the very faint scent on it, leading beyond the gate, that he had been following so long. He sat down again and put his nose through the bars, and after a minute he whined.

It was a small sound, but Peter heard it.

"That dog," he said.

The editor whirled round, saying, "What dog?" and saw him.

"I was going to let you know about him, only I forgot," said Peter. "He came up a while ago, and I can't get rid of him. I don't know how he got here. The Committee didn't give me any warning and there's nothing about him in the paper."

"He wasn't on the bulletin," said the editor. "Must have been a slip-up somewhere."

"I don't think so," said Peter. "Dogs don't often come here. Only one other since I've been here, as a matter of fact. What kind of a dog is he any way? I never saw anything like him." He sounded troubled and put out, and the editor grinned, knowing he didn't meant it.

"I never was much of a dog man," he said. "But that's a likely-looking foxhound. He must have followed somebody's scent up here. Hi, boy!" he said. "What's your name? Bob? Spot? Duke?"

The hound lowered his head a little, wrinkled his nose, and wagged his tail across the stone.

"Say," said the editor. "Why don't I put an ad in the Lost and Found? I've never had anything to put there before. But you better bring him in and keep him here till the owner claims him."

"I can't do that," said Peter. "It's against the Law."

"No dogs. Say, I always thought it was funny there were no dogs here. What happens to them?"

"They get removed," said Peter. "They just go."

"That don't seem right," the young editor said. He ruffled his black hair with his hand. "Say, Saint," he asked, "who made this law anyway?"

"It's in Revelations. John wasn't a dog man, as you call it. Back in Galilee we didn't think much of dogs, you see. They were mostly pariahs."

"I see," said the editor. His blue eyes sparkled. "But say! Why can't I put it in the news? And write an editorial? By golly, I haven't had anything to raise a cause on since I got here."

Peter shook his head dubiously.

"It's risky," he said.

"It's a free country," exclaimed the editor. "At least nobody's told me different. Now probably there's nothing would mean so much to the owner of that dog as finding him up here. You get a genuine dog man and this business of passing the love of women is just hooey to him."

"Hooey?" Peter asked quietly.

"It just means he likes dogs better than anything. And this is a good dog. I tell you. He's cold-tracked this fellow, whoever he is, Lord knows how.

Besides, he's only one dog, and look at the way the rabbits have been getting into the manna in the public garden. I'm not a dog man, as I said before, but believe me, Saint, it's a pretty thing on a frosty morning to hear a good hound high-tailing a fox across the hills."

"We don't have frost here, Don."

"Well," said the editor, "frost or no frost, I'm going to do it. I'll have to work quick to get it in before the forms close. See you later."

"Wait," said Peter. "What's the weather report say?"

The editor gave a short laugh.

"What do you think? Fair, moderate winds, little change in temperature. Those twerps up in the bureau don't even bother to read the barometer any more. They just play pinochle all day, and the boy runs that report off on the mimeograph machine."

"*I* think there's a wind making up in the outer heavens," Peter said. "When we get a real one, it just about blows the gate stone away. That poor animal wouldn't last a minute."

The editor whistled. "We'll have to work fast." Then, suddenly his eye blazed. "All my life I wanted to get out an extra. I never had a chance, running a weekly. Now, by holy, I will."

He went off up the avenue on the dead run. Even Peter, watching him go, felt excited.

"Nice dog," he said to the hound; and the hound, at the deep gentle voice, gulped in his tongue and twitched his haunches. The whipping of his tail on the gate stone made a companionable sound for the old man. His beard folded on his chest and he nodded a little.

III

He was dozing quietly when the hound barked.

It was a deep, vibrant note that anyone who knew dogs would have expected the minute he saw the spring of those ribs; it was mellow, like honey in the throat. Peter woke up tingling with the sound of it and turned to see the hound swaying the whole hind half of himself with his tail.

Then a high loud voice shouted, "Mose, by Jeepers! What the hell you doing here, you poor dumb fool?"

Peter turned to see a stocky, short-legged man who stuck out more than was ordinary, both in front and behind. He had on a gray flannel shirt, and blue denim pants, and a pair of lumberman's rubber packs on his feet, with the tops laced only to the ankle. There was a hole in the front of his felt hat where the block had worn through. He wasn't, on the whole, what you might expect to see walking on that Avenue. But Peter has seen queer people come to Heaven and he said mildly, "Do you know this dog?"

"Sure," said the stout man. "I hunted with him round Hawkinsville for the last seven years. It's old Mose. Real smart dog. He'd hunt for anybody."

"Mose?" said Peter. "For Moses, I suppose."

"Maybe. He could track anything through hell and high water."

"Moses went through some pretty high water," said Peter. "What's your name?"

"Freem Brock. What's yours?"

Peter did not trouble to answer, for he was looking at the hound; and he was thinking he had seen some people come to Heaven's gate and look pleased, and some come and look shy, and some frightened, and some a little shamefaced, and some satisfied, and some sad (maybe with memories they couldn't leave on earth), and some jubilant, and a whole quartette still singing "Adeline" just the way they were when the hotel fell on their necks in the earthquake. But in all his career at the gate he had never seen anyone express such pure, unstifled joy as this rawboned hound.

"Was he your dog?" he asked Freeman Brock.

"Naw," said Freem. "He belonged to Pat Haskell." He leaned his shoulder against the gatepost and crossed one foot over the other. "Stop that yawping," he said to Mose, and Mose lay down, wagging. "Maybe you ain't never been in Hawkinsville," he said to Peter. "It's a real pretty village right over the Black River. Pat kept store there and he let anybody take Mose that wanted to. Pretty often I did. He liked coming with me because I let him run foxes. I'm kind of a fox hunter," he said, blowing out his breath. "Oh, I like rabbit hunting all right, but there's no money in it. . . . Say," he broke off, "you didn't tell me what your name was."

"Peter," said the old man.

"Well, Pete, two years ago was Mose's best season. Seventy-seven fox was shot ahead of him. I shot thirty-seven of them myself. Five crosses and two blacks in the lot. Yes, sir. I heard those black foxes had got away from the fur farm and I took Mose right over there. I made three hundred and fifty dollars out of them hides."

"He was a good dog, then?" asked Peter.

"Best foxhound in seven counties," said Freem Brock. He kicked the gate with his heel in front of Mose's nose and Mose let his ears droop. "He was a fool to hunt. I don't see no fox signs up here. Plenty rabbits in the Park. But there ain't nobody with a gun. I wish I'd brought my old Ithaca along."

"You can't kill things here," said Peter.

"That's funny. Why not?"

"They're already dead."

"Well, I know that. But it beats me how I got here. I never did nothing to get sent to this sort of place. Hell, I killed them farm foxes and I poached up the railroad in the *pre*-serve. But I never done anything bad."

"No," said St. Peter. "We know that."

"I got drunk, maybe. But there's other people done the same before me."

"Yes, Freem."

"Well, what the devil did I get sent here for, Pete?"

"Do you remember when the little girl was sick and the town doctor wouldn't come out at night on a town case, and you went over to town and made him come?"

"Said I'd knock his teeth out," said Freem, brightening.

"Yes. He came. And the girl was taken care of," said Peter.

"Aw," Freem said, "I didn't know what I was doing. I was just mad. Well, maybe I'd had a drink, but it was a cold night, see? I didn't knock his teeth out. He left them in the glass." He looked at the old man. "Jeepers," he said. "And they sent me here for that?"

Peter looked puzzled.

"Wasn't it a good reason?" he asked. "It's not such a bad place."

"Not so bad as I thought it was going to be. But people don't want to talk to me. I tried to talk to an old timber-beast named Boone down the road. But he asked me if I ever shot an Indian, and when I said no he went along. You're the only feller I've seen that was willing to talk to me," he said, turning to the old man. "I don't seem to miss likker up here, but there's nowhere I can get to buy some tobacco."

Peter said, "You don't have to buy things in Heaven."

"Heaven?" said Freeman Brock. "Say, is that what this is?" He looked frightened all at once. "That's what the matter is, I don't belong here. I ain't the kind to come here. There must have been a mistake somewhere." He took hold of Peter's arm. "Listen," he said urgently. "Do you know how to work that gate?"

"I do," said Peter. "But I can't let you out."

"I got to get out."

Peter's voice grew gentler.

"You'll like it here after a while, Freem."

"You let me out."

"You couldn't go anywhere outside," Peter said.

Freem looked through the bars at the outer heavens and watched a couple of stars like water lilies floating by below. He said slowly, "We'd go some place."

Peter said, "You mean you'd go out there with that dog?"

Freem flushed.

"I and Mose have had some good times," he said.

At the sound of his name, Mose's nose lifted.

Peter looked down at the ground. With the end of his shepherd's staff he thoughtfully made a cross and then another overlapping it and put an X in the upper left-hand corner. Freem looked down to see what he was doing.

"You couldn't let Mose in, could you, Pete?"

Peter sighed and rubbed out the pattern with his sandal.

"I'm sorry," he said. "The Committee don't allow dogs."

"What'll happen to the poor brute, Pete?"

Peter shook his head.

"If you ask me," Freem said loudly, "I think this is a hell of a place."

"What's that you said?"

Peter glanced up.

"Hello, Don," he said. "Meet Freem Brock. This is the editor of the paper," he said to Freem. "His name's Don."

"What was that you said about Heaven being a hell of a place?" asked the editor.

Freem drew a long breath. He took a look at old Mose lying outside the gate with his big nose resting squashed up and sideways against the bottom crossbar; he looked at the outer heavens, and he looked at the editor.

"Listen," he said. "That hound followed me up here. Pete says he can't let him in. He says I can't go out to where Mose is. I only been in jail twice," he said, "but I liked it better than this."

The editor said, "You'd go out there?"

"Give me a chance."

"What a story!" said the editor. "I've got my extra on the Avenue now. The cherubs will be coming this way soon. It's all about the hound, but this stuff is the genuine goods. Guest prefers to leave Heaven. Affection for old hunting dog prime factor in his decision. It's human interest. I tell you it'll shake the Committee. By holy, I'll have an editorial in my next edition calling for a celestial referendum."

"Wait," said Peter. "What's the weather report?"

"What do you think? Fair, moderate winds, little change in temperature. But the Central Office is making up a hurricane for the South Pacific and it's due to go by pretty soon. We got to hurry, Saint."

He pounded away up the Avenue, leaving a little trail of star dust in his wake.

Freem Brock turned on Saint Peter.

"He called you something," he said.

Peter nodded.

"Saint."

"I remember about you now. Say, you're a big shot here. Why can't you let Mose in?"

Peter shook his head.

"I'm no big shot, Freem. If I was, maybe—"

His voice was drowned out by a shrieking up the Avenue.

"Extry! Extry! Special Edition. Read all about it. Dog outside Heaven's Gate. Dog outside . . ."

A couple of cherubs were coming down the thoroughfare, using their wings to make time. When he saw them, Freem Brock started. His shoulders began to itch self-consciously and he put a hand inside his shirt.

"My gracious," he said.

Peter, watching him, nodded.

"Everybody gets them. You'll get used to them after a while. They're handy, too, on a hot day."

"For the love of Pete," said Freem.

"Read all about it! Dog outside Heaven's Gate. Lost Dog waiting outside . . ."

"He ain't lost!" cried Freem. "He never got lost in his life."

"'Committee at fault,'" read Peter. "Thomas Aquinas isn't going to like that," he said.

"It don't prove nothing," said Freem.

"Mister, please," said a feminine voice. "The editor sent me down. Would you answer some questions?"

"Naw," said Freem, turning to look at a young woman with red hair and a gold pencil in her hand. "Well, what do you want to know, lady?"

The young woman had melting brown eyes. She looked at the hound. "Isn't he cute?" she asked. "What's his name?"

"Mose," said Freem. "He's a cute hound all right."

"Best in seven counties," said Peter.

"May I quote you on that, Saint?"

"Yes," said Peter. "You can say I think the dog ought to be let in." His face was pink over his white beard. "You can say a hurricane is going to pass, and that before I see that animal blown off by it I'll go out there myself—I and my friend Freem. Some say I'm a has-been, but I've got some standing with the public yet."

The girl with red hair was writing furiously with a little gold glitter of her pencil. "Oh," she said.

"Say I'm going out too," said Freem. "I and Pete."

"Oh," she said. "What's your name?"

"Freeman Brock, Route 5, Boonville, New York, U.S.A."

"Thanks," she said breathlessly.

"How much longer before we got that hurricane coming?" asked Freem.

"I don't know," said the old man, anxiously. "I hope Don can work fast."

"Extry! Owner found. Saint Peter goes outside with hound, Moses. Committee bluff called. Read all about it."

"How does Don manage it so fast?" said Peter. "It's like a miracle."

"It's science," said Freem. "Hey!" he yelled at a cherub.

They took the wet sheet, unheeding of the gold ink that stuck to their fingers.

"They've got your picture here, Pete."

"Have they?" Peter asked. He sounded pleased. "Let's see."

It showed Peter standing at the gate.

"It ain't bad," said Freem. He was impressed. "You really meant it?" he asked. Peter nodded.

"By cripus," Freem said slowly, "you're a pal."

Saint Peter was silent for a moment. In all the time he had minded Heaven's Gate, no man had ever called him a pal before.

IV

Outside the gate, old Mose got up on his haunches. He was a weather-wise dog, and now he turned his nose outwards. The first puff of wind came like a slap in the face, pulling his ears back, and then it passed. He glanced over his shoulder and saw Freem and the old man staring at each other. Neither of them had noticed him at all. He pressed himself against the bars and lifted his nose and howled.

At his howl both men turned.

There was a clear gray point way off along the reach of the wall, and the whine in the sky took up where Mose's howl had ended.

Peter drew in his breath.

"Come on, Freem," he said, and opened the gate.

Freeman Brock hesitated. He was scared now. He could see that a real wind was coming, and the landing outside looked almighty small to him. But he was still mad, and he couldn't let an old man like Peter call his bluff.

"All right," he said. "Here goes."

He stepped out, and Mose jumped up on him, and licked his face.

"Get down, darn you," he said. "I never could break him of that trick," he explained shamefacedly to Peter. Peter smiled, closing the gate behind him with a firm hand. Its gong-like note echoed through Heaven just as the third edition burst upon the Avenue.

Freeman Brock was frightened. He glanced back through the bars, and Heaven looked good to him. Up the Avenue a crowd was gathering. A couple of lanky, brown-faced men were in front. They started towards the gate.

Then the wind took hold of him and he grasped the bars and looked outward. He could see the hurricane coming like an express train running through infinity. It had a noise like an express train. He understood suddenly just how the victim of a crossing accident must feel.

He glanced at Peter.

The old Saint was standing composedly, leaning on his staff with one hand, while with the other he drew Mose close between his legs. His white robe fluttered tight against his shanks and his beard bent sidewise like the hound's ears. He had faced lack of faith in others; what was worse, he had faced it in himself; and a hurricane, after all, was not so much. He turned to smile at Freem. "Don't be afraid," he said.

"O.K.," said Freem, but he couldn't let go the gate.

Old Mose, shivering almost hard enough to rattle, reached up and licked Peter's hand.

One of the brown-faced men said, "That's a likely-looking hound. He the one I read about in the paper?"

"Yep," said Freem. He had to holler now.

Daniel Boone said, "Let us timber-beasts come out with you, Saint, will you?"

Peter smiled. He opened the gate with a wave of his hand, and ten or a dozen timber-beasts—Carson, Bridger, Nat Foster—all crowded through, and started shaking hands with him and Freeman Brock. With them was a thin, mild-eyed man.

"My name's Francis," he said to Freem when his turn came. "From Assisi."

"He's all right," Daniel Boone explained. "He wasn't much of a shot, but he knows critters. We better get holt of each other, boys."

It seemed queer to Freem. Here he was going to get blown to eternity and he didn't even know where it was, but all of a sudden he felt better than he ever had in his life. Then he felt a squirming round his legs and there was Mose, sitting on his feet, the way he would on his snowshoes in cold weather when they stopped for a sandwich on earth. He reached down and took hold of Mose's ears.

"Let her blow to blazes," he thought.

She blew.

The hurricane was on them. The nose of it went by, sweeping the wall silver. There was no more time for talk. No voices could live outside Heaven's gate. If a man had said a word, the next man to hear it would have been some poor heathen aborigine on an island in the Pacific Ocean, and he wouldn't have known what it meant.

The men on the gate stone were crammed against the bars. The wind dragged them bodily to the left, and for a minute it looked as if Jim Bridger were going, but they caught him back. There were a lot of the stoutest hands that ever swung an axe in that bunch holding on to Heaven's gate, and they weren't letting go for any hurricane—not yet.

But Freem Brock could see it couldn't last that way. He didn't care, though. He was in good company, and that was what counted the most. He wasn't a praying man, but he felt his heart swell with gratitude, and he took hold hard of the collar of Mose and felt the license riveted on. A queer thing to think of, a New York State dog license up there. He managed to look down at it, and he saw that it had turned to gold, with the collar gold under it. The wind tore at him as he saw it. The heart of the hurricane was on him now like a million devils' fingers.

"Well, Mose," he thought.

And then in the blur of his thoughts a dazzling bright light came down and he felt the gate at his back opening and he and Peter and Francis and Daniel and the boys were all drawn back into the peace of Heaven, and a quiet voice belonging to a quiet man said, "Let the dog come in."

V

They were sitting together, Freem and Peter, by the gate, reading the paper in the morning warmth, and Peter was having an easy time with the editor's new type arrangement. "Gridley," he was reading the upper-case names, "Griscome, Godolphin, Habblestick, Hafey, Hanlon, Hartwell, Haskell . . ."

"Haskell," said Freem. "Not Pat?"

"Yes," said Peter. "Late of Hawkinsville."

"Not in big type?"

"Yes."

"Well, I'll be . . . Well, that twerp. Think of that. Old Pat."

Peter smiled.

"By holy," said Freem. "Ain't he going to be amazed when he finds Mose up here?'"

"How's Mose doing?"

"He's all right now," said Freem. "He's been chasing the rabbits. I guess he's up there now. The dew's good."

"He didn't look so well, I thought," Peter said.

"Well, that was at first," said Freem. "You see, the rabbits just keep going up in the trees and he couldn't get a real run on any of them. There, he's got one started now."

Peter glanced up from the paper.

Old Mose was doing a slow bark, kind of low, working out the scent from the start. He picked up pace for a while, and then he seemed to strike a regular knot. His barks were deep and patient.

And then, all of a sudden, his voice broke out—that deep, ringing, honey-throated baying that Freem used to listen to in the late afternoon on the sand hills over the Black River. It went away through the public gardens and out beyond the city, the notes running together and fading and swelling and fading out.

"He's pushing him pretty fast," said Freem. "He's going to get pretty good on these rabbits."

The baying swelled again; it came back, ringing like bells. People in the gardens stopped to look up and smile. The sound of it gave Peter a warm tingling feeling.

Freem yawned.

"Might as well wait here till Pat Haskell comes in," he said.

It was pleasant by the gate, under the black and yellow parasol. It made a shade like a flower on the hot star dust. They didn't have to talk, beyond just, now and then, dropping a word between them as they sat.

After a while they heard a dog panting and saw old Mose tracking down the street. He came over to their corner and lay down at their feet, lolling a long tongue. He looked good, a little fat, but lazy and contented. After a minute, though, he got up to shift himself around, and paused as he sat down, and raised a hind leg, and scratched himself behind his wings.

The Care and Training of a Dog

BY E. B. WHITE

THE RICHES OF E. B. White go on forever. Essayist, poet, storyteller, White's delights include articles and stories in *The New Yorker, Atlantic Monthly,* and *Harper's Magazine, Charlotte's Web* and *Stuart Little* and seventeen other books, and collections of letters and essays. Many years after his death he is still amusing, entertaining, and delighting readers.

After retiring to his farm in Maine, White lived a pastoral life, alternately tending his animals, working in his garden, and writing. He was ably abetted in all those endeavors by one or more dogs.

White was a devoted dog fancier, owner, and admirer. He makes no pretense about being a dog trainer. In a different essay which mentions his dog, he says, "Fred was an unbeliever. He worshiped no personal God, no Supreme Being. He certainly did not worship *me.*"

★　★　★　★　★

THERE IS A BOOK out called *Dog Training Made Easy* and it was sent to me the other day by the publisher, who rightly guessed that it would catch my eye. I like to read books on dog training. Being the owner of dachshunds, to me a book on dog discipline becomes a volume of inspired humor. Every sentence is a riot. Some day, if I ever get a chance, I shall write a book, or warning, on the character and temperament of the dachshund and why he can't be trained and shouldn't be. I would rather train a striped zebra to balance an Indian club than induce a dachshund to heed my slightest command.

For a number of years past I have been agreeably encumbered by a very large and dissolute dachshund named Fred. Of all the dogs whom I have served I've never known one who understood so much of what I say or held it in such deep contempt. When I address Fred I never have to raise either my voice or my hopes. He even disobeys me when I instruct him in something that he wants to do. And when I answer his peremptory scratch at the door and hold the door open for him to walk through, he stops in the middle and lights a cigarette, just to hold me up.

"Shopping for a puppy presents a number of problems," writes Mr. William Cary Duncan, author of *Dog Training Made Easy*. Well, shopping for a puppy has never presented many problems for me, as most of the puppies and dogs that have entered my life (and there have been scores of them) were not the result of a shopping trip but an act of God. The first puppy I owned, when I was about nine years old, was not shopped for—it was born to the collie bitch of the postman of my older sister, who sent it to me by express from Washington, D.C., in a little crate containing, in addition to the puppy, a bar of Peters' chocolate and a ripe frankfurter. And the puppy I own now was not shopped for but was won in a raffle. Between these two extremes there have been many puppies, mostly unshopped for. It is not so much that I acquired dogs as it is that dogs acquire me. Maybe they even shop for me, I don't know. If they do I assume they have many problems, because they certainly always arrive with plenty, which they then turn over to me.

The possession of a dog today is a different thing from the possession of a dog at the turn of the century, when one's dog was fed on mashed potato and brown gravy and lived in a doghouse with an arched portal. Today a dog is fed on scraped beef and Vitamin B_1 and lives in bed with you.

An awful lot of nonsense has been written about dogs by persons who don't know them very well, and the attempt to elevate the purebred to a position of national elegance has been, in the main, a success. Dogs used to mate with other dogs rather casually in my day, and the results were discouraging to the American Kennel Club but entirely satisfactory to small boys who liked puppies. In my suburban town, "respectable" people didn't keep she-dogs. One's washerwoman might keep a bitch, or one's lawn cutter, but not one's next door neighbor.

The prejudice against females made a deep impression on me, and I grew up thinking that there was something indecent and unclean about she-things in general. The word bitch of course was never used in polite families. One day a little mutt followed me home from school, and after much talk I persuaded my parents to let me keep it—at least until the owner turned up or advertised for it. It dwelt among us only one night. Next morning my father took me aside and in a low voice said: "My son, I don't know whether you realize it, but that dog is a female. It'll have to go."

"But why does it have to?" I asked.

"They're a nuisance," he replied, embarrassed. "We'd have all the other dogs in the neighborhood around here all the time."

That sounded like an idyllic arrangement to me, but I could tell from my father's voice that the stray dog was doomed. We turned her out and she went off toward the more liberal section of town. This sort of incident must have been happening to thousands of American youngsters in those days, and we grew up to find that it had been permanently added to the record by Dorothy Parker in her short story "Mr. Durant."

On our block, in the days of my innocence, there were in addition to my collie, a pug dog, a dachshund named Brun, a fox terrier named Sunny who spent many years studying one croquet ball, a red setter, and a St. Bernard who carried his mistress's handbag, shuffling along in a stately fashion with the drool running out both sides of his jaws. I was scared of this St. Bernard because of his size, and never passed his house without dread. The dachshund was old, surly, and disagreeable, and was endlessly burying bones in the flower border of the DeVries's yard. I should very much doubt if any of those animals ever had its temperature taken rectally, ever was fed raw meat or tomato juice, ever was given distemper inoculations, or ever saw the whites of a veterinary's eyes. They were brought up on chicken bones and gravy and left-over cereal, and were all fine dogs. Most of them never saw the inside of their owner's houses—they knew their place.

The "problem" of caring for a dog has been unnecessarily complicated. Take the matter of housebreaking. In the suburbia of those lovely post-Victorian days of which I write the question of housebreaking a puppy was met with the simple bold courage characteristic of our forefathers. You simply kept the house away from the puppy. This was not only the simplest way, it was the only practical way, just as it is today. Our parents were in possession of a vital secret—a secret which has been all but lost to the world: the knowledge that a puppy will live and thrive without ever crossing the threshold of a dwelling house, at least till he's big enough so he doesn't wet the rug.

Although our fathers and mothers very sensibly never permitted a puppy to come into the house, they made up for this indignity by always calling the puppy "Sir." In those days a dog didn't expect anything very elaborate in the way of food or medical care, but he did expect to be addressed civilly.

Mr. Duncan discusses housebreaking at some length and assumes, as do all writers of dog books, that the owner of a puppy has little else to do except own the puppy. It is Mr. Duncan's theory that puppies have a sense of modesty and don't like to be stared at when they are doing something. When you are walking the dog, he says, you must "appear utterly uninterested" as you approach some favorite spot. This, as any city dweller knows, is a big order. Anybody who has ever tried to synchronize a puppy's bowels with a rigid office schedule knows that one's interest in the small phenomena of early morning sometimes reaches fever pitch. A dog owner may feign disinterest, but his masque will not suffice. Nothing is more comical than the look on the face of a person at the upper end of a dog leash, pretending not to know what is going on at the lower.

A really companionable and indispensable dog is an accident of nature. You can't get it by breeding for it, and you can't buy it with money. It just happens along. Out of the vast sea of assorted dogs that I have had dealings with, by far the noblest, the best, and the most important was the first, the one my sister sent me in a crate. He was an old-style collie, beautifully marked, with a blunt nose, and great natural gentleness and intelligence. When I got him he was what I badly needed. I think probably all these other dogs of mine have just been a groping toward that old dream. I've never dared get another collie for fear the comparison would be too uncomfortable. I can still see my first dog in all the moods and situations that memory has filed him away in, but I think of him oftenest as he used to be right after breakfast on the back porch, listlessly eating up a dish of petrified oatmeal rather than hurt my feelings. For six years he met me at the same place after school and convoyed me home—a service he thought up himself. A boy doesn't forget that sort of association. It is a monstrous trick of fate that now, settled in the country and with sheep to take care of, I am obliged to do my shepherding with the grotesque and sometimes underhanded assistance of two dachshunds and a wire-haired fox terrier.

Mallard-Pool-Mutt

From *The Dog Who Wouldn't Be*

BY FARLEY MOWAT

F ARLEY MOWAT HAS TWO faces—one is very serious. Among other scholarly works, he writes tellingly of the history and tribulations of the Inuit and other Indian tribes of the far, frozen North in touching books like *People of the Deer.*

Mowat's alternate face is that of the dedicated naturalist and raconteur of such laugh-out-loud tales as *Never Cry Wolf* and *Owls in the Family.* But he is most enticing as the young animal lover growing up on the Canadian plains with parents so understanding as to let him, for example, keep two full-grown owls in the house.

The Dog Who Wouldn't Be, from which this chapter is taken, is a delightful story of Mowat's youth and the perverse character of Mutt, the title dog.

★　★　★　★　★

I HAD SUPPOSED THAT after the fiascos of that first week of hunting, Mutt would be banned from all further expeditions. It seemed a logical supposition, even though logic was often the stranger in our home. Consequently I was thoroughly startled one morning to find the relative positions of the antagonists in our family's battle of the sexes reversed. At breakfast Mother elaborated on her new theme that Mutt was far too sensible to waste his time hunting game birds; and Father replied with the surprising statement that he could train any dog to do anything, and that Mutt could, and would, become the "best damn bird dog in the west!" I thought that my father was being more than usually rash, but he thought otherwise, and so throughout the rest of that season Mutt accompanied us on every shooting trip, and he and Father struggled with one another in a conflict that at times reached epic proportions.

The trouble was that Mutt, having discovered the joys of cattle running, infinitely preferred cows to birds. The task of weaning him away from cattle chasing to an interest in game birds seemed hopeless. Yet Father persevered with such determination that toward the end of the season he began to see some meager prospect of success. On those rare occasions when Mutt allowed us to shoot a bird we would force the corpse into his jaws, or hang it, albatrosslike, about his neck, for him to bring back to the car. He deeply resented this business, for the feathers of upland game birds made him sneeze, and the oily taste of duck feathers evidently gave him a mild form of nausea. Eventually, however, he was persuaded to pick up a dead Hungarian partridge of his own volition, but he did this only because Father had made it clear to him that there would be no more cow chasing that day if he refused to humor us. Finally, on a day in early October, he stumbled on a dead partridge, without having it pointed out to him, and, probably because there were no cows in sight and he was bored, he picked it up and brought it back. That first real retrieve was not an unqualified success, since Mutt did not have what dog fanciers refer to as a "tender mouth." When we received the partridge we got no more than a bloody handful of feathers. We did not dare complain.

Being determinedly optimistic, we took this incident as a hopeful sign, and redoubled our efforts. But Mutt remained primarily a cow chaser; and it was not until the final week end of the hunting season that the tide began to turn.

As the result of a book-distributing plan which he had organized, my father had become acquainted with an odd assortment of people scattered all through the province. One of these was a Ukrainian immigrant named Paul Sazalisky. Paul owned two sections on the shores of an immense slough known as Middle Lake that lies well to the east of Saskatoon. On Thursday of the last week of the season, Paul phoned Father to report that huge flocks of Canada geese were massing on the lake. He invited us to come out and try our luck.

That was a frigid journey. Snow already lay upon the ground and the north wind was so bitter that Mutt did not leap out after cattle even once. He stayed huddled up on the floor boards over the manifold heater, inhaling gusts of hot air and carbon monoxide.

We arrived at Middle Lake in the early evening and found a wasteland that even to our eyes seemed the essence of desolation. Not a tree pierced the gray emptiness. The roads had subsided into freezing gumbo tracks and they seemed to meander without hope across a lunar landscape. The search for Paul's farm was long and agonizing.

Paul's house, when at last we found it, turned out to be a clay-plastered shanty perched like a wart upon the face of the whitened plains. It was unprepossessing in appearance. There were only two rooms, each with a single tiny window—yet it held Paul, his wife, his wife's parents, Paul's seven children, and two cousins who had been recruited to help with the pigs. The pigs, as we soon discovered, were the mainstay of the establishment, and their aroma was everywhere. It seemed to me to be a singularly unpleasant odor too—far worse than that usually associated with pigs. But there was a good reason for the peculiarly powerful properties of that memorable stench.

Like most of the immigrants who came from middle Europe in response to the lure of free land in Canada, Paul was an astute and farsighted fellow. As soon as he had taken over his homestead on the shores of Middle Lake, he made a thorough assessment of the natural resources at his disposal. He soon discovered that a narrow channel which flowed through his property, connecting the two main arms of Middle Lake, was crowded with enormous suckers. There was no commercial market for these soft-fleshed fish, so they had remained undisturbed until Paul came, and saw, and was inspired. Paul concluded that if the fish could not be marketed in their present form, their flesh might very well be sold if it was converted into a more acceptable product—such as pork.

He surprised his wheat-farming neighbors by going into the pig business on a large scale.

He acquired three dip nets, and he began to raise hogs on suckers. The hogs prospered almost unbelievably on this pure protein diet, reaching marketable weight in about two thirds the length of time required by corn-fed swine. They bred with abandon, and their progeny were insatiable for fish.

Paul was a bit of a mystery locally. None of his neighbors knew about the fish, and there were two good reasons for Paul's reticence. First of all, he had no wish to share a good thing with duller folk; and secondly, he had sometimes tasted fish-fed swine in the Ukraine. Because of this experience he chose to ship his hogs all the way to Winnipeg, disdaining the more accessible local markets, and cheerfully shouldering the extra freight costs. The local people thought that this was foolish, but Paul saw no reason to explain that he had chosen Winnipeg because it would be practically impossible for retail butchers in that large city to trace the origin of certain hams and sides of bacon which seemed to have been cured in cod-liver oil.

In later years Paul became a powerful and respected figure in the west. He was of the stuff from which great men are made.

He was still in the preliminary stages of his career when we knew him and he had few physical amenities to offer guests. Nevertheless, when Eardlie drew up at his door, he took us to the bosom of his family.

That is to say he took Father and me to the family bosom. Mutt refused to be taken. Sniffing the heavy air about the cabin with ill-concealed disgust, he at first refused even to leave the car. He sat on the seat, his nose dripping, saying "Faugh!" at frequent intervals. It was not until full darkness had brought with it the breath of winter, and the wailing of the coyotes, that he came scratching at the cabin door.

We three slept on the floor, as did most of Paul's family, for there was only one bed in the place. The floor had its advantages since the air at the lower levels contained some oxygen. There was none too much and, since neither of the two windows could be opened, the trickle of fresh air that found its way under the door was soon lost in a swirl of nameless other gases. Our lungs worked overtime, and we sweated profusely, for the stove remained volcanic the night through.

For Father and me it was a difficult experience. For Mutt it was sheer hell. Gasping for breath, he squirmed about the floor, seeking relief and finding none. Finally he thrust his nose under my armpit and resigned himself to what seemed like certain suffocation.

For once in his life Mutt was delighted to rise before the sun. When Mrs. Sazalisky opened the door at 4 A.M. to get some poplar billets with which to cook our breakfast, Mutt staggered from the room moaning audibly. He had not yet fully recovered an hour later when Paul guided us down to the soggy shores of the lake and out along a low mud spit.

At the tip of the spit Paul had previously dug two foxholes for us. There was water in the holes, and it was ice-encrusted. The mud was stiff and frigid. There was a nasty wind out of the northwest and, although it was still too dark to see, we could feel the sharp bite of driven snow in our faces.

Paul left us after a murmured injunction to keep an eye out for flocks coming from behind, and we three settled down to wait until dawn.

In retrospect I cannot recall ever having been so cold. Not even the excitement of waiting for my first shot at a goose could keep the blood flowing to my numb extremities. As for Mutt, he was soon beyond all feeling. We had found a sack for him to lie on, but it did him little good. He began to shiver extravagantly, and then to snuffle, and finally his teeth began to chatter. Father and I were surprised by this, for neither of us had ever heard a dog's teeth chatter before. We had not thought that such a thing was possible. Nevertheless, all through that interminable wait Mutt's teeth rang like a cascade of gravel. He was so cold that he no longer even complained, and we recognized this as a bad sign, for when Mutt could not complain he was near the last extremity.

The dawn, when it came at last, was gray and somber. The sky lightened so imperceptibly that we could hardly detect the coming of the morning. Father and I strained our eyes over the wind-driven water and then, suddenly, we heard the sounds of wings. Cold was forgotten. We crouched in the flooded holes and flexed our numb fingers in their shooting gloves.

Father saw them first. He nudged me sharply and I half turned my head to behold a spectacle of incomparable grandeur. Out of the gray storm scud, like ghostly ships, a hundred whistling swans drove down upon us on their heavy wings. They passed directly overhead, not half a gunshot from us, and we were lost beyond time and space in a moment of unparalleled majesty and mystery. Then they were gone, and the snow eddies once again obscured our straining vision.

It would not have mattered greatly after that if we had seen no other living thing all day, nor fired a single shot. But the swans were only the leaders of a multitude. The windy silence of the mud spit was soon pierced by the sonorous cries of seemingly endless flocks of geese that drifted wraithlike overhead. They were flying low that day, so we could see them clearly. Snow geese, startlingly white of breast, with jet-black wing tips, beat past the point, and small bands of waveys kept formation with them like outriders. The honkers came close behind, and as the rush of air through their great pinions sounded harsh above the wind, Father and I stood up and raised our guns. A flight came low directly over us, and we fired as one. The sound of the shots seemed puny, and was lost at once in that immensity of wind and water.

It was pure mischance that one of the birds was hit, for, as we admitted to each other later, neither of us had really aimed at those magnificent gray presences. Nevertheless, one of them fell, appearing gigantic and primeval in the tenuous light as it spiraled sharply down. It struck the water a hundred yards from shore and we saw with dismay that it had only been winged, for it swam off at once, with neck outthrust, after the vanishing flock.

We ran to the shore, and we were frantic. It was not entirely the prospect of losing the goose that distracted us; rather it was the knowledge that we could not leave that great bird to perish slowly amidst the gathering ice. We had no boat. Paul had promised to return after dawn with a little dugout; but there was no sign of him, and the goose was now swimming strongly toward the outer limit of our vision.

We had quite forgotten Mutt. We were astounded when he suddenly appeared beside us, cast one brief glance at the disappearing bird, and leaped into the bitter waters.

To this day I have no idea what prompted him. Perhaps it was because the goose, being very large, seemed more worthy of his efforts than any duck had ever been. Perhaps he was simply so cold and miserable that the death wish was upon him. But I do not really believe either of these explanations. I think my mother was right, and that somewhere in his inscrutable ancestry a memory had at long last come to life.

The snow flurries had grown heavier and Mutt and the goose soon vanished from our view. We waited through interminable minutes, and when he did not reappear we began to be frightened for him. We called, but if he heard us down the wind, he did not respond. At length Father ran off down the mud spit to seek Paul and the boat, leaving me alone with a growing certainty that I had seen my dog for the last time.

The relief was almost overwhelming when, some minutes later, I caught a glimpse of Mutt returning out of the lowering scud. He was swimming hard, but the wind and the seas were against him and it was some time before I could see him clearly. He had the goose firmly by one wing, but the honker was fighting fiercely. It seemed inconceivable that Mutt could succeed in bringing it to shore and I was convinced that he would drown before my very eyes. Many times he was driven completely under water, yet each time, when he emerged, his grip upon the goose remained unbroken. The goose buffeted him across the face with its uninjured wing; it jumped on his head; it attempted to fly; it attempted to dive; yet Mutt held on.

When he was still twenty feet from shore I could bear the strain no longer and I waded out into the shallows until I was hip-deep. Mutt saw me and turned my way. When he came within reach I grabbed the goose from him and discovered that it was as formidable as it appeared to be. It was all I could do to haul it ashore, and I suffered a buffeting in the process that left my legs and arms bruised for many a day.

Paul and Father arrived in the little boat a short time later. They hurried ashore and Paul stood looking down at Mutt, who was now swathed in my hunting coat. I was sitting on the goose, and barely managing to keep it under control.

"By God!" Paul said, and there was awe in his voice. "By God! You shoot the *big* gray goose! And dat dam' dog—he bring him back? By God! I don't believe!"

Mutt wriggled under the coat and one eye opened. Life was returning; for if there was one thing that could stir him from the edge of the grave itself, it was honest praise. He must have recognized Paul's incredulity as the highest praise indeed.

We carried him back to the cabin and when Mrs. Sazalisky heard the story, she gave him a hero's welcome. He was placed beside the red-hot stove and fed enormous quantities of steaming goulash. Only when he had begun to burp uncontrollably from the combination of too much heat and too much food, did his hostess desist from filling his plate.

We all made much of him, both then and later when we returned home. Never before had Mutt received such adulation, and he found it good. We could not anticipate it at the time, but when the hunting season rolled around a year later, we were to discover that cows, gophers, and even cats (during the shooting season at least) had been erased forever from his list of loves.

Once Mutt had made up his mind to be a bird dog, there was no further question of his being "trained." Nothing could have been more superfluous than the attempt. If any training was done at all, then it was Father and I who were the trainees. For Mutt soon displayed an incredible array of hidden talents. And if he was completely unorthodox, he was indisputably brilliant in his new career.

The nature of this new Mutt became apparent on opening day of the duck season in the following year.

By coincidence we had returned once more to the slough where Mutt had disgraced himself on his first hunting expedition. That slough, still nameless then, is now renowned to sportsmen throughout the west as Mallard-Pool-Mutt, and this is the tale of how it got its name.

We did not sleep out on this occasion, but drove direct from home, arriving just in time to hurry into the blind before day broke. We had Mutt on a leash, for his exploit at Middle Lake had not completely erased our memory of the debacle which had resulted from his first visit to the slough. We had hopes that he would redeem himself this time—but we were cautious. We even considered the advisability of muzzling him so that he would not scream the ducks away again; but this ignominy would have been too much for him to bear, and we risked his voice.

It was a different dawn, and yet the same as that which we had seen two years before. Once more the red glare of the morning sun fell on the immaculate mirror of the pond; and once more there was a pair of ducks—pintails this time—sleepily dabbling among the long reeds by the shore. The same pungent odor of salt and muck—an odor that is tasted rather than smelled—rose to us on the edgings of gray mist along the borders of the slough. And the same taut expectation lay upon us as we waited for the morning flight.

The flight, too, came as it had done before, and as it had probably done since this slough was born. Out of the northern sky, half lit up now, the sound of its approach was like a rush of wind.

We crouched lower in the blind and my grip tightened warningly on Mutt's collar. Once more I felt him tremble under my hand, and I was vaguely aware that he was making odd little whimpering cries deep in his throat. But my attention was on the approaching flocks.

They came in with a great "whoosh" as the leaders thrust out their feet and struck and shattered the calm surface of the pool. They came in such numbers that it seemed the slough would be too small to hold them all—and still they came.

There was no premature fusillade this time. Father and I were no longer tyros—and Mutt was securely tethered. We stood up together and the crash of the guns echoed like the hint of distant thunder amidst a swirling hurricane of stiff and frantic wings. It was all over in less than a minute. The sky was clear above us and the silence had returned. Out on the slough eight ducks remained, and five of them were greenhead drakes.

Mutt was almost tearing the leash from my hands as we left the blind. "Let him go," my father said. "He can't do any harm now. Let's see what he makes of this."

I slipped the leash. Mutt went through the band of muck and sedge at the water's edge like a kangaroo, in great ungainly leaps. The last jump took him well into deep water, and he began churning forward like an old-fashioned stern-wheeler. There was a wild, almost mad glint in his eyes and he had the look of impetuous resolution about him that belongs naturally to a charging buffalo.

Father and I stared at each other, and then at Mutt, in dumb amaze. But when we saw him reach the first dead bird, snap his teeth in a wing tip, and start for shore with it, we knew that we had found us a retrieving dog.

What Mutt had done up to this point was, of course, no more than any good bird dog would have done. But the events that followed unmistakably presaged the flowering of his unique genius.

The signs were blurred at first, for though he brought the first dead duck to shore all right, he made no attempt to deliver it promptly into our hands. He simply dropped it on the verge and turned at once to make the next retrieve.

However, as long as he brought the ducks to land, we saw no reason to complain—at least we saw no reason until he had retrieved the three dead ducks and had begun work on the remaining five, all of which were still quite active.

Then he began to have difficulties. It took him several minutes to swim-down the first cripple, but eventually he managed to catch it by a wing tip and drag it to shore. He deposited it unceremoniously, and at once leaped back into the water. Hard on his heels, the duck followed suit. Mutt did not notice, for his attention was already fixed on another duck in mid-pond.

It was a very large slough, and very soft and treacherous near the edge. Try as we might, neither Father nor I could manage to be on hand when Mutt brought the cripples in. Neither could we put the wounded birds out of their pain, as we should have liked to do, since we were not able to get within gunshot of them. It was all up to Mutt.

By the time he had retrieved fifteen out of the original eight ducks, he was beginning to grow annoyed. His first fresh enthusiasm was wearing thin, but his brain was beginning to function. The next duck he brought ashore followed the routine already established by it and its fellows and, as soon as Mutt's back was turned, waddled into the pond. This time Mutt kept a wary eye cocked over his shoulder, and he saw that he was being had.

Father and I were at the far end of the pond, and we watched to see how he would react now that he knew the worst. Treading water in mid-pond, he turned and stared at us with a look of mingled scorn and disgust, as if to say: "What on earth's the matter with you? You've got legs, haven't you? Expect me to do *all* the work?"

The situation suddenly struck us as being vastly amusing, and we began to laugh. Mutt never could stand being laughed at, though he enjoyed being laughed with; and he turned his back and began to swim to the far end of the pond. We thought for a moment he had abandoned the ducks and was about to take himself off. We were wrong.

With not so much as another glance in our direction, he swam to the far side of the slough, turned about, and painstakingly began to herd all the crippled ducks toward our end of the pond.

When all of them, save one old greenhead which skillfully evaded the roundup by diving, were within easy shotgun range of our position, Mutt turned and swam nonchalantly away again.

We did our duty, but with a strong feeling of unreality upon us. "Do you think he did that on purpose?" Father asked me in awe-struck tones.

Mutt had now gone back for the remaining mallard. This one was a magnificent drake, perhaps the leader of the flight, and he was cunning with his years. His injury must have been slight, for it was all Mutt could do to close the gap between them. And then, when Mutt was near enough to lunge, his teeth snapped shut on nothing but a mouthful of water. The drake had dived again.

We watched as, three times, the drake evaded capture in this manner, leaving Mutt to swim in aimless circles on the surface.

The old bird chose his water, and stayed well away from shore, for he knew about guns. We concluded finally that this was one duck we would not get, and we decided to call Mutt in.

He was growing very weary. As his coat became increasingly water-logged he swam lower and lower, and his speed diminished to the point where he could just manage to overhaul the drake, and that was all. Nevertheless, he ignored us when we called to him, gently at first, and then in commanding tones. We began to be afraid that, in this willful obstinacy, he would drown himself. Father had already begun to strip off his hunting jacket and boots, ready to effect a rescue, when the incredible thing happened.

Mutt had closed with his quarry for the fifth time. The duck waited, and at the last instant again upended and disappeared.

This time Mutt also disappeared.

A swirl of muddy water marked his passing, and in the center of the swirl there was a whitish blob that twisted back and forth lethargically. I recognized it as the tip of Mutt's tail, held aloft by the remaining buoyancy in his long feathers.

Father was already wading through the muck when my startled yell halted him. Together we stood and stared, and could not credit the reality of what we saw.

Mutt had reappeared. Weed festooned his face, and his eyes were bulging horribly. He gasped for breath and floundered heavily. But between his front teeth was the tip of the drake's wing.

When at last Mutt lay before us, panting and half drowned, we were a humbled and penitent man and boy. I rolled the leash up in my hand and, catching Father's glance, I turned and threw it with all my strength far out into the slough.

It sank with hardly a ripple in the still depths of Mallard-Pool-Mutt.

Gone Wrong

BY P. G. WODEHOUSE

BORN AND EDUCATED in England, P(elham) G(renville) Wodehouse made a lifetime career of spoofing the British aristocracy. "He maintained his enormous popularity with nearly 100 novels depicting amusing characters in absurd and intricate situations," according to informed sources. Maybe the best known of his large cast of hilariously bumbling Brits were the useless Bertie Wooster and his most capable butler, Jeeves.

He brought us a fine eye and ear, was highly observant, and had the ability to deflate artifice with a few well-placed words. As a longtime resident of the United States, he occasionally directed his gaze at American quirks. His tale of the dog who "went Hollywood" was written while he was living in Hollywood, working as a scriptwriter. It is a Wodehouse gem, displaying in a few short pages his talent for making us laugh by pointing out the sham.

★　★　★　★　★

HOLLYWOOD IS A GOOD place for dogs. At least, when I say Hollywood, I mean Beverly Hills. Hollywood itself is a noisome spot, where no self-respecting dog would live, but Beverly Hills is different. It is an oasis in a rather depressing countryside, consisting of a series of parallel roads with nice houses dotted along at intervals. Each house has a lawn in front of it, running unfenced down to the pavement, and on each lawn sits a dog. And, as you pass, each dog comes down to the edge of its lawn and chats with you.

Stiffy, when I first saw him, was not on his lawn. He was out in the road, dodging a motor and laughing his head off. Presently he came trotting back, took a sniff at me, decided that I smelled all right, and became friendly.

Stiffy was a sort of bull-terrier, with variations. His hind legs were pure black, his body white with a few black stripes. He looked like a member of some football club, and he was as charming and unaffected a dog as I have ever met. As nobody in this motor-ridden place ever takes a dog for a walk, for nobody ever goes for a walk, he was delighted to meet a genuine pedestrian. He came with me all the way to Wilshire Boulevard, which involved my carrying him across three crowded streets, and from that day there were no reserves between us.

He was a mine of gossip about the neighbors. It was Stiffy who, by telling me the secret in the life of the Peke at 1005 Benedict Canyon Drive, enabled me to get the goods on the latter and force him to treat me as an equal. It seems that this Peke, though outwardly a tough egg and standing no nonsense from postmen, tradesmen and the like, is not really the terror he appears on the surface.

A week or so ago, the Peke's mistress went away for a holiday, and the Peke, as usual, slept in her room. At seven the next morning it occurred to the master of the house to go in and see how he was getting on. It is the habit of the master of the house, on going to bed, to tie a black bandage over his eyes in order to keep the light from them. This bandage he omitted to remove, with the result that the Peke, seeing a masked stranger entering, uttered one panic-stricken howl and shot under the bed, from which it required all the persuasion of the entire household to remove him.

"Gave me a good laugh, that did," said Stiffy.

It was he, too, who told me of the Sealyham at No. 415 rolling in the box of toffee and getting it all over the curtains. In short, if there was one dog of my acquaintance on whom I felt I could rely for real companionship, it was Stiffy. Always absolutely himself. Never an ounce of side about him.

And then one morning the tragedy burst upon me. Without warning, too, which made it all the worse.

I was on my way down to the village for tobacco; and, passing Stiffy's lawn and seeing him curled up on it, I yoo-hooed to him without a second thought. I was particularly anxious to pass the time of day, for I had seen nothing of him for some weeks. For some reason, his lawn had always been empty when I had come by.

So I shouted to him, and then a strange thing happened. Usually, on these occasions, he would leap across the lawn in two bounds and be licking my face before you could say "What ho!" But now he scarcely moved. As he heard my voice, he raised his head slowly, opened his eyes very wide, turned his head so that his profile was exposed to an imaginary camera, and, having held the position for a moment, relaxed again. Finally he rose, and, walking in an abominably affected way, came mincing towards me.

"Hullo, Stiffy," I said.

His manner was cold.

"*Mister* Stiffy, I prefer to be called," he replied. "That," he went on with an ill-assumed carelessness, "is how Izzy always addresses me."

"Izzy?"

"Isadore Wertheimer, the production manager of the Bigger and Better."

"Bigger and Better what?" I asked, perplexed.

"Studio, of course, you poor chump," he snapped, in a rather more natural tone. "I'm with the B. and B. now."

"You are?" I said weakly.

He yawned.

"Yes," he said. "Doing a picture with Clarry."

"Clarry?"

"Clara Svelte. A nice little thing. I could wish no better support. I see no reason why I should not use her in my next, unless this girl Garbo is as good as they say. I am having Greta watched closely, with a view to taking her on. That Swedish accent is a bit of a drawback, of course, but I could carry her. And now, my dear fellow," said Stiffy, "I know you will excuse me. I have to save my voice. And my man will be along in a moment with the car to take me to the lot. So glad to have seen you."

He nodded distantly and curled up in a ball. And I walked on.

I started this article by saying that Hollywood is a good place for dogs. I have changed my mind. As far as the climate and surroundings go, it may be excellent, but there are always those fatal studios in the background; and, since that wire-haired terrier made such a hit in Ronald Colman's last picture, the executives are beginning to consider a canine interest essential to a film. They have spoiled Stiffy. It is perfectly sickening to see that dog now. A few days ago

I was present when a friendly Aberdeen trotted up to fraternize with him, and I have never witnessed anything more repulsive than the way in which he registered Aristocratic Disdain.

However, I am told that his contract runs out next month. If it is not renewed, the old Stiffy may return.

The Bloodhounds of Broadway

BY DAMON RUNYON

THE QUINTESSENTIAL NEW YORKER, the biographer of Broadway, the columnist who kept tens of millions of people informed about "what's playin' at the Roxy," was indeed born in Manhattan—Kansas—and grew up in Pueblo, Colorado. Nonetheless, he had his finger on the pulse of the Big Apple, kept America delighted and amused at the trials and tribulations of a host of innovatively named characters in his daily newspaper column, and wrote the story for one of Broadway's finest musicals, *Guys and Dolls.*

Finally, Runyon turned his talents toward dogs, and we are graced with the sight of bloodhounds running down Broadway.

★ ★ ★ ★ ★

ONE MORNING ALONG ABOUT four bells, I am standing in front of Mindy's restaurant on Broadway with a guy by the name of Regret, who has this name because it seems he wins a very large bet the year the Whitney filly, Regret, grabs the Kentucky Derby, and can never forget it, which is maybe because it is the only very large bet he ever wins in his life.

What this guy's real name is I never hear, and anyway names make no difference to me, especially on Broadway, because the chances are that no matter what name a guy has, it is not his square name. So, as far as I am concerned, Regret is as good a name as any other for this guy I am talking about, who is a fat guy, and very gabby, though generally he is talking about nothing but horses, and how he gets beat three dirty noses the day before at Belmont, or wherever the horses are running.

In all the years I know Regret he must get beat ten thousand noses, and always they are dirty noses, to hear him tell it. In fact, I never once hear him say he is beat a clean nose, but of course this is only the way horse racing guys talk. What Regret does for a living besides betting on horses I do not know, but he seems to do pretty well at it, because he is always around and about, and generally well dressed, and with a lot of big cigars sticking up out of his vest pocket.

It is generally pretty quiet on Broadway along about four bells in the morning, because at such an hour the citizens are mostly in speak-easies, and night clubs, and on this morning I am talking about it is very quiet, indeed, except for a guy by the name of Marvin Clay hollering at a young doll because she will not get into a taxicab with him to go to his apartment. But of course Regret and I do not pay much attention to such a scene, except that Regret remarks that the young doll seems to have more sense than you will expect to see in a doll loose on Broadway at four bells in the morning, because it is well known to one and all that any doll who goes to Marvin Clay's apartment, either has no brains whatever, or wishes to go there.

This Marvin Clay is a very prominent society guy, who is a great hand for hanging out in night clubs, and he has plenty of scratch which comes down to him from his old man, who makes it out of railroads and one thing and another. But Marvin Clay is a most obnoxious character, being loud and ungentlemanly at all times, on account of having all this scratch, and being always very rough and abusive with young dolls such as work in night clubs, and who have to stand for such treatment from Marvin Clay because he is a very good customer.

He is generally in evening clothes, as he is seldom around and about except in the evening, and he is maybe fifty years old, and has a very ugly mugg, which is covered with blotches, and pimples, but of course a guy who has as much scratch as Marvin Clay does not have to be so very handsome, at that, and he is very welcome indeed wherever he goes on Broadway. Personally, I wish no part of such a guy as Marvin Clay, although I suppose in my time on Broadway I must see a thousand guys like him, and there will always be guys like Marvin Clay on Broadway as long as they have old men to make plenty of scratch out of railroads to keep them going.

Well, by and by Marvin Clay gets the doll in the taxicab, and away they go, and it is all quiet again on Broadway, and Regret and I stand there speaking of this and that, and one thing and another, when along comes a very strange looking guy leading two very strange looking dogs. The guy is so thin I figure he must be about two pounds lighter than a stack of wheats. He has a long nose, and a sad face, and he is wearing a floppy old black felt hat, and he has on a flannel shirt, and baggy corduroy pants, and a see-more coat, which is a coat that lets you see more hip pockets than coat.

Personally, I never see a stranger looking guy on Broadway, and I wish to say I see some very strange looking guys on Broadway in my day. But if the guy is strange looking, the dogs are even stranger looking, because they have big heads, and jowls that hang down like an old-time faro bank dealer's, and long ears the size of bed sheets. Furthermore, they have wrinkled faces, and big, round eyes that seem so sad I half expect to see them bust out crying.

The dogs are a sort of black and yellow in color, and have long tails, and they are so thin you can see their ribs sticking out of their hides. I can see at once that the dogs and the guy leading them can use a few Hamburgers very nicely, but then so can a lot of other guys on Broadway at this time, leaving out the dogs.

Well, Regret is much interested in the dogs right away, because he is a guy who is very fond of animals of all kinds, and nothing will do but he must stop the guy and start asking questions about what sort of dogs they are, and in fact I am also anxious to hear myself, because while I see many a pooch in my time I never see anything like these.

"They is bloodhounds," the sad looking guy says in a very sad voice, and with one of these accents such as Southern guys always have. "They is man-tracking bloodhounds from Georgia."

Now of course both Regret and me know what bloodhounds are because we see such animals chasing Eliza across the ice in Uncle Tom's Cabin
when we are young squirts, but this is the first time either of us meet up with
any bloodhounds personally, especially on Broadway. So we get to talking quite
a bit to the guy, and his story is as sad as his face, and makes us both feel very
sorry for him.

In fact, the first thing we know we have him and the bloodhounds in
Mindy's and are feeding one and all big steaks, although Mindy puts up an
awful squawk about us bringing the dogs in, and asks us what we think he is
running, anyway. When Regret starts to tell him, Mindy says never mind, but
not to bring any more Shetland ponies into his joint again as long as we live.

Well, it seems that the sad looking guy's name is John Wangle, and he
comes from a town down in Georgia where his uncle is the high sheriff, and
one of the bloodhounds' name is Nip, and the other is Tuck, and they are both
trained from infancy to track down guys such as lags who escape from the
county pokey . . . and one thing and another, and after John Wangle gets the
kinks out of his belly on Mindy's steaks, and starts talking good, you must either figure him a high class liar, or the hounds the greatest man-trackers the
world ever sees.

Now, looking at the dogs after they swallow six big sirloins apiece, and
a lot of matzoths, which Mindy has left over from the Jewish holidays, and a
joblot of goulash from the dinner bill, and some other odds and ends, the best I
can figure them is hearty eaters, because they are now lying down on the floor
with their faces hidden behind their ears, and are snoring so loud you can
scarcely hear yourself think.

How John Wangle comes to be in New York with these bloodhounds
is quite a story, indeed. It seems that a New York guy drifts into John's old
home town in Georgia when the bloodhounds are tracking . . . and this guy
figures it will be a wonderful idea to take John Wangle and the dogs to New
York and hire them out to the movies to track down the villains in the pictures. But when they get to New York, it seems that movies have other
arrangements for tracking down their villains, and the guy runs out of scratch
and blows away, leaving John Wangle and the bloodhounds stranded.

So here John Wangle is with Nip and Tuck in New York, and they are
all living together in one room in a tenement house over in West Forty-ninth
Street, and things are pretty tough with them, because John does not know
how to get back to Georgia unless he walks, and he hears the walking is no
good south of Roanoke. When I ask him why he does not write to his uncle,

the high sheriff down there in Georgia, John Wangle says there are two reasons, one being that he cannot write, and the other that his uncle cannot read.

Then I ask him why he does not sell the bloodhounds, and he says it is because the market for bloodhounds is very quiet in New York, and furthermore if he goes back to Georgia without the bloodhounds, his uncle is apt to knock his ears down. Anyway, John Wangle says he personally loves Nip and Tuck very dearly, and in fact he says it is only his great love for them that keeps him from eating one or the other, and maybe both, the past week, when his hunger is very great indeed.

Well, I never before see Regret so much interested in any situation as he is in John Wangle and the bloodhounds, but personally I am getting very tired of them, because the one that is called Nip finally wakes up and starts chewing on my leg, thinking it is maybe more steak, and when I kick him in the snoot, John Wangle scowls at me, and Regret says only very mean guys are unkind to dumb animals.

But to show you that John Wangle and his bloodhounds are not so dumb, they come moseying along past Mindy's every morning after this at about the same time, and Regret is always there ready to feed them, although he now has to take the grub out on the sidewalk, as Mindy will not allow the hounds in the joint again. Naturally Nip and Tuck become very fond of Regret, but they are by no means as fond of him as John Wangle, because John is commencing to fat up very nicely, and the bloodhounds are also taking on weight.

Now what happens but Regret does not show up in front of Mindy's for several mornings hand running, because it seems that Regret makes a very nice score for himself one day against the horses, and buys himself a brand new Tuxedo, and starts stepping out around the night clubs, and especially around Miss Missouri Martin's Three Hundred Club, where there are many beautiful young dolls who dance around with no more clothes on them than will make a pad for a crutch, and it is well known that Regret dearly loves such scenes.

Furthermore, I hear reports around and about of Regret becoming very fond of a doll by the name of Miss Lovey Lou, who works in Miss Missouri Martin's Three Hundred Club, and of him getting in some kind of a jam with Marvin Clay over this doll, and smacking Marvin Clay in the kisser, so I figure Regret is getting a little simple, as guys who hang around Broadway long enough are bound to do. Now, when John Wangle and Nip and Tuck come around looking for a handout, there is nothing much doing for them, as nobody else around Mindy's feels any great interest in bloodhounds, especially such interest as will cause them to buy steaks, and soon Nip and Tuck are commencing to look very sad again, and John Wangle is downcast more than somewhat.

It is early morning again, and warm, and a number of citizens are out in front of Mindy's as usual, breathing the fresh air, when along comes a police inspector by the name of McNamara, who is a friend of mine, with a bunch of plain clothes coppers with him, and Inspector McNamara tells me he is on his way to investigate a situation in an apartment house over in West Fifty-fourth Street, about three blocks away, where it seems a guy is shot, and not having anything else to do, I go with them, although as a rule I do not care to associate with coppers, because it arouses criticism from other citizens.

Well, who is the guy who is shot but Marvin Clay, and he is stretched out on the floor in the living room of his apartment in evening clothes, with his shirt front covered with blood, and after Inspector McNamara takes a close peek at him, he sees that Marvin Clay is plugged smack dab in the chest, and that he seems to be fairly dead. Furthermore, there seems to be no clue whatever to who does the shooting, and Inspector McNamara says it is undoubtedly a very great mystery, and will be duck soup for the newspapers, especially as they do not have a good shooting mystery for several days.

Well, of course all this is none of my business, but all of a sudden I happen to think of John Wangle and his bloodhounds, and it seems to me it will be a great opportunity for them, so I say to the Inspector as follows:

"Listen, Mac," I say, "there is a guy here with a pair of man-tracking bloodhounds from Georgia who are very expert in tracking down matters such as this, and," I say, "maybe they can track down the rascal who shoots Marvin Clay, because the trail must be hotter than mustard right now."

Well, afterwards I hear there is much indignation over my suggestion, because many citizens feel that the party who shoots Marvin Clay is entitled to more consideration than being tracked with bloodhounds. In fact, some think the party is entitled to a medal, but this discussion does not come up until later.

Anyway, at first the Inspector does not think much of my idea, and the other coppers are very skeptical, and claim that the best way to do under the circumstances is to arrest everybody in sight and hold them as material witnesses for a month or so, but the trouble is there is nobody in sight to arrest at this time, except maybe me, and the Inspector is a broad-minded guy, and finally he says all right, bring on the bloodhounds.

So I hasten back to Mindy's, and sure enough John Wangle and Nip and Tuck are out on the sidewalk peering at every passing face in the hope that maybe one of these faces will belong to Regret. It is a very pathetic sight, indeed, but John Wangle cheers up when I explain about Marvin Clay to him, and hurries back to the apartment house with me so fast that he stretches Nip's neck a foot, and is pulling Tuck along on his stomach half the time.

Well, when we get back to the apartment, John Wangle leads Nip and Tuck up to Marvin Clay, and they snuffle him all over, because it seems bloodhounds are quite accustomed to dead guys. Then John Wangle unhooks their leashes, and yells something at them, and the hounds begin snuffling all around and about the joint, with Inspector McNamara and the other coppers watching with great interest. All of a sudden Nip and Tuck go busting out of the apartment and into the street, with John Wangle after them, and all the rest of us after John Wangle. They head across Fifty-fourth Street back to Broadway, and the next thing anybody knows they are doing plenty of snuffling around in front of Mindy's.

By and by they take off up Broadway with their snozzles to the sidewalk, and we follow them very excited, because even the coppers now admit that it seems to be a sure thing they are red hot on the trail of the party who shoots Marvin Clay. At first Nip and Tuck are walking, but pretty soon they break into a lope, and there we are loping after them, John Wangle, the Inspector, and me, and the coppers.

Naturally, such a sight as this attracts quite some attention as we go along from any citizens stirring at this hour, and by and by milkmen are climbing down off their wagons, and scavenger guys are leaving their trucks standing where they are, and newsboys are dropping everything, and one and all joining in the chase, so by the time we hit Broadway and Fifty-sixth there is quite a delegation following the hounds with John Wangle in front, just behind Nip and Tuck, and yelling at them now and then as follows:

"Hold to it, boys!"

At Fifty-sixth the hounds turn east off Broadway and stop at the door of what seems to be an old garage, this door being closed very tight, and Nip and Tuck seem to wish to get through this door, so the Inspector and the coppers kick the door open, and who is in the garage having a big crap game but many prominent citizens of Broadway. Naturally, these citizens are greatly astonished at seeing the bloodhounds, and the rest of us, especially the coppers, and they start running every which way trying to get out of the joint, because crap shooting is quite illegal in these parts.

But the Inspector only says Ah-ha, and starts jotting down names in a note book as if it is something he will refer to later, and Nip and Tuck are out of the joint almost as soon as they get in and are snuffling on down Fifty-sixth.

They stop at four more doors in Fifty-sixth Street along, and when the coppers kick open these doors they find they are nothing but speakeasies, although one is a hop joint, and the citizens in these places are greatly put out by the excitement, especially as Inspector McNamara keeps jotting down things in his note book.

Finally the Inspector starts glaring very fiercely at the coppers with us, and anybody can see that he is much displeased to find so much illegality going on in this district, and the coppers are starting in to hate Nip and Tuck quite freely, and one copper says to me like this:

"Why," he says, "these mutts are nothing but stool pigeons."

Well, naturally, the noise of John Wangle's yelling, and the gabble of the mob following the hounds makes quite a disturbance, and arouses many of the neighbors in the apartment houses and hotels in the side streets, especially as this is summer, and most everybody has their windows open.

In fact, we see many touseled heads poked out of window, and hear guys and dolls inquiring as follows:

"What is going on?"

It seems that when word gets about that bloodhounds are tracking down a wrongdoer it causes great uneasiness all through the Fifties, and in fact I afterwards hear that three guys are taken to the Polyclinic suffering with broken ankles and severe bruises from hopping out of windows in the hotels we pass in the chase, or from falling off of fire escapes.

Well, all of a sudden Nip and Tuck swing back into Seventh Avenue, and pop into the entrance of a small apartment house, and go tearing up the stairs to the first floor, and when we get there these bloodhounds are scratching vigorously at the door of Apartment B-2, and going woofle-woofle, and we are all greatly excited, indeed, but the door opens, and who is standing there but a doll by the name of Maud Milligan, who is well known to one and all as the ever-loving doll of Big Nig, the crap shooter, who is down in Hot Springs at this time taking the waters, or whatever it is guys take in Hot Springs.

Now, Maud Milligan is not such a doll as I will care to have any part of, being red-headed, and very stern, and I am glad Nip and Tuck do not waste any more time in her apartment than it takes for them to run through her living room and across her bed, because Maud is commencing to put the old eye on such of us present as she happens to know. But Nip and Tuck are in and out of the joint before you can say scat, because it is only a two-room apartment, at that, and we on our way down the stairs and back into Seventh Avenue again while Inspector McNamara is still jotting down something in his note book.

Finally where do these hounds wind up, with about four hundred citizens behind them, and everybody perspiring quite freely indeed from the exercise, but at the door of Miss Missouri Martin's Three Hundred Club, and the doorman, who is a guy by the name of Soldier Sweeney, tries to shoo them away, but Nip runs between the Soldier's legs and upsets him, and Tuck steps in the Soldier's eye in trotting over him, and most of the crowd behind the hounds tread on him in passing, so the old Soldier is pretty well flattened out at the finish.

Nip and Tuck are now more excited than somewhat, and are going zoople-zoople in loud voices as they bust into the Three Hundred Club with John Wangle and the law, and all these citizens behind them. There is a very large crowd present and Miss Missouri Martin is squatted on the back of a chair in the middle of the dance floor when we enter, and is about to start her show when she sees the mob surge in, and at first she is greatly pleased because she thinks new business arrives, and if there is anything Miss Missouri Martin dearly loves, it is new business.

But before she can say hello, sucker, or anything else whatever, Nip runs under her chair, thinking maybe he is a dachshund, and dumps Miss Missouri Martin on the dance floor, and she lays there squawking no little, while the next thing anybody knows, Nip and Tuck are over in one corner of the joint, and are eagerly crawling up and down a fat guy who is sitting there with a doll alongside of him, and who is the fat guy but Regret!

Well, as Nip and Tuck rush at Regret he naturally gets up to defend himself, but they both hit him at the same time, and over he goes on top of the doll who is with him, and who seems to be nobody but Miss Lovey Lou. She is getting quite a squashing with Regret's heft spread out over her, and she is screaming quite some, especially when Nip lets out a foot of tongue and washes her make-up off her face, reaching for Regret. In fact, Miss Lovey Lou seems to be more afraid of the bloodhounds than she does of being squashed to death, for when John Wangle and I hasten to her rescue and pull her out from under Regret she is moaning as follows:

"Oh, do not let them devour me—I will confess."

Well, as nobody but me and John Wangle seem to hear this crack, because everybody else is busy trying to split out Regret and the bloodhounds, and as John Wangle does not seem to understand what Miss Lovey Lou is mumbling about, I shove her off into the crowd, and on back into the kitchen, which is now quite deserted, what with all the help being out watching the muss in the corner, and I say to her like this:

"What is it you confess?" I say. "Is it about Marvin Clay?"

"Yes," she says. "It is about him. He is a pig," she says. "I shoot him, and I am glad of it. He is not satisfied with what he does to me two years ago, but he tries his deviltry on my baby sister. He has her in his apartment and when I find it out and go to get her, he says he will not let her go. So I shoot him. With my brother's pistol," she says, "and I take my baby sister home with me, and I hope he is dead, and gone where he belongs."

"Well, now," I say, "I am not going to give you any argument as to where Marvin Clay belongs, but," I say, "you skip out of here and go on home, and wait until we can do something about this situation, while I go back and help Regret, who seems to be in a tough spot."

"Oh, do not let these terrible dogs eat him up," she says, and with this she takes the breeze and I return to the other room to find there is much confusion, indeed, because it seems that Regret is now very indignant at Nip and Tuck, especially when he discovers that one of them plants his big old paw right on the front of Regret's shirt bosom, leaving a dirty mark. So when he struggles to his feet, Regret starts letting go with both hands, and he is by no means a bad puncher for a guy who does not do much punching as a rule. In fact, he flattens Nip with a right hand to the jaw, and knocks Tuck plumb across the room with a left hook.

Well, poor Tuck slides over the slick dance floor into Miss Missouri Martin just as she is getting to her feet again, and bowls her over once more, but Miss Missouri Martin is also indignant by this time, and she gets up and kicks Tuck in a most unladylike manner. Of course, Tuck does not know so much about Miss Martin, but he is pretty sure his old friend Regret is only playing with him, so back he goes to Regret with his tongue out, and his tail wagging, and there is no telling how long this may go on if John Wangle does not step in and grab both hounds, while Inspector McNamara puts the arm on Regret and tells him he is under arrest for shooting Marvin Clay.

Well, of course everybody can see at once that Regret must be the guilty party all right, especially when it is remembered that he once has trouble with Marvin Clay, and one and all present are looking at Regret in great disgust, and saying you can see by his face that he is nothing but a degenerate type.

Furthermore, Inspector McNamara makes a speech to Miss Missouri Martin's customers in which he congratulates John Wangle and Nip and Tuck on their wonderful work in tracking down this terrible criminal, and at the same time putting in a few boosts for the police department, while Regret stands there paying very little attention to what the Inspector is saying, but trying to edge himself over close enough to Nip and Tuck to give them the old foot.

Well, the customers applaud what Inspector McNamara says, and Miss Missouri Martin gets up a collection of over two C's for John Wangle and his hounds, not counting what she holds out for herself. Also the chef comes forward and takes John Wangle and Nip and Tuck back into the kitchen, and stuffs them full of food, although personally I will just as soon not have any of the food they serve in the Three Hundred Club.

They take Regret to the jail house, and he does not seem to understand why he is under arrest, but he knows it has something to do with Nip and Tuck and he tries to bribe one of the coppers to put the bloodhounds in the same cell with him for awhile, though naturally the copper will not consider such a proposition. While Regret is being booked at the jail house, word comes around that Marvin Clay is not only not dead, but the chances are he will get well, which he finally does, at that.

Moreover, he finally bails Regret out, and not only refuses to prosecute him but skips the country as soon as he is able to move, although Regret lays in the sneezer for several weeks, at that, never letting on after he learns the real situation that he is not the party who plugs Marvin Clay. Naturally, Miss Lovey Lou is very grateful to Regret for his wonderful sacrifice, and will no doubt become his ever-loving wife in a minute, if Regret thinks to ask her, but it seems Regret finds himself brooding so much over the idea of an ever-loving wife who is so handy with a roscoe that he never really asks.

In the meantime, John Wangle and Nip and Tuck go back to Georgia on the dough collected by Miss Missouri Martin, and with a big reputation as man-trackers. So this is all there is to the story, except that one night I run into Regret with a suit case in his hand, and he is perspiring very freely, although it is not so hot, at that, and when I ask him if he is going away, he says this is indeed his general idea. Moreover, he says he is going very far away. Naturally, I ask him why this is, and Regret says to me as follows:

"Well," he says, "ever since Big Nig, the crap shooter, comes back from Hot Springs, and hears how the bloodhounds track the shooter of Marvin Clay, he is walking up and down looking at me out of the corner of his eye. In fact," Regret says, "I can see that Big Nig is studying something over in his mind, and while Big Nig is a guy who is not such a fast thinker as others, I am afraid he may finally think himself to a bad conclusion.

"I am afraid," Regret says, "that Big Nig will think himself to the conclusion that Nip and Tuck are tracking me instead of the shooter, as many evilminded guys are already whispering around and about, and that he may get the wrong idea about the trail leading to Maud Milligan's door."

How to Raise a Dog

BY JACK ALAN

F ROM BLANCHE SAUNDERS'S THEORIES to the monks of Skete and their ideas, it's easy to find books on training your dog. After all, there are thousands of them out there. Rewards, reinforcement, let-'em-figure-it-out-themselves: doggie psychiatrists and behavioral "experts" will happily put you on the right path. Theirs.

Jack Alan has another approach—he let his dog train *him*. And it seems to be working very nicely. Next thing you know, we'll be seeing a book from Gilbert.

★ ★ ★ ★ ★

DOG OWNERS, ARISE! Too long has the actual head of your family not even paid an income tax. Too long have you tried to conceal from your dog the fact that he really owns you. Too long have you searched in vain for the counsel you so sorely need when, panting and tongue hanging out, you fall back into the nearest chair and finally admit to yourself that the lively little fellow isn't going to sit up and beg, hasn't the slightest intention of leaving that frayed end of the tapestry alone, and is unshakeably convinced that the mathematical center of the living-room rug is the Comfort Station Supreme.

You can expect no help from dog books or dog doctors. In this all-important emergency, all they do is back away, muttering incoherent statements about Training and Psychology. And you are left holding the bag, one end of which has already been chewed away, like everything else you own.

I am no expert. I might as well tell you right now that I generally go to sleep with a large, greasy bone under my pillow because I have failed to sway my dog in his opinion that there isn't a better spot in town for bone hiding. My house is thoroughly dog-broken. But I do not intend to leave my fellow man with his dog having the upper paw in the household.

I believe my predicament to be an average one, a valuable case history. I will show you how I deal with my dog. Maybe you will be able to discover where along the line something went terribly, terribly wrong.

Things started badly when I bought him. I didn't select him, he selected me. When I went to the kennel, I had decided definitely against buying four or five puppies, as I wanted to do. Phyllis claims that this is too many for a small apartment. Cunningly, however, I planned to get around this by getting as much dog as possible for my money—a Great Dane.

I looked critically at the batch of puppies, which, while only three months old, were the size of Airedales. Then one detached himself from the mob. He had a lot of filling out to do. He took, I noticed, several steps before his skin started moving along with him. He galloped over, sat down heavily on my feet, and looked me over carefully. I couldn't move, so I had to look at him, too. He was obviously admiring me. His next step was to take my trouser leg in his mouth and shake it, possibly to test the quality of the material. Then he gave several pleased body wiggles, attempted to climb up on me, and washed my hand thoroughly with a salmon-pink tongue. Then he sat down again on my feet and admired me some more.

I had been chosen.

Several months have passed, and we have learned much about each other. Neither of us regrets his choice, although my training methods seem to lack something.

I have found that the very first step must be to Gain His Confidence. To accomplish this, I sit on the floor next to him and say, "*Good* little dog!" This is a flat lie and he knows it, being well aware that he is neither little nor good. He backs away several feet, presses himself close to the floor, and turns up his eyes at me with a wary "You-are-up-to-something-tricky-and-I'm-not-going-to-like-it" expression.

I reach out reassuringly and pat his nearest paw. He withdraws the paw and licks it off fastidiously.

I attempt now to get his attention by cupping both hands and saying coyly: "Guess what I've got here?"

Showing signs of interest, he nuzzles into my hands. I am caught flat-footed with nothing in them. I run to get a dog biscuit to absolve myself. Meanwhile he stalks off bitterly to a corner of the room, tenses his forelegs, digs a hole in the carpet, and lies down in it.

I now change my approach, deciding to try the Great Big Playmate tactic. Crouching on all fours, I advance on him, barking several times with mock ferocity. He decides to humor me by pretending he thinks I'm a huge, dangerous dog. With a happy yelp, he flashes around a chair and dashes upon me from behind. Since he weighs roughly eighty-two pounds at the moment, I am now flat on the floor with him on top of me. He wants to pretend he is shaking me by the neck. This is too difficult unless he actually does shake me by the back of the neck. So he does.

I get up and brush myself off. I brush him off me, too, several times. I have now succeeded in gaining his confidence and showing him that I am a regular fellow who doesn't mind a good, clean romp, so I am through. But he isn't. He likes it too well to quit. He gets my tie in his teeth and hangs from it. It is some time before I get my breath.

He still refuses to stop. It is therefore time for me to Punish Him. I decide to lock him in the bathroom. This consists of the following steps:

1. He instantly senses my purpose and scrambles into the bedroom and under the bed.
2. I rush after him and say, "Come out from under there this minute!"
3. He doesn't.

4. I get down on the floor and look under the bed. We face each other. I blink, which gives him the round.
5. I mutter several dire threats. So does he.
6. I hold out my handkerchief, hoping he will grab it and pull, thereby enabling me to drag him out.
7. He grabs it and pulls.
8. We are now both under the bed.
9. I seize him firmly and wriggle out.
10. A head bumps severely against the box spring. It is not his.
11. I shove and pull him into the bathroom and back out, closing the door.
12. I stop closing the door to avoid catching his nose in it.
13. I shove him back and close the door, catching my hand in it.
14. We both howl simultaneously.

Returning to the living room, tired but victorious (look up Pyrrhic in any good encyclopedia), I now proceed to describe my dog to you. He is still a puppy, seven months old. He is a good dog to have for a case history because, although a thoroughbred, he has a character which is practically a cross section of that of America's dogs.

Although large and getting larger, it is his opinion that he is a lapdog and as such entitled to climb on my chair whether I am in it or not. When I can catch him to give him a bath, he emerges as a dull gold in color with a mouth fringed with black. This mouth is already large enough to contain my arm and, when I am giving him a bath, does. Like all his breed, he has a short coat, but he sheds it with the success of the collie. He has a way of searching out tidbits in his food which probably reveals that in spite of his pedigree he contains a trace of ant-eater. He has a beery sort of baritone. And he is very democratic in his ideas about love.

When I first got him I called him Gilbert, the name I still introduce him by. The only word he will always answer to, however, is Food, so I generally call him that.

Food, or Gilbert, is still in the bathroom, you will recall. This is my golden opportunity to get something to eat unbeknownst to him. Let me explain.

Since I have known Gilbert, I have had few square meals at home. This is because Gilbert is an adept at a quiet, effective sort of bullying. When I am eating, he is too wily to use strong-arm tactics, realizing that force will be answered with force. He therefore just looks at me tragically. He keeps looking at me. He meditates on man's inhumanity to dog. He sighs. Beginning to feel like a heartless gourmand, I transfer my little morsel of food to my mouth. His glance never wavers. He drools slowly.

As a result, I spend a large part of my time at my dinner table chewing things up a little for Gilbert. Then I give them to him, cursing.

But now that Gilbert is in the bathroom, I turn on the radio full blast and enter the kitchen singing loudly, hoping that both noises will distract him.

It is a losing game. Gilbert, who would sleep soundly through a collision with another planet, easily detects the noiseless opening of the electric icebox. No sooner do I reach a guilty hand to a roast-beef bone than Gilbert utters a series of agonized cries, giving the entire neighborhood the impression that I am murdering him by inches. In self-defense I rush to the bathroom to make him stop.

He is very happy as I open the door, particularly since a well-timed move enables him to snatch the beef bone from my hand and rush back to the bathroom.

I am about to follow him to get back my bone when the doorbell rings.

It is Mrs. Garble, a middle-aged woman I do not like. She is the president of Phyllis' club. She is also a cat lover. She expresses relief at being able to come in for once and not have that great brute of a dog jumping all over her. Looking nervously, she asks where he is. I tell her.

"What in the world is he doing in the bathroom?" she says.

"Well, really, Mrs. Garble," I reply primly, "he *said* he wanted to wash his hands."

This keeps her quiet for a moment. It then develops that she wants to see Phyllis, who isn't home. She looks at the carpet, which has no more than a normal amount of Gilbert's hair on it.

"Goodness gracious!" she says, clucking, "I don't see *how* you can keep a great Dane in a city apartment! Why, I'd just as soon keep a horse in one!"

I bristle and stifle a desire to say, "Oh, so you don't think I ought to keep my horse, either?"

Gilbert chooses this moment to enter. And not, to my surprise, with his usual attitude, which practically says, "Oh my chin and whiskers! What wonderful things have I been missing!" Instead, he comes in with measured dignity. He casts a sedate glance at Mrs. Garble.

"He seems to be getting much better manners," she says grudgingly. "You certainly are training him to behave like a gentleman!"

I decide that Mrs. Garble, too, seems to be getting better manners. I warm toward her, as I do to all types of characters who have a kind word to say for Gilbert. I even toy with the idea of giving her a drink.

I watch with paternal pride as Gilbert walks slowly over to her. He sniffs at her leg in a genteel way. I beam reassuringly. Mrs. Garble smiles back uncertainly. Gilbert seems about to walk past her. He doesn't. He stops. Trained to observe such matters, I suddenly notice an uncertain attitude, a slight quivering of the muscles of Gilbert's left hind leg.

"GILBERT!" I cry, in the nick of time.

There is no need to go into the next five minutes. It will serve no purpose for me to repeat my weak explanation to the outraged Mrs. Garble that Gilbert, being still in the experimental stage, was merely about to test out a comparatively new idea. And that there was no personal malice or intended criticism involved.

Gilbert and I are alone again—and it is definitely time for me to Take Him Out.

Gilbert *loves* to go out. Five, seven times a day he responds with mad joy to the rattle of his chain, dances with impatience as I attach his collar, and, in a series of chamoislike bounds, precipitates me to our apartment elevator, permitting me to touch the corridor with my feet only intermittently on the way.

If Gilbert is in luck, there will be another passenger in the elevator. This is a stout, very short gentleman with a red face who lives on the floor above us. He is generally on his way to some formal affair. There is something about his frock coats and silk hats which brings out Gilbert's warmest feelings of affection.

It takes Gilbert no time at all to place both his paws on the little man's carefully groomed shoulders. Gilbert's tongue then quickly and deftly leaves a long moist streak from chin to forehead, as Gilbert's body deposits large amounts of hair on the faultless apparel.

The little man's face now becomes even redder, because he does not Understand Dogs. I know he doesn't, because the very first time this occurred, I said to him reassuringly, "It's all right, he is friendly."

To which he replied: "I'm not."

Since then all we say to each other is "Look out!"

Once we have left the elevator and passed through the lobby—a passage too swift for the average vision—Gilbert and I find ourselves outside. It is now that my problems begin and Gilbert's end. This is because we spend a lot of time standing by trees, lampposts, and pillars. It is not the fact that Gilbert is generally standing on one more leg than I am which makes my position more difficult than his. It is rather that I am far more conscious than he of the famous girls' finishing school on our block. Since its dismissal times seem to coincide with our airings, it bothers me to feel that there are hundreds of pretty young girls in the world who believe I spend my entire time standing by upright columns.

It is therefore frequently necessary for me to pretend that I do not know Gilbert. This is difficult, because of the stout chain which connects us. There are various attitudes, however, which I assume:

1. That I happen to be out with a chain and a careless dog got caught in it.
2. That a dog happened to be out with a chain and *I* got caught in it.
3. That a chain happened to be out and the dog and I both got caught in it.

Between lampposts, Gilbert and I walk along with dignity. With as much dignity as possible, that is, considering that we are walking in the gutter.

Sometimes we pause in the gutter and turn around rapidly many times. Then one of us reads a newspaper, while the finishing school, which we are directly in front of, conducts a fire drill.

I could go on interminably. Maybe you think I have already. But anyway, we are agreed that my dog-handling methods are not ideal. Now let me give you some information which is really practical in case you plan to have a dog. Let us examine Gilbert's habits, his point of view, his psychology. I know all about them and it does me no good, but it may forewarn you abut your own dog.

I have observed many of Gilbert's moods. They are, I believe, fairly common to his race. Here are a few of them:

1. *The Hooray-Hooray-a-New-Day's-Dawning! Mood.* This manifests itself twice a day. Once at six in the morning, at which time Gilbert lands heavily on my stomach, knocking both breath and sleep out of me. And a second time at a few moments past midnight, just after he has been bedded down, at which time he insists that I throw his rubber bone for him, or take him out with my coat over my pajamas. There must be some way to stop this.
2. *The Aren't-I-Supposed-to-Have-Any-Normal-Instincts-at-All? Mood.* This is caused simply by the fact that Gilbert is devoid of a sense of shame and I am not. It often results in our not speaking to each other and also in other people not speaking to me. There is no way to avoid this.

3. *The I-Was-Asleep-and-Some-Bad-Man-Must-Have-Come-in-and-Torn-that-Blue-Bedspread-to-Bits Attitude.* This is accompanied by a brazen, hypocritical simulation if overweening joy at my entrance and is unconvincing because of the large piece of blue cloth which Gilbert is unconsciously carrying on his dewlap. One method of avoiding this is always to leave your bed bare to the springs until retiring.

All right. Now that I have revealed my relationship to my dog in all its squalor, the curious may inquire why I have a dog at all. The curious may, but not the wise.

The answer, of course, is simple. In Gilbert I have found a being to whom I am superior in many ways, in spite of the fact that Phyllis insists that a lot more people stop to admire him than me on the street. Gilbert cannot drive a car. I can. Gilbert cannot wash dishes, pour drinks for people, run errands, or do dozens of other things around the house Phyllis considers necessary. Above all, Gilbert is a living, breathing answer to her contention that I am the most inefficient form of life yet devised.

He is also the finest dog in town, even if he did tear up the very best parts of this piece.

Rex

BY D. H. LAWRENCE

A COAL MINER'S SON from the bleak and gloomy wastes of Nottinghamshire, D. H. Lawrence was a sickly child, an angry teenager, and a turbulent and disturbed grown man. The grim colliery towns his family moved into and out of were not the kind of background which one would expect to nurture a writer, especially one whose works often explored the fine relationship between human beings and the natural world. Still there was some softness somewhere, as shown in this story.

Clearly, "Rex" is autobiographical; clearly, it takes place in a brutal world; and clearly, Lawrence loved Rex—flaws and all.

★ ★ ★ ★ ★

SINCE EVERY FAMILY HAS its black sheep, it almost follows that every man must have a sooty uncle. Lucky if he hasn't two. However, it is only with my mother's brother that we are concerned. She had loved him dearly when he was a little blond boy. When he grew up black, she was always vowing she would never speak to him again. Yet when he put in an appearance, after years of absence, she invariably received him in a festive mood, and was even flirty with him.

He rolled up one day in a dog-cart, when I was a small boy. He was large and bullet-headed and blustering, and this time, sporty. Sometimes he was rather literary, sometimes colored with business. But this time he was in checks, and was sporty. We viewed him from a distance.

The upshot was, would we rear a pup for him. Now my mother detested animals about the house. She could not bear the mix-up of human with animal life. Yet she consented to bring up the pup.

My uncle had taken a large, vulgar public-house in a large and vulgar town. It came to pass that I must fetch the pup. Strange for me, a member of the Band of Hope, to enter the big, noisy, smelly plate-glass and mahogany public-house. It was called The Good Omen. Strange to have my uncle towering over me in the passage, shouting "Hello Johnny, what d'yer want?" He didn't know me. Strange to think he was my mother's brother, and that he had his bouts when he read Browning aloud with emotion and *éclat*.

I was given tea in a narrow, uncomfortable sort of living-room, half kitchen. Curious that such a palatial pub should show such miserable private accommodations, but so it was. There was I, unhappy, and glad to escape with the soft fat pup. It was winter-time, and I wore a big-flapped black overcoat, half cloak. Under the cloak-sleeves I hid the puppy, who trembled. It was Saturday, and the train was crowded, and he whimpered under my coat. I sat in mortal fear of being hauled out for traveling without a dog-ticket. However, we arrived, and my torments were for nothing.

The others were wildly excited over the puppy. He was small and fat and white, with a brown-and-black head: a fox terrier. My father said he had a lemon head—some such mysterious technical phraseology. It wasn't lemon at all, but colored like a field bee. And he had a black spot at the root of his spine.

It was Saturday night—bath-night. He crawled on the hearth-rug like a fat white tea-cup, and licked the bare toes that had just been bathed.

"He ought to be called Spot," said one. But that was too ordinary. It was a great question, what to call him.

"Call him Rex—the King," said my mother, looking down on the fat, animated little tea-cup, who was chewing my sister's little toe and making her squeal with joy and tickles. We took the name in all seriousness.

"Rex—the King!" We thought it was just right. Not for years did I realize that it was a sarcasm on my mother's part. She must have wasted some twenty years or more of irony, on our incurable naïveté.

It wasn't a successful name, really. Because my father, and all the people in the street, failed completely to pronounce the monosyllable Rex. They all said Rax. And it always distressed me. It always suggested to me seaweed, and rack-and-ruin. Poor Rex!

We loved him dearly. The first night we woke to hear him weeping and whinneying in loneliness at the foot of the stairs. When it could be borne no more, I slipped down for him, and he slept under the sheets.

"I won't have that little beast in the beds. Beds are not for dogs," declared my mother callously.

"He's as good as we are," we cried, injured.

"Whether he is or not, he's not going in the beds."

I think now, my mother scorned us for our lack of pride. We were a little infra dig., we children.

The second night, however, Rex wept the same and in the same way was comforted. The third night we heard our father plod downstairs, heard several slaps administered to the yelping, dismayed puppy, and heard the amiable, but to us heartless voice saying "Shut it then! Shut thy noise, 'st hear? Stop in thy basket, stop there!"

"It's a shame!" we shouted, in muffled rebellion, from the sheets.

"I'll give you shame, if you don't hold your noise and go to sleep," called our mother from her room. Whereupon we shed angry tears and went to sleep. But there was a tension.

"Such a houseful of idiots would make me detest the little beast, even if he was better than he is," said my mother.

But as a matter of fact, she did not detest Rexie at all. She only had to pretend to do so, to balance our adoration. And in truth, she did not care for close contact with animals. She was too fastidious. My father, however, would take on a real dog's voice, talking to the puppy: a funny, high, sing-song falsetto which he seemed to produce at the top of his head. "'S a pretty little dog! 's a pretty little doggy!-ay!-yes!-Wag thy strunt, then! Wag thy strunt, Raxie!-Ha-ha! Nay, tha munna—" This last as the puppy, wild with excitement at the strange falsetto voice, licked my father's nostrils and bit my father's nose with his sharp little teeth.

" 'E makes blood come," said my father.

"Serves you right for being so silly with him," said my mother. It was odd to see her as she watched the man, my father, crouching and talking to the little dog and laughing strangely when the little creature bit his nose and tousled his beard. What does a woman think of her husband at such a moment?

My mother amused herself over the names we called him.

"He's an angel—he's a little butterfly—Rexie, my sweet!"

"Sweet! A dirty little object!" interpolated my mother. She and he had a feud from the first. Of course he chewed boots and worried our stockings and swallowed our garters. The moment we took off our stockings he would dart away with one, we after him. Then as he hung, growling vociferously, at one end of the stocking, we at the other, we would cry:

"Look at him, mother! He'll make holes in it again." Whereupon my mother darted at him and spanked him sharply.

"Let go, Sir, you destructive little fiend!"

But he didn't let go. He began to growl with real rage, and hung on viciously. Mite as he was, he defied her with a manly fury. He did not hate her, nor she him. But they had one long battle with one another.

"I'll teach you, my Jockey! Do you think I'm going to spend my life darning after your destructive little teeth! I'll show you if I will!"

But Rexie only growled more viciously. They both became really angry, whilst we children expostulated earnestly with both. He would not let her take the stocking from him.

"You should tell him properly, mother. He won't be driven," we said.

"I'll drive him further than he bargains for. I'll drive him out of my sight forever, that I will," declared my mother, truly angry. He would put her into a real temper, with his tiny, growling defiance.

"He's sweet! A Rexie, a little Rexie!"

"A filthy little nuisance! Don't think I'll put up with him."

And to tell the truth, he was dirty at first. How could he be otherwise, so young! But my mother hated him for it. And perhaps this was the real start of their hostility. For he lived in the house with us. He would wrinkle his nose and show his tiny dagger-teeth in fury when he was thwarted, and his growls of real battle-rage against my mother rejoiced us as much as they angered her. But at last she caught him in flagrante. She pounced on him, rubbed his nose in the mess, and flung him out into the yard. He yelped with shame and disgust and indignation. I shall never forget the sight of him as he rolled over, then tried to turn his head away from the disgust of his own muzzle, shaking his little snout with a sort of horror, and trying to sneeze it off. My sister gave a yell of despair, and dashed out with a rag and a pan of water, weeping wildly. She sat in the middle of the yard with the befouled puppy, and shedding bitter tears she wiped him and washed him clean. Loudly she reproached my mother. "Look how much bigger you are than he is. It's a shame, it's a shame!"

"You ridiculous little lunatic, you've undone all the good it would do him, with your soft ways. Why is my life made a curse with animals! Haven't I enough as it is—"

There was a subdued tension afterwards. Rex was a little white chasm between us and our parent.

He became clean. But then another tragedy loomed. He must be docked. His floating puppy-tail must be docked short. This time my father was the enemy. My mother agreed with us that it was an unnecessary cruelty. But my father was adamant. "The dog'll look a fool all his life, if he's not docked." And there was no getting away from it. To add to the horror, poor Rex's tail must be *bitten* off. Why bitten? we asked aghast. We were assured that biting was the only way. A man would take the little tail and just nip it through with his teeth, at a certain joint. My father lifted his lips and bared his incisors, to suit the description. We shuddered. But we were in the hands of fate.

Rex was carried away, and a man called Rowbotham bit off the superfluity of his tail in the Nags Head, for a quart of best and bitter. We lamented our poor diminished puppy, but agreed to find him more manly and *comme il faut*. We should always have been ashamed of his little whip of a tail, if it had not been shortened. My father said it had made a man out of him.

Perhaps it had. For now his true nature came out. And his true nature, like so much else, was dual. First he was a fierce, canine little beast, a beast of rapine and blood. He longed to hunt, savagely. He lusted to set his teeth in his prey. It was no joke with him. The old canine Adam stood first in him, the dog with fangs and glaring eyes. He flew at us when we annoyed him. He flew at all intruders, particularly the postman. He was almost a peril to the neighborhood. But not quite. Because close second in his nature stood that fatal need to love, the *besoin d'aimer* which at last makes an end of liberty. He had a terrible, terrible necessity to love, and this trammelled the native, savage hunting beast which he was. He was torn between two great impulses: the native impulse to hunt and kill, and the strange, secondary, supervening impulse to love and obey. If he had been left to my father and mother, he would have run wild and got himself shot. As it was, he loved us children with a fierce, joyous love. And we loved him.

When we came home from school we would see him standing at the end of the entry, cocking his head wistfully at the open country in front of him, and meditating whether to be off or not: a white, inquiring little figure, with green savage freedom in front of him. A cry from a far distance from one of us, and like a bullet he hurled himself down the road, in a mad game. Seeing him coming, my sister invariably turned and fled, shrieking with delighted terror. And he would leap straight up her back, and bite her and tear her clothes. But it was only an ecstasy of savage love, and she knew it. She didn't care if he tore her pinafores. But my mother did.

My mother was maddened by him. He was a little demon. At the least provocation, he flew. You had only to sweep the floor, and he bristled and sprang at the broom. Nor would he let go. With his scruff erect and his nostrils snorting rage, he would turn up the whites of his eyes at my mother, as she wrestled at the other end of the broom. "Leave go, Sir; leave go!" She wrestled and stamped her foot, and he answered with horrid growls. In the end it was she who had to let go. Then she flew at him, and he flew at her. All the time we had him he was within a hair's-breadth of savagely biting her. And she knew it. Yet he always kept sufficient self-control.

We children loved his temper. We would drag the bones from his mouth, and put him into such paroxysms of rage that he would twist his head right over and lay it on the ground upside-down, because he didn't know what to do with himself, the savage was so strong in him and he must fly at us. "He'll fly at your throat one of these days," said my father. Neither he nor my mother dared have touched Rex's bone. It was enough to see him bristle and roll the whites of his eyes when they came near. How near he must have been to driving his teeth right into us cannot be told. He was a horrid sight, snarling and crouching at us. But we only laughed and rebuked him. And he would whimper in the sheer torment of his need to attack us.

He never did hurt us. He never hurt anybody, though the neighborhood was terrified of him. But he took to hunting. To my mother's disgust, he would bring large dead bleeding rats and lay them on the hearth-rug, and she had to take them up on a shovel. For he would not remove them. Occasionally he brought a mangled rabbit, and sometimes, alas, fragmentary poultry. We were in terror of prosecution. Once he came home bloody and feathery and rather sheepish-looking. We cleaned him and questioned him and abused him. Next day we heard of six dead ducks. Thank heaven no one had seen him.

But he was disobedient. If he saw a hen he was off, and calling would not bring him back. He was worst of all with my father, who would take him walks on Sunday morning. My mother would not walk a yard with him. Once, walking with my father, he rushed off at some sheep in a field. My father yelled in vain. The dog was at the sheep, and meant business. My father crawled through the hedge, and was upon him in time. And now the man was in a paroxysm of rage. He dragged the little beast into the road and thrashed him with a walking stick.

"Do you know you're thrashing that dog unmercifully?" said a passer-by.

"Ay, an' mean to," shouted my father.

The curious thing was that Rex did not respect my father any the more for the beatings he had from him. He took much more heed of us children, always.

But he let us down also. One fatal Saturday he disappeared. We hunted and called, but no Rex. We were bathed, and it was bed-time, but we would not go to bed. Instead we sat in a row in our night-dresses on the sofa, and wept without stopping. This drove our mother mad.

"Am I going to put up with it? Am I? And all for that hateful little beast of a dog! He shall go! If he's not gone now, he shall go."

Our father came in late, looking rather queer, with his hat over his eye. But in his staccato tippled fashion he tried to be consoling.

"Never mind, my duckie, I s'll look for him in the morning."

Sunday came—oh, such a Sunday. We cried, and didn't eat. We scoured the land, and for the first time realized how empty and wide the earth is, when you're looking for something. My father walked for many miles—all in vain. Sunday dinner, with rhubarb pudding, I remember, and an atmosphere of abject misery that was unbearable.

"Never," said my mother, "never shall an animal set foot in this house again, while I live. I knew what it would be! I knew."

The day wore on, and it was the black gloom of bed-time when we heard a scratch and an impudent little whine at the door. In trotted Rex, mud-black, disreputable, and impudent. His air of off-hand "how d'ye do!" was indescribable. He trotted round with suffisance, wagging his tail as if to say, "Yes, I've come back. But I didn't need to. I can carry on remarkably well by myself." Then he walked into his water, and drank noisily and ostentatiously. It was rather a slap in the eye for us.

He disappeared once or twice in this fashion. We never knew where he went. And we began to feel that his heart was not so golden as we had imagined it.

But one fatal day reappeared my uncle and the dog-cart. He whistled to Rex, and Rex trotted up. But when he wanted to examine the lusty, sturdy dog, Rex became suddenly still, then sprang free. Quite jauntily he trotted round—but out of reach of my uncle. He leaped up, licking our faces, and trying to make us play.

"Why what ha' you done wi' the dog—you've made a fool of him. He's softer than grease. You've ruined him. You've made a damned fool of him," shouted my uncle.

Rex was captured and hauled off to the dog-cart and tied to the seat. He was in a frenzy. He yelped and shrieked and struggled, and was hit on the head, hard, with the butt-end of my uncle's whip, which only made him struggle more frantically. So we saw him driven away, our beloved Rex, frantically, madly fighting to get to us from the high dog-cart, and being knocked down, whilst we stood in the street in mute despair.

After which, black tears, and a little wound which is still alive in our hearts.

I saw Rex only once again, when I had to call just once at The Good Omen. He must have heard my voice, for he was upon me in the passage before I knew where I was. And in the instant I knew how he loved us. He really loved us. And in the same instant there was my uncle with a whip, beating and kicking him back, and Rex cowering, bristling, snarling.

My uncle swore many oaths, how we had ruined the dog for ever, made him vicious, spoiled him for showing purposes, and been altogether a pack of mard-soft fools not fit to be trusted with any dog but a gutter-mongrel.

Poor Rex! We heard his temper was incurably vicious, and he had to be shot.

And it was our fault. We had loved him too much, and he had loved us too much. We never had another pet.

It is a strange thing, love. Nothing but love has made the dog lose his wild freedom, to become the servant of man. And this very servility or completeness of love makes him a term of deepest contempt.—"You dog!"

We should not have loved Rex so much, and he should not have loved us. There should have been a measure. We tended, all of us, to overstep the limits of our own natures. He should have stayed outside human limits; we should have stayed outside canine. Nothing is more fatal than the disaster of too much love. My uncle was right, we had ruined the dog.

My uncle was a fool, for all that.

A Bird Like Christmas

BY DATUS C. PROPER

VEN IF HUNTING ISN'T a fancy of yours, I think you'll wish you could be out on this crisp December day with Datus Proper, his dog Trooper, and his sense of, and appreciation for, the natural world around him. A long-time contributor to *Field & Stream* magazine, Proper brings us a fresh look at bird hunting and the brilliantly colored pheasant he seeks.

If you can't be with him as he walks the fields, breathing deep and just enjoying the time and place, then come along as he tells us about it. It's nearly as good as being there.

★   ★   ★   ★   ★

YOU NEVER HUNT ALONE when you take your dog along. At least, you never feel alone if you have a dog who likes to hunt with you. There are dogs who don't care for human interference, and they are happier than their people, because the dogs get to hunt birds while the people spend their time hunting dogs. Hunting birds is much more fun than hunting dogs.

When Trooper and I were younger, it took us awhile to decide that we could get more birds when we were both hunting in the same acre. This realization brought about a compromise. For my part, I agreed to stop hunting according to the principles of Euclidean geometry. Some time before Trooper I had persuaded myself that a square field should be hunted in a pattern with 90-degree angles, missing no corners or tangles of briars, and that every pheasant would run all the way to the end of a hedgerow. I was better at geometry than at smelling pheasants. Trooper explained that the way to find birds was to look where his nose was pointing, or a few yards farther on. Trooper is a German shorthaired pointer who failed geometry, but nothing is wrong with his nose.

Trooper's discovery was that I shoot better than he can. I don't shoot as well as a lot of the boys at the skeet range, but they seldom come hunting with us, and between me and Trooper there is no comparison. Trooper has now become the opposite of gun shy, whatever you call that. The skeet range makes him unhappy because with so much shooting there are bound to be dead pheasants all over the place, yet I never let him out of the car to retrieve.

I forgot to tell you that Trooper is also a retriever when he's allowed to be. He's delighted to bring me half of every pheasant he finds—the bony half, which is dry and hard to swallow anyhow. Clearly a fair deal, when you consider that with all the loops he runs, he probably hunts 30 miles to my 10. Trooper has never understood why I make him point dead instead of practicing his retrieves. But he bears no ill will, and when he hears my gun go off—even at mile 28—his old joints stop aching and he runs like a puppy to the place where the bird ought to fall, frequently arriving at about the same time. His hope is that the pheasant will try to run. Trooper is allowed to retrieve runners. My wife cooks some abbreviated pheasants that we'd be ashamed to serve to guests, but at least we don't leave many wounded birds out there for the foxes.

Take one day last season, for instance. It was the third Saturday in December, and we weren't hunting for Christmas dinner, because a rooster for that occasion had already been hanging in a cold corner for a week, building up flavor. We just wanted a bird to justify the week's sitting around; to go with a bottle of red wine, for New Year's; and to keep the place looking right after Christmas dinner. A cock pheasant has every color you could want for the short days. You could deck out a balsam fir with his feathers and they'd look prettier than the ornaments your kid made at school.

I was, however, a little concerned about the weather forecast—the gusty northwest winds, not the part about the chill factor of 10 below zero. Cold I can dress for, and Trooper doesn't care as long as he's dry, running, and finding a sniff of pheasant now and then. But holding a pheasant (or any other bird) is tough for a dog when it's windy.

Turned out the day wasn't as bad as it sounded to the disc jockey in his heated booth. The wind didn't blow all the time and the storm coming through from Montana had beaten the haze, giving us a Montana sun instead of the distant orange, fluorescent glow that sometimes passes for daylight here in the mid-Atlantic.

You're a hunter, I guess, so I don't have to tell you what it feels like to whistle up your dog and hike off across the fields after a week of commuting through a dingy city. A step becomes a stride, and fields that were cramped in the green four months ago now stretch on to the sky in corn stubble and yellow grass. Winter fields are endless, for a fellow with hunting permission, even if he has to turn corners and climb barbed-wire fences to keep from reaching a stopping point. And it is a little spooky—if you believe that humans and other animals are far apart—to see that your dog shares your stupid grin. His ears flap back, he runs in unprofitable circles, and he clears tall rosebushes in a single bound.

Trooper's first hedgerow had some splendid smells, and I reckoned we'd find birds in it, because last year we had shot a rooster right here and found two hens killed by a goshawk that had eaten only the intestines and pieces of thigh—just the bits that Trooper prefers. Perhaps the other predators have figured out something that humans are too squeamish to understand.

Trooper got a little carried away by whatever he was smelling and beat me to the end of the hedgerow. I saw a flicker of something bright running out ahead of him and thought, *oh, indecent dog, you are going to bust the bird*. But Trooper didn't. He didn't even bust the fox, which is what had been making the smells. She—must have been a she, to be in that kind of mood—came running back to play. She flirted her long tail and dared him to chase her. He did.

In another corner of the field, where the fox had not been, Trooper found the correct smells. They were in the only decent patch of grass around, and pheasants do love tall grass. We had a point.

Now, Trooper is not a dog who just stands there when a bird is encountered, waiting for someone to come up and do the necessary. His eyes bug out; he nearly stops breathing; his tail stands up and quivers; his body emits wavelengths that say: *shut up and sit still, bird, till the boss comes up and makes you into a Christmas decoration*. Mostly they do sit still, when Trooper is that close.

Seven of them sit this time. I can't blame Trooper for pointing hens, and he doesn't blame me when I fail to shoot as they flush, one after another, leaving a hunter undergoing withdrawal symptoms. I have never tried any other drug that required withdrawal, so I don't know much about cold turkey, but it can't get much shakier than hot hen pheasants.

You hear of dogs that grow surly if the boss fails to get off a shot, or misses, but Trooper just figures it's a chance to do the thing all over again. So off we rush, hoping the hens will lead us to where the cocks are hiding. It usually doesn't work, but it's as good as any other idea I have, and at least hens can be counted on for abundant winter points. The other good thing about them is that they will still be around in spring to produce eggs, half of which will contain incipient roosters. Maybe that's why I can hunt pheasants right through the holidays and find just as many the next year.

Some of the hens have, I think, lit in a brushy hedgerow. Thither I go. Elsewhere Trooper goes. I whistle. He persists in sniffing around the edges of a woodlot that is clearly too thin to shelter pheasants. Clearly to me, that is. Guess who is right. Before Trooper can locate and point, a rooster swirls out of the trees at full flap, heading toward the field we just abandoned. I told you I was a slow learner. We go back to Field One and hunt it for half an hour, finding only a hen who flew that way at the first flush. The rooster has, no doubt, gone several fields farther—a nasty habit roosters have after the first bangs of November.

Then we walk. And walk, and walk. Both of us are a little weaker of knee than we were at sunup, but I am not at the hallucinatory stage yet, so the pheasants had better watch out. As a pheasant hunter I have fewer talents than Trooper, but I do have long legs, toes that point straight forward, and a disposition to follow them until the matter of New Year's dinner had been resolved.

A possible resolution appears, at last, in a high, dense, bramble patch that has grown over a fence bordering corn stubble. We come up from the downhill side and Trooper points. There is no way over the fence without a long detour, so I have to come up from below and behind Trooper, which is precisely the wrong way to approach a dog pointing pheasants. With both adversaries on one side, the bird naturally flushes on the other, and there is no shot to be had through the bramble jungle. The cock stays low for 50 yards, then rises toward dim horizons—snowy ring resplendent below evergreen head, red wattles rampant, orange breast aflame, tail pennants flouting the idiot with a shotgun. No wonder that bird is still alive on December 21. But I think there is a way to get him surrounded next weekend: Trooper will come up from below again, while I will cross the fence well back from the brambles and tiptoe in from the top.

Which makes this a good place to observe that pheasant hunting is a different thing from pheasant shooting. Pheasant shooting is what we do (with luck) during the first hours of opening day, or (with money) on shooting preserves, or (with an airplane ticket and much money) on the other side of the Atlantic.

As to the shooting part, I can manage to miss under most circumstances. When, after a lot of hunting, a shot that I can make does offer itself, I am not disappointed. I am, on the contrary, profoundly thankful that Trooper found the pheasant and then stopped to wait for me. There are enough of the other kind of shots, at 40 yards through the woodlot, with my left foot in the greenbriars.

Pheasants have been hunted, one way or another, for millennia, and by now they do it all. They run, and they stop. They flush wild and they sit tighter than woodcock, while hunters walk past. Mostly pheasants do what's best for their survival, given recent experiences with men and dogs. If they happen to make a long, sneaky trail for Trooper to puzzle out, and if at the end of that trail they hide away where no one has found them before, then he and I think we're doing something which is about as good as hunting gets. Hunting, not shooting.

Of course, there are also days like the Saturday last season, when we were limping toward evening without a feather in the game pocket. I was limping, at least. Trooper was still ranging, but it was near sundown when he went on point, off in the distance. Before I could get close a covey of bob-whites flushed and passed me, almost out of range, headed for an impenetrable patch of second-growth woods. I took a shot with the left barrel, and while nothing fell, I thought that one bird landed too soon, in thick grass at the edge of the woods. On the remote chance that it had been hit I ran to the spot and stood there while Trooper hunted dead. I didn't want to spoil any scent by moving around. Then, after a few minutes, I slumped on a limestone outcrop while Trooper kept at work. When he finally locked up, his nose was pointed down at the ground. I walked in to pick up what I thought would be a dead 7-ounce quail, and out flushed a 3-pound cock pheasant in excellent flying condition. I was ready: had been for a long time.

By now, it seemed clear to me that there was no bobwhite around, but Trooper did not want to leave the tall grass. Probably just wanted to enjoy his recent triumph; another of his defects, like sticky retrieves. So I sagged onto the soft rock again. And Trooper pointed again. When I reached him he broke point, ran 30 yards, and pointed a second time. I trotted up and he went off 50 yards to a third point. Poor old dog had been running so long that his over-heated brain was producing fantasies. But this time, when I circled in from the side, the fantasy jumped into the air and cackled off, setting sun flickering through fanned-out wing feathers. We headed for the car with two big birds bulging my game pocket so it felt like Santa's pack, and now both of us could afford to limp.

Those two roosters had held still for walking, running, waiting, grass-kicking, shooting, cussing, whistle-blowing, bell-ringing, and dog-calling. All of it took place within a few yards of the birds—sometimes a few feet. They did not move until the dog had them accurately located. You can figure how much chance I'd have had without Trooper.

But that, I suppose, is merely practical. Nothing tastes better than a pheasant, but Trooper and I really hunt together because we have the same cells down the middle of our backs. When he is pointing something close, a ridge of hair along his spine ruffles. My back hairs fell out during the last Pleistocene, but the cells where the hair ought to be still work fine; so there I am, out in the suntanned field backing my pointer. He makes mistakes, but he doesn't lie. Something is going to happen when I take a few steps. Probably it's a hen; maybe it's the farmer's cat; and once or twice a day it's a big bird decorated like a Christmas tree.

Man's (Sportswriter's) Best Friend

From a column by Red Smith in the *New York Herald Tribune*

BY SPARSE GREY HACKLE

BEST KNOWN AS AN ANGLER, fishing writer, and environmental ac-
tivist, Sparse Grey Hackle was also an animal lover. He was extremely fond of dogs—so much so that puppies who cried at night
from loneliness didn't stay lonely long. More than once Sparse was
discovered dozing in his armchair with a puppy blissfully asleep in his lap.

Sparse Grey Hackle was my father and he and my mother had an ongoing discussion about the definition of spoiling as regards to puppies. Father's
voice was louder, so he won. He was solely responsible for the bad habits of all
our dogs.

I can personally attest that this tale of Boy is only partially exaggerated.

★ ★ ★ ★ ★

LET US GIVE THANKS for blessings large and small, namely: the log in the fireplace, the ribbon in the typewriter, the fried bologna on the festive board, and, above all, the United States mail. Without the postman there would be no letters from Mr. Sparse Grey Hackle, gentleman, sportsman, and friend of all sportswriters in need. In need of a holiday, that is. With an unfailing sense of timing, Mr. Hackle writes:

"Our mutual friend Mr. Big George Evans is just back from a week's woodcock shooting in Maine with Boy. Boy is a 65-pound, jet-propelled pointer who doesn't like automobiles. He publicly insults the cars of George's visitors, and when traveling he whizzes around inside George's Pontiac like a misguided missile, treading on George's countenance and jumping on the accelerator.

"So before starting on this long trip, George consulted the vet.

" 'Sure,' said the vet, 'give him these tranquilizers when he gets restless.'

Houdini with Liver-Colored Spots

"I cannot get a coherent account of what happened, beyond the statement that, although Boy habitually eats pillows, furniture, briefcases, and parts of the milkman, he does not and will not eat tranquilizers. In the end, George took the tranquilizers himself.

"The first night in Maine, the cabin turned colder than a curb broker's heart"—Mr. Hackle works in Wall Street—"and Boy decided to sleep in the bed. Not with his master, but instead of him. The next night, George put an old sweatshirt on Boy and tied it securely around the dog's waist. It looked a bit improbable, but it kept Boy warm.

"In the morning George drove into town and locked Boy, still wearing the sweatshirt, in the car while he went to breakfast. Now, I do not expect you to believe that a pointer measuring 2 feet tall at the shoulder and 10 inches across the chest can unlatch, push open, and climb through the ventilator window of a 1953 Pontiac.

"I will merely bet you 10 bucks that this one can and, as soon as George had crossed the street, did.

Bright College Years

"Certain invalids were tottering down the main street of Cherryfield on their way to the dispensary for their morning dose of health-restoring bitters. They leaped violently upon beholding a liver-colored dog wearing a Notre Dame sweatshirt extruding through the ventilator window of a car. They departed rapidly, looking straight ahead and muttering.

"Boy paid them no heed. He walked directly to a parked automobile and insulted it. George did not notice whether the car had Oklahoma license plates but I think it likely, for that was the day you-know-who defeated you-know-whom at football.

"The sweatshirt and the affronted car are no longer available, but I can produce the dog and the Pontiac anytime you produce the 10 bucks."

Every Dog Should Own a Man

BY COREY FORD

SOMEWHERE IN THE ENVIRONS of Hanover, New Hampshire, is the Corey Ford Rugby Field. Humorist and sportsman Corey Ford was writer-in-residence at Dartmouth College for some years—and clearly had some other sporting influences as well.

Ford also wrote regularly for Field & Stream magazine, being the proponent of the Lower Forty Shooting, Angling, and Inside Straight Club. It's obvious that he also had a lurking fondness for dogs . . . especially those who owned him.

★ ★ ★ ★ ★

EVERY DOG SHOULD HAVE a man of his own. There is nothing like a well-behaved person around the house to spread the dog's blanket for him, or bring him his supper when he comes home man-tired at night.

For example, I happen to belong to an English setter who acquired me when he was about six months old and has been training me quite successfully ever since. He has taught me to shake hands with him and fetch his ball. I've learned to not to tug at the leash when he takes me for a walk. I am completely housebroken, and I make him a devoted companion.

The first problem a dog faces is to pick out the right man—a gay and affectionate disposition is more important than an expensive pedigree. I do not happen to be registered but my setter is just as fond of me as though I came from a long line of blue bloods. Also, since a dog is judged by the man he leads, it is a good idea to walk the man up and down a couple of times to make sure his action is free and he has springy hindquarters.

The next question is whether the dog and man should share the house together. Some dogs prefer a kennel because it is more sanitary, but my setter decided at the start that he'd move right in the house with me. I can get into any of the chairs I want except the big overstuffed chair in the living room, which is his.

Training a man takes time. Some men are a little slow to respond, but a dog who makes allowances and tries to put himself in the man's place will be rewarded with a loyal pal. Men are apt to be high-strung and sensitive, and a dog who loses his temper will only break a man's spirit.

Punishment should be meted out sparingly—more can be accomplished by a reproachful look than by flying off the handle. My setter has never raised a paw to me, but he has cured me almost entirely of the habit of running away. When he sees me start to pick up my suitcase he just lies down on the floor with his chin in his forepaws and gazes at me sadly. Usually I wind up by canceling my train reservations.

The first thing to teach a man is to stay at heel. For this lesson the dog should hook one end of a leash to his collar and loop the other end around the man's wrist so he cannot get away. Start down the street slowly, pausing at each telephone pole until the man realizes that he's under control. He may tug and yank at first, but this can be discouraged by slipping deftly between his legs and winding the leash around his ankles. If the man tries to run ahead, brace all four feet and halt suddenly, thus jerking him flat on his back. After a few such experiences the man will follow his dog with docility. Remember, however, that all such efforts at discipline must be treated as sport, and after a man has sprawled on the sidewalk the dog should lick his face to show him it was all in fun.

Every man should learn to retrieve a rubber ball. The way my setter taught me this trick was simple. He would lie in the center of the floor while I carried the ball to the far side of the room and rolled it toward him, uttering the word "Fetch!" He would watch the ball carefully as it rolled past him under the sofa. I would then get the ball from under the sofa and roll it past him again, giving the same command, "Fetch!"

This lesson would be repeated until the setter was asleep. After I got so I would retrieve the ball every time I said "Fetch!" my dog substituted other articles for me to pick up, such as an old marrow bone or a piece of paper he found in the wastebasket.

The matter of physical conditioning is important. A man whose carriage is faulty, and who slouches and droops his tail, is a reflection of the dog who owns him. The best way to get him in shape is to work him constantly and never give him a chance to relax. Racing him up and down the street at the end of a leash is a great conditioner. If he attempts to slump in the easy chair when he gets back, the dog should leap into it ahead of him and force him to sit in a straight-backed chair to improve his posture. And be sure to get him several times a night to go out for a walk, especially if it is raining.

Equally important is diet. Certain liquids such as beer have a tendency to bloat a man, and a dog should teach him restraint by jumping up at him and spilling his drink, or tactfully knocking the glass off the table with a sweep of his tail.

Not every dog who tries to bring up a man is as successful as my setter. The answer lies in understanding. The dog must be patient and not work himself up into a tantrum if his man can't learn to chase rabbits or wriggle under fences as well as a dog does. After all, as my setter says, it's hard to teach an old man new tricks.

A Dog's Tale

BY MARK TWAIN

THERE'S JUST SOMETHING ABOUT talking dog-talk that tempts all sorts of writers. This device of sounding like a dog has seduced writers from William Cowper to Barbara Bush, but too often the results are less than winning. Timothy Foote calls it "that trickiest of techniques, a narrative told by the dog himself."

Yet when one of America's leading humorists sets his mind to it, he hits the right notes: pathos, gentle humor, and the kind of language that feels right for a dog-told story. There are smiles in this story and tears, some harsh reality and some obvious make-believe—all deftly rendered with a master's touch.

★ ★ ★ ★ ★

1

MY FATHER WAS A ST. BERNARD, my mother was a collie, but I am a Presbyterian. This is what my mother told me, I do not know these nice distinctions myself. To me they are only fine large words meaning nothing. My mother had a fondness for such; she liked to say them, and see other dogs look surprised and envious, as wondering how she got so much education. But, indeed, it was not real education; it was only show: she got the words by listening in the dining-room and drawing-room when there was company, and by going with the children to Sunday-school and listening there; and whenever she heard a large word she said it over to herself many times, and so was able to keep it until there was a dogmatic gathering in the neighborhood, then she would get it off, and surprise and distress them all, from pocket-pup to mastiff, which rewarded her for all her trouble. If there was a stranger he was nearly sure to be suspicious, and when he got his breath again he would ask her what it meant. And she always told him. He was never expecting this but thought he would catch her; so when she told him, he was the one that looked ashamed, whereas he had thought it was going to be she. The others were always waiting for this, and glad of it and proud of her, for they knew what was going to happen, because they had had experience. When she told the meaning of a big word they were all so taken up with admiration that it never occurred to any dog to doubt if it was the right one; and that was natural, because, for one thing, she answered up so promptly that it seemed like a dictionary speaking, and for another thing, where could they find out whether it was right or not? For she was the only cultivated dog there was. By and by, when I was older, she brought home the word Unintellectual, one time, and worked it pretty hard all the week at different gatherings, making much unhappiness and despondency; and it was at this time that I noticed that during that week she was asked for the meaning at eight different assemblages, and flashed out a fresh definition every time, which showed me that she had more presence of mind than culture, though I said nothing, of course. She had one word which she always kept on hand, and ready, like a life-preserver, a kind of emergency word to strap on when she was likely to get washed overboard in a sudden way—that was the word Synonymous. When she happened to fetch out a long word which had had its day weeks before and its prepared meanings gone to her dump-pile, if there was a stranger there of course it knocked him groggy for a couple of minutes, then he would come to, and by that time she would be away down wind on another tack, and not expecting anything; so when he'd hail and ask her to cash in, I (the only dog on the inside of her game) could see her canvas flicker a moment—but only just a moment—then it would belly out taut and full, and she would say, as calm as a summer's day, "It's synonymous with supererogation," or some godless long reptile of a word like that, and go placidly about and skim away on the next tack, perfectly comfortable, you know, and leave that stranger looking profane and embarrassed, and the initiated slatting the floor with their tails in unison and their faces transfigured with a holy joy.

And it was the same with phrases. She would drag home a whole phrase, if it had a grand sound, and play it six nights and two matinees, and explain it a new way every time—which she had to, for all she cared for was the phrase; she wasn't interested in what it meant, and knew those dogs hadn't wit enough to catch her, anyway. Yes, she was a daisy! She got so she wasn't afraid of anything, she had such confidence in the ignorance of those creatures. She even brought anecdotes that she had heard the family and the dinner-guests laugh and shout over; and as a rule she got the nub of one chestnut hitched onto another chestnut, where, of course, it didn't fit and hadn't any point; and when she delivered the nub she fell over and rolled on the floor and laughed and barked in the most insane way, while I could see that she was wondering to herself why it didn't seem as funny as it did when she first heard it. But no harm was done; the others rolled and barked too, privately ashamed of themselves for not seeing the point, and never suspecting that the fault was not with them and there wasn't any to see. You can see by these things that she was of a rather vain and frivolous character; still, she had virtues, and enough to make up, I think. She had a kind heart and gentle ways, and never harbored resentments for injuries done her, but put them easily out of her mind and forgot them; and she taught her children her kindly way, and from her we learned also to be brave and prompt in time of danger, and not to run away, but face the peril that threatened friend or stranger, and help him the best we could without stopping to think what the cost might be to us. And she taught us not by words only, but by example, and that is the best way and the surest and the most lasting. Why, the brave things she did, the splendid things! She was just a soldier; and so modest about it—well, you couldn't help admiring her, and you couldn't help imitating her; not even a King Charles spaniel could remain entirely despicable in her society. So, as you see, there was more to her than her education.

2

When I was well grown, at last, I was sold and taken away, and I never saw her again. She was broken-hearted, and so was I, and we cried; but she comforted me as well as she could, and said we were sent into this world for a wise and good purpose, and must do our duties without repining, take our life as we might find it, live it for the best good of others, and never mind about the results; they were not our affair. She said men who did like this would have a noble and beautiful reward by and by in another world, and although we animals would not go there, to do well and right without reward would give to our brief lives a worthiness and dignity which in itself would be a reward. She had gathered these things from time to time when she had gone to the Sunday-school with the children, and had laid them up in her memory more carefully than she had done with those other words and phrases; and she had studied them deeply, for her good and ours. One may see by this that she had a wise and thoughtful head, for all there was so much lightness and vanity in it.

So we said our farewells, and looked our last upon each other through our tears; and the last thing she said—keeping it for the last to make me remember it the better, I think—was, "In memory of me, when there is a time of danger to another do not think of yourself, think of your mother, and do as she would do."

Do you think I could forget that? No.

3

It was such a charming home!—my new one; a fine great house, with pictures, and delicate decorations, and rich furniture, and no gloom anywhere, but all the wilderness of dainty colors lit up with flooding sunshine; and the spacious grounds around it, and the great garden—oh, greensward, and noble trees, and flowers, no end! And I was the same as a member of the family; and they loved me, and petted me, and did not give me a new name, but called me by my old one that was dear to me because my mother had given it me—Aileen Mavoureen. She got it out of song; and the Grays knew that song, and said it was a beautiful name.

Mrs. Gray was thirty, and so sweet and so lovely, you cannot imagine it; and Sadie was ten, and just like her mother, just a darling slender little copy of her, with auburn tails down her back, and short frocks; and the baby was a year old, and plump and dimpled, and fond of me, and never could get enough of hauling on my tail, and hugging me, and laughing out its innocent happiness; and Mr. Gray was thirty-eight, and tall and slender and handsome, a little bald in front, alert, quick in his movements, business-like, prompt, decided, unsentimental, and with that kind of trim-chiseled face that just seems to glint and sparkle with frosty intellectuality! He was a renowned scientist. I do not know what the word means, but my mother would know how to use it and get effects. She would know how to depress a rat-terrier with it and make a lap-dog look sorry he came. But that is not the best one; the best one was Laboratory. My mother could organize a Trust on that one that would skin the tax-collars off the whole herd. The laboratory was not a book, or a picture, or a place to wash your hands in, as the college president's dog said—no, that is the lavatory; the laboratory is quite different, and is filled with jars, and bottles, and electrics, and wires, and strange machines; and every week other scientists came there and sat in the place, and used the machines, and discussed, and made what they called experiments and discoveries; and often I came, too, and stood around and listened, and tried to learn, for the sake of my mother, and in loving memory of her, although it was a pain to me, as realizing what she was losing out of her life and I gaining nothing at all; for try as I might, I was never able to make anything out of it at all.

Other times I lay on the floor in the mistress's work-room and slept, she gently using me for a foot-stool, knowing it pleased me, for it was a caress; other times I spent an hour in the nursery, and got well tousled and made happy; other times I watched by the crib there, when the baby was asleep and the nurse out for a few minutes on the baby's affairs; other times I romped and raced through the grounds and the garden with Sadie till we were tired out, then slumbered on the grass in the shade of a tree while she read her book; other times I went visiting among the neighbor dogs—for there were some most pleasant ones not far away, and one very handsome and courteous and graceful one, a curly-haired Irish setter by the name of Robin Adair, who was a Presbyterian like me, and belonged to the Scotch minister.

The servants in our house were all kind to me and were fond of me, and so, as you see, mine was a pleasant life. There could not be a happier dog than I was, nor a gratefuler one. I will say this for myself, for it is only the truth: I tried in all ways to do well and right, and honor my mother's memory and her teachings, and earn the happiness that had come to me, as best I could.

By and by came my little puppy, and then my cup was full, my happiness was perfect. It was the dearest little waddling thing, and so smooth and soft and velvety, and had such cunning little awkward paws, and such affectionate eyes, and such a sweet and innocent face; and it made me so proud to see how the children and their mother adored it, and fondled it, and exclaimed over every little wonderful thing it did. It did seem to me that life was just too lovely to—

Then came the winter. One day I was standing a watch in the nursery. That is to say, I was asleep on the bed. The baby was asleep in the crib, which was alongside the bed, on the side next the fireplace. It was the kind of crib that has a lofty tent over it made of gauzy stuff that you can see through. The nurse was out, and we two sleepers were alone. A spark from the wood-fire was shot out, and it lit on the slope of the tent. I suppose a quiet interval followed, then a scream from the baby awoke me, and there was that tent flaming up toward the ceiling! Before I could think, I sprang to the floor in my fright, and in a second was half-way to the door; but in the next half-second my mother's farewell was sounding in my ears, and I was back on the bed again. I reached my head through the flames and dragged the baby out by the waist-band, and tugged it along, and we fell to the floor together in a cloud of smoke; I snatched a new hold, and dragged the screaming little creature along and out at the door and around the bend of the hall, and was still tugging away, all excited and happy and proud, when the master's voice shouted:

"Begone you cursed beast!" and I jumped to save myself; but he was furiously quick, and chased me up, striking furiously at me with his cane, I dodging this way and that, in terror, and at last a strong blow fell upon my left foreleg, which made me shriek and fall, for the moment, helpless; the cane went up for another blow, but never descended, for the nurse's voice rang wildly out, "The nursery's on fire!" and the master rushed away in that direction, and my other bones were saved.

The pain was cruel, but, no matter, I must not lose any time; he might come back at any moment; so I limped on three legs to the other end of the hall, where there was a dark little stairway leading up into a garret where old boxes and such things were kept, as I had heard say, and where people seldom went. I managed to climb up there, then I searched my way through the dark among the piles of things, and hid in the secretest place I could find. It was foolish to be afraid there, yet still I was; so afraid that I held in and hardly even whimpered, though it would have been such a comfort to whimper, because that eases the pain, you know. But I could lick my leg, and that did some good.

For half an hour there was a commotion downstairs, and shoutings, and rushing footsteps, and then there was quiet again. Quiet for some minutes, and that was grateful to my spirit, for then my fears began to go down; and fears are worse than pains—oh, much worse.

Then came a sound that froze me. They were calling me—calling me by name—hunting for me!

It was muffled by distance, but that could not take the terror out of it, and it was the most dreadful sound to me that I had ever heard. It went all about, everywhere, down there: along the halls, through all the rooms, in both stories, and in the basement and the cellar; then outside, and farther and farther away—then back, and all about the house again, and I thought it would never, never stop. But at last it did, hours and hours after the vague twilight of the garret had long ago been blotted out by black darkness.

Then in that blessed stillness my terrors fell little by little away, and I was at peace and slept. It was a good rest I had, but I woke before the twilight had come again. I was feeling fairly comfortable, and I could think out a plan now. I made a very good one; which was, to creep down, all the way down the back stairs, and hide behind the cellar door, and slip out and escape when the iceman came at dawn, while he was inside filling the refrigerator; then I would hide all day, and start on my journey when night came; my journey to—well, anywhere where they would not know me and betray me to the master. I was feeling almost cheerful now; then suddenly I thought: Why, what would life be without my puppy!

That was despair. There was no plan for me; I saw that; I must stay where I was; stay, and wait, and take what might come—it was not my affair; that was what life is—my mother had said it. Then—well, then the calling began again! All my sorrows came back. I said to myself, the master will never forgive. I did not know what I had done to make him so bitter and so unforgiving, yet I judged it was something a dog could not understand, but which was clear to a man and dreadful.

They called and called—days and nights, it seemed to me. So long that the hunger and thirst near drove me mad, and I recognized that I was getting very weak. When you are this way you sleep a great deal, and I did. Once I woke in an awful fright—it seemed to me that the calling was right there in the garret! And so it was: it was Sadie's voice, and she was crying; my name was falling from her lips all broken, poor thing, and I could not believe my ears for the joy of it when I heard her say:

"Come back to us—oh, come back to us, and forgive—it is all so sad without our—"

I broke in with *such* a grateful little yelp, and the next moment Sadie was plunging and stumbling through the darkness and the lumber and shouting for the family to hear, "She's found, she's found!"

The days that followed—well, they were wonderful. The mother and Sadie and the servants—why, they just seemed to worship me. They couldn't seem to make me a bed that was fine enough; and as for food, they couldn't be satisfied with anything but game and delicacies that were out of season; and every day the friends and neighbors flocked in to hear about my heroism—that was the name they called it by, and it means agriculture. I remember my mother pulling it on a kennel once, and explaining it in that way, but didn't say what agriculture was, except that it was synonymous with intramural incandescence; and a dozen times a day Mrs. Gray and Sadie would tell the tale to new-comers, and say I risked my life to save the baby's, and both of us had burns to prove it, and then the company would pass me around and pet me and exclaim about me, and you could see the pride in the eyes of Sadie and her mother; and when the people wanted to know what made me limp, they looked ashamed and changed the subject, and sometimes when people hunted them this way and that way with questions about it, it looked to me as if they were going to cry.

And this was not all the glory; no, the master's friends came, a whole twenty of the most distinguished people, and had me in the laboratory, and discussed me as if I was a kind of discovery; and some of them said it was wonderful in a dumb beast, the finest exhibition of instinct they could call to mind; but the master said, with vehemence, "It's far above instinct; it's REASON, and many a man, privileged to be saved and go with you and me to a better world by right of its possession, has less of it than this poor silly quadruped that's foreordained to perish"; and then he laughed, and said: "Why, look at me—I'm a sarcasm! Bless you, with all my grand intelligence, the only think I inferred was that the dog had gone mad and was destroying the child, whereas but for the beast's intelligence—it's REASON, I tell you!—the child would have perished!"

They disputed and disputed, and *I* was the very center of subject of it all, and I wished my mother could know that this grand honor had come to me; it would have made her proud.

Then they discussed optics, as they called it, and whether a certain injury to the brain would produce blindness or not, but they could not agree about it, and said they must test it by experiment by and by; and next they discussed plants, and that interested me, because in the summer Sadie and I had planted seeds—I helped her dig the holes, you know—and after days and days a little shrub or a flower came up there, and it was a wonder how that could happen; but it did, and I wished I could talk—I would have told those people about it and shown them how much I knew, and been all alive with the subject; but I didn't care for the optics; it was dull, and when they came back to it again it bored me, and I went to sleep.

Pretty soon it was spring, and sunny and pleasant and lovely, and the sweet mother and the children patted me and the puppy good-by, and went away on a journey and a visit to their kin, and the master wasn't any company for us, but we played together and had good times, and the servants were kind and friendly, so we got along quite happily and counted the days and waited for the family.

And one day those men came again, and said, now for the test, and they took the puppy to the laboratory, and I limped three-leggedly along, too, feeling proud, for any attention shown to the puppy was a pleasure to me, of course. They discussed and experimented, and then suddenly the puppy shrieked, and they set him on the floor, and he went staggering around, with his head all bloody, and the master clapped his hands and shouted:

"There, I've won—confess it! He's as blind as a bat!"

And they all said:

"It's so—you've proved your theory, and suffering humanity owes you a great debt from henceforth," and they crowded around him, and wrung his hand cordially and thankfully, and praised him.

But I hardly saw or heard these things, for I ran at once to my little darling, and snuggled close to it where it lay, and licked the blood, and it put its head against mine, whimpering softly, and I knew in my heart it was a comfort to it in its pain and trouble to feel its mother's touch, though it could not see me. Then it dropped down, presently, and its little velvet nose rested upon the floor, and it was still, and did not move any more. Soon the master stopped discussing a moment, and rang in the footman, and said, "Bury it in the far corner of the garden," and then went on with the discussion, and I trotted after the footman, very happy and grateful, for I knew the puppy was out of its pain now, because it was asleep. We went far down the garden to the farthest end, where the children and the nurse and the puppy and I used to play in the summer in the shade of a great elm, and there the footman dug a hole, and I saw he was going to plant the puppy, and I was glad, because it would grow and come up a fine handsome dog, like Robin Adair, and be a beautiful surprise for the family when they came home; so I tried to help him dig, but my lame leg was no good, being stiff, you know, and you have to have two, or it is no use. When the footman had finished and covered little Robin up, he patted my head, and there were tears in his eyes, and he said: "Poor little doggie, you saved *his* child!"

I have watched two whole weeks, and he doesn't come up! This last week a fright has been stealing upon me. I think there is something terrible about this. I do not know what it is, but the fear makes me sick, and I cannot eat, though the servants bring me the best of food; and they pet me so, and even come in the night, and cry, and say, "Poor doggie—do give it up and come home; *don't* break our hearts!" and all this terrifies me the more, and makes me sure something has happened. And I am so weak; since yesterday I cannot stand on my feet anymore. And within this hour the servants, looking toward the sun where it was sinking out of sight and the night chill coming on, said things I could not understand, but they carried something cold to my heart.

"Those poor creatures! They do not suspect. They will come home in the morning, and eagerly ask for the little doggie that did the brave deed, and who of us will be strong enough to say the truth to them: 'The humble little friend is gone where go the beasts that perish.' "

The Sword in the Stone

From *The Once and Future King*

BY T. H. WHITE

I N HIS SEARCH for authenticity, T. H. White once wrote to a friend asking for information on where he could find a suit of armor. White was about to start on his Arthurian legend opus *The Once and Future King* and wanted to know how it felt to ride a horse, swing a sword, pull a bow, or just walk in armor. Sadly, he was too large a man to fit in any medieval armor that might have come his way.

 That commitment lends an extraordinary sense of reality to what is essentially a fairy tale. Our selection is from *The Sword in the Stone,* one of the four books that make up *The Once and Future King,* and is the telling of the early days of King Arthur (herein known as "Wart"): his upbringing, his magical tutor Merlyn, and his life before being unveiled as the Saxon savior.

 The uncommon mixture of modern-day speech and thought with the trappings and emotions of a medieval boar hunt make this excerpt a unique pleasure.

★ ★ ★ ★ ★

THE WART GOT UP EARLY next morning. He made a determined effort the moment he woke, threw off the great bearskin run under which he slept, and plunged his body into the biting air. He dressed furiously, trembling, skipping about to keep warm, and hissing blue breaths to himself as if he were grooming a horse. He broke the ice in a basin and dipped his face in it with a grimace like eating something sour, said A-a-ah, and rubbed his stinging cheeks vigorously with a towel. Then he felt quite warm again and scampered off to the emergency kennels, to watch the King's huntsman making his last arrangements.

Master William Twyti turned out in daylight to be a shriveled, harassed-looking man, with an expression of melancholy on his face. All his life he had been forced to pursue various animals for the royal table, and, when he had caught them, to cut them up into proper joints. He was more than half a butcher. He had to know what parts the hounds should eat, and what parts should be given to his assistants. He had to cut everything up handsomely, leaving two vertebrae on the tail to make the chine look attractive, and almost ever since he could remember he had been either pursuing a hart or cutting it up into helpings.

He was not particularly fond of doing this. The harts and hinds in their herds, the boars in their singulars, the skulks of foxes, the richesses of martens, the bevies of roes, the cetes of badgers and the routs of wolves—all came to him more or less as something which you either skinned or flayed and then took home to cook. You could talk to him about os and argos, suet and grease, croteys, fewmets and fiants, but he only looked polite. He knew that you were showing off your knowledge of these words, which were to him a business. You could talk about a mighty boar which had nearly slashed you last winter, but he only stared at you with his distant eyes. He had been slashed sixteen times by mighty boars, and his legs had white weals of shiny flesh that stretched right up to his ribs. While you talked, he got on with whatever part of his profession he had in hand. There was only one thing which could move Master William Twyti. Summer or winter, snow or shine, he was running or galloping after boars and harts, and all the time his soul was somewhere else. Mention a *hare* to Master Twyti and, although he would still go on galloping after the wretched hart which seemed to be his destiny, he would gallop with one eye over his shoulder yearning for puss. It was the only thing he ever talked about. He was always being sent to one castle or another, all over England, and when he was there the local servants would fête him and keep his glass filled and ask him about his greatest hunts. He would answer distractedly in monosyllables. But if anybody mentioned a huske of hares he was all attention, and then he would thump his glass upon the table and discourse upon the marvels of this astonishing beast, declaring that you could never blow a menee for it, because the same hare could at one time be male and another time female, while it carried grease and croteyed and gnawed, which things no beast on earth did except it.

Wart watched the great man in silence for some time, then went indoors to see if there was any hope of breakfast. He found that there was, for the whole castle was suffering from the same sort of nervous excitement which had got him out of bed so early, and even Merlyn had dressed himself in a pair of breeches which had been fashionable some centuries later with the University Beagles.

Boar-hunting was fun. It was nothing like badger-digging or covert-shooting or fox-hunting today. Perhaps the nearest thing to it would be ferreting for rabbits—except that you used dogs instead of ferrets, had a boar that easily might kill you, instead of a rabbit, and carried a boar-spear upon which your life depended instead of a gun. They did not usually hunt the boar on horseback. Perhaps the reason for this was that the boar season happened in the two winter months, when the old English snow would be liable to ball in your horse's hoofs and render galloping too dangerous. The result was that you were yourself on foot, armed only with steel, against an adversary who weighed a good deal more than you did and who could unseam you from the nave to the chaps, and set your head upon his battlements. There was only one rule in boar-hunting. It was: Hold on. If the boar charged, you had to drop on one knee and present your boar-spear in his direction. You held the butt of it with your right hand on the ground to take the shock, while you stretched your left arm to its fullest extent and kept the point toward the charging boar. The spear was as sharp as a razor, and it had a cross-piece about eighteen inches away from the point. This cross-piece or horizontal bar prevented the spear from going more than eighteen inches into his chest. Without the cross-piece, a charging boar would have been capable of rushing right up the spear, even if it did go through him, and getting at the hunter like that. But with the cross-piece he was held away from you at a spear's length, with eighteen inches of steel inside him. It was in this situation that you had to hold on.

He weighed between ten and twenty score, and his one object in life was to heave and weave and sidestep, until he could get at his assailant and champ him into chops, while the assailant's one object was not to let go of the spear, clasped tight under his arm, until somebody had come to finish him off. If he could keep hold of his end of the weapon, while the other end was stuck in the boar, he knew that there was at least a spear's length between them, however much the boar ran him round the forest. You may be able to understand, if you think this over, why all the sportsmen of the castle got up early for the Boxing Day Meet, and ate their breakfast with a certain amount of sup-pressed feeling.

"Ah," said Sir Grummore, gnawing a pork chop which he held in his fingers, "down in time for breakfast, hey?"

"Yes, I am," said the Wart.

"Fine huntin' mornin'," said Sir Grummore. "Got your spear sharp, hey?"

"Yes, I have, thank you," said the Wart. He went over to the sideboard to get a chop for himself.

"Come on, Pellinore," said Sir Ector. "Have a few of these chickens. You're eatin' nothin' this mornin'."

King Pellinore said "I don't think I will, thank you all the same. I don't think I feel quite the thing, this morning, what?"

Sir Grummore took his nose out of his chop and inquired sharply, "Nerves?"

"Oh, no," cried King Pellinore. "Oh, no, really not that, what? I think I must have taken something last night that disagreed with me."

"Nonsense, my dear fellah," said Sir Ector, "here you are, just you have a few chickens to keep your strength up."

He helped the unfortunate King to two or three capons, and the latter sat down miserably at the end of the table, trying to swallow a few bits of them.

"Need them," said Sir Grummore meaningly, "by the end of the day, I dare say."

"Do you think so?"

"Know so," said Sir Grummore, and winked at his host.

The Wart noticed that Sir Ector and Sir Grummore were eating with rather exaggerated gusto. He did not feel that he could manage more than one chop himself, and, as for Kay, he had stayed away from the breakfast-room altogether.

When breakfast was over, and Master Twyti had been consulted, the Boxing Day cavalcade moved off to the Meet. Perhaps the hounds would have seemed rather a mixed pack to a master of hounds today. There were half a dozen black and white alaunts, which looked like greyhounds with the heads of bull-terriers or worse. These, which were the proper hounds for boars, wore muzzles because of their ferocity. The gaze-hounds, of which there were two taken just in case, were in reality nothing but greyhounds according to modern language, while the lymers were a sort of mixture between the bloodhound and the red setter of today. The latter had collars on, and were led with straps. The braches were like beagles, and trotted along with the master in the way that beagles always have trotted, and a charming way it is.

With the hounds went the foot-people. Merlyn, in his running breeches, looked rather like Lord Baden-Powell except, of course, that the latter did not wear a beard. Sir Ector was dressed in "sensible" leather clothes—it was not considered sporting to hunt in armor—and he walked beside Master Twyti with that bothered and important expression which has always been worn by masters of hounds. Sir Grummore, just behind, was puffing and asking everybody whether they had sharpened their spears. King Pellinore had dropped back among the villagers, feeling that there was safety in numbers. All the villagers were there, every male soul on the estate from Hob the austringer down to old Wat with no nose, every man carrying a spear or a pitchfork or a worn scythe blade on a stout pole. Even some of the young women who were courting had come out, with baskets of provisions for the men. It was a regular Boxing Day Meet.

At the edge of the forest the last follower joined up. He was a tall, distinguished-looking person dressed in green, and he carried a seven-foot bow.

"Good morning, Master," he said pleasantly to Sir Ector.

"Ah, yes," said Sir Ector. "Yes, yes, good mornin', eh? Yes, good mornin'."

He led the gentleman in green aside and said in a loud whisper that could be heard by everybody, "For heaven's sake, my dear fellow, do be careful. This is the King's own huntsman, and those two other chaps are King Pellinore and Sir Grummore. Now do be a good chap, my dear fellow, and don't say anything controversial, will you, old boy, there's a good chap?"

"Certainly I won't," said the green man reassuringly, "but I think you had better introduce me to them."

Sir Ector blushed deeply and called out: "Ah, Grummore, come over here a minute will you? I want to introduce a friend of mine, old chap, a chap called Wood, old chap—Wood with a W, you know, not an H. Yes, and this is King Pellinore. Master Wood—King Pellinore."

"Hail," said King Pellinore, who had not quite got out of the habit when nervous.

"How do?" said Sir Grummore. "No relation to Robin Hood I suppose?"

"Oh, not in the least," interrupted Sir Ector hastily. "Double you, double owe, dee, you know, like the stuff they make furniture out of—furniture, you know, and spears, and—well—spears, you know, and furniture."

"How do you do?" said Robin.

"Hail," said King Pellinore.

"Well," said Sir Grummore, "it is funny you should both wear green."

"Yes, it is funny, isn't it?" said Sir Ector anxiously. "He wears it in mournin' for an aunt of his, who died by fallin' out of a tree."

"Beg pardon, I'm sure," said Sir Grummore, grieved at having touched upon this tender subject—and all was well.

"Now then, Mr. Wood," said Sir Ector when he had recovered. "Where shall we go for our first draw?"

As soon as this question had been put, Master Twyti was fetched into the conversation, and a brief confabulation followed in which all sorts of technical terms like "lesses" were bandied about. Then there was a long walk in the wintry forest, and the fun began.

Wart had lost the panicky feeling which had taken hold of his stomach when he was breaking his fast. The exercise and the snow-wind had breathed him, so that his eyes sparkled almost as brilliantly as the frost crystals in the white winter sunlight, and his blood raced with the excitement of the chase. He watched the lymerer who held the two bloodhound dogs on their leashes, and saw the dogs straining more and more as the boar's lair was approached. He saw how, one by one and ending with the gazehounds—who did not hunt by scent—the various hounds became uneasy and began to whimper with desire. He noticed Robin pause and pick up some lesses, which he handed to Master Twyti, and then the whole cavalcade came to a halt. They had reached the dangerous spot.

Boar-hunting was like cub-hunting to this extent, that the boar was attempted to be held up. The object of the hunt was to kill him as quickly as possible. Wart took up his position in the circle round the monster's lair, and knelt down on one knee in the snow, with the handle of his spear couched on the ground, ready for emergencies. He felt the hush which fell upon the company, and saw Master Twyti wave silently to the lymerer to uncouple his hounds. The two lymers plunged immediately into the covert which the hunters surrounded. They ran mute.

There were five long minutes during which nothing happened. The hearts beat thunderously in the circle, and a small vein on the side of each neck throbbed in harmony with each heart. The heads turned quickly from side to side, as each man assured himself of his neighbors, and the breath of life steamed away on the north wind sweetly, as each realized how beautiful life was, which a reeking tusk might, in a few seconds, rape away from one or another of them if things went wrong.

The boar did not express his fury with his voice. There was no uproar in the covert or yelping from the lymers. Only, about a hundred yards away from the Wart, there was suddenly a black creature standing on the edge of the clearing. It did not seem to be a boar particularly, not in the first seconds that it stood there. It had come too quickly to seem to be anything. It was charging Sir Grummore before the Wart had recognized what it was.

The black thing rushed over the white snow, throwing up little puffs of it. Sir Grummore—also looking black against the snow—turned a quick somersault in a larger puff. A kind of grunt, but no noise of falling, came clearly on the north wind, and then the boar was gone. When it was gone, but not before, the Wart knew certain things about it—things which he had not had time to notice while the boar was there. He remembered the rank mane of bristles standing upright on its razor back, one flash of a sour tush, the staring ribs, the head held low, and the red flame from a piggy eye.

Sir Grummore got up, dusting snow out of himself unhurt, blaming his spear. A few drops of blood were to be seen frothing on the white earth. Master Twyti put his horn to his lips. The alaunts were uncoupled as the exciting notes of the menee began to ring through the forest, and then the whole scene began to move. The lymers which had reared the boar—the proper word for dislodging—were allowed to pursue him to make them keen on their work. The braches gave musical tongue. The alaunts galloped baying through the drifts. Everybody began to shout and run.

"Avoy, avoy," cried the foot-people. "Shahou, shahou! Avaunt, sire, avaunt!"

"Swef, swef!" cried Master Twyti anxiously. "Now, now, gentlemen, give the hounds room, if you please."

"I say, I say!" cried King Pellinore. "Did anybody see which way he went? What an exciting day, what? Sa sa cy avaunt, cy sa avaunt, sa cy avaunt!"

"Hold hard, Pellinore!" cried Sir Ector. "'Ware hounds, man, 'ware hounds. Can't catch him yourself, you know. Il est hault. Il est hault!"

And "Til est ho," echoed the foot-people. "Tilly-ho," sang the trees. "Tally-ho," murmured the distant snow-drifts as the heavy branches, disturbed by the vibrations, slid noiseless puffs of sparkling powder to the muffled earth.

The Wart found himself running with Master Twyti.

It was like beagling in a way, except that it was beagling in a forest where it was sometimes difficult even to move. Everything depended on the music of the hounds and the various notes which the huntsman could blow to tell where he was and what he was doing. Without these the whole field would have been lost in two minutes—and even with them about half of it was lost in three.

Wart stuck to Twyti like a burr. He could move as quickly as the huntsman because, although the latter had the experience of a life-time, he himself was smaller to get through obstacles and had, moreover, been taught by Maid Marian. He noticed that Robin kept up too, but soon the grunting of Sir Ector and the baa-ing of King Pellinore were left behind. Sir Grummore had given in early, having had most of the breath knocked out of him by the boar, and stood far in the rear declaring that his spear could no longer be quite sharp. Kay had stayed with him, so that he should not get lost. The foot-people had been early mislaid because they did not understand the notes of the horn. Merlyn had torn his breeches and stopped to mend them up by magic.

The sergeant had thrown out his chest so far in crying Tally-ho and telling everybody which way they ought to run that he had lost all sense of place, and was leading a disconsolate party of villagers, in Indian file, at the double, with knees up, in the wrong direction. Hob was still in the running.

"Swef, swef," panted the huntsman, addressing the Wart as if he had been a hound. "Not so fast, master, they are going off the line."

Even as he spoke, Wart noticed that the hound music was weaker and more querulous.

"Stop," said Robin, "or we may tumble over him."

The music died away.

"Swef, swef!" shouted Master Twyti at the top of his voice. "Sto arere, so howe, so howe!" He swung his baldrick in front of him, and, lifting the horn to his lips, began to blow a recheat.

There was a single note from one of the lymers.

"Hoo arere," cried the huntsman.

The lymer's note grew in confidence, faltered, then rose to the full bay.

"Hoo arere! Here how, amy. Hark to Beaumont the valiant! Ho moy, ho moy, hole, hole, hole, hole."

The lymer was taken up by the tenor bells of the braches. The noises grew to a crescendo of excitement as the blood-thirsty thunder of the alaunts pealed through the lesser notes.

"They have him," said Twyti briefly, and the three humans began to run again, while the huntsman blew encouragement with Trou-rou-root.

In a small bushment the grimly boar stood at bay. He had got his hindquarters into the nook of a tree blown down by a gale, in an impregnable position. He stood on the defensive with his upper lip writhed back in a snarl. The blood of Sir Grummore's gash welled fatly among the bristles of his shoulder and down his leg, while the foam of his chops dropped on the blushing snow and melted it. His small eyes darted in every direction. The hounds stood round, yelling at his mask, and Beaumont, with his back broken, writhed at his feet. He paid no further attention to the living hound, which could do him no harm. He was black, flaming and bloody.

"So-ho," said the huntsman.

He advanced with his spear held in front of him, and the hounds, encouraged by their master, stepped forward with him pace by pace.

The scene changed as suddenly as a house of cards falling down. The boar was not at bay any more, but charging Master Twyti. As it charged, the alaunts closed in, seizing it fiercely by the shoulder or throat or leg, so that what surged down on the huntsman was not one boar but a bundle of animals. He dared not use his spear for fear of hurting the dogs. The bundle rolled forward unchecked, as if the hounds did not impede it at all. Twyti began to reverse his spear, to keep the charge off with its butt end, but even as he reversed it the tussle was upon him. He sprang back, tripped over a root, and the battle closed on top. The Wart pranced around the edge, waving his own spear in an agony, but there was nowhere were he dared to thrust it in. Robin dropped his spear, drew his falchion in the same movement, stepped into the huddle of snarls, and calmly picked an alaunt up by the leg. The dog did not let go, but there was space were its body had been. Into this space the falchion went slowly, once, twice, thrice. The whole superstructure stumbled, recovered itself, stumbled again, and sank down ponderously on its left side. The hunt was over.

Master Twyti drew one leg slowly from under the boar, stood up, took hold of his knee with his right hand, moved it inquiringly in various directions, nodded to himself and stretched his back straight. Then he picked up his spear without saying anything and limped over to Beaumont. He knelt down beside him and took his head on his lap. He stroked Beaumont's head and said, "Hark to Beaumont. Softly, Beaumont, mon amy. Oyez à Beaumont the valiant. Swef, le douce Beaumont, swef, swef." Beaumont licked his hand but could not wag his tail. The huntsman nodded to Robin, who was standing behind, and held the hound's eyes with his own. He said, "Good dog, Beaumont the valiant, sleep now, old friend Beaumont, good old dog." Then Robin's falchion let Beaumont out of this world, to run free with Orion and roll among the stars.

The Wart did not like to watch Master Twyti for a moment. The strange, leathery man stood up without saying anything and whipped the hounds off the corpse of the boar as he was accustomed to do. He put his horn to his lips and blew the four long notes of the mort without a quaver. But he was blowing the notes for a different reason, and he startled the Wart because he seemed to be crying.

The mort brought most of the stragglers up in due time. Hob was there already and Sir Ector came next, whacking the brambles aside with his boar-spear, puffing importantly and shouting, "Well done, Twyti. Splendid hunt, very. That's the way to chase a beast of venery, I will say. What does he weigh?" The others dribbled in by batches, King Pellinore bounding along and crying out, "Tally-ho! Tally-ho! Tally-ho!" in ignorance that the hunt was done. When informed of this, he stopped and said "Tally-ho, what?" in a feeble voice, then relapsed into silence. Even the sergeant's Indian file arrived in the end, still doubling with knees up, and were halted in the clearing while the sergeant explained to them with great satisfaction that if it had not been for him, all would have been lost. Merlyn appeared holding up his running shorts, having failed in his magic. Sir Grummore came stumping along with Kay, saying that it had been one of the finest points he had ever seen run, although he had not seen it, and then the butcher's business of the "undoing" was proceeded with apace.

Over this there was a bit of excitement. King Pellinore, who had really been scarcely himself all day, made the fatal mistake of asking when the hounds were going to be given their quarry. Now, as everybody knows, a quarry is a reward of entrails, etc., which is given to the hounds on the hide of the dead beast (sur le quir), and, as everybody else knows, a slain boar is not skinned. It is disembowelled without the hide being taken off, and, since there can be no hide, there can be no quarry. We all know that the hounds are rewarded with a fouail, or mixture of bowels and bread cooked over a fire, and, of course, poor King Pellinore had used the wrong word.

So King Pellinore was bent over the dead beast amid loud huzzas, and the protesting monarch was given a hearty smack with a sword blade by Sir Ector. The King then said, "I think you are all a lot of beastly cads," and wandered off mumbling into the forest.

The boar was undone, the hounds rewarded, and the foot-people, standing about in chattering groups because they would have got wet if they had sat down in the snow, ate the provisions which the young women had brought in baskets. A small barrel of wine which had been thoughtfully provided by Sir Ector was broached, and a good drink was had by all. The boar's feet were tied together, a pole was slipped between his legs, and two men hoisted it upon their shoulders. William Twyti stood back, and courteously blew the prise.

It was at this moment that King Pellinore reappeared. Even before he came into view they could hear him crashing in the undergrowth and calling out, "I say, I say! Come here at once! A most dreadful thing has happened!" He appeared dramatically upon the edge of the clearing, just as a disturbed branch, whose burden was too heavy, emptied a couple of hundredweight of snow on his head. King Pellinore paid no attention. He climbed out of the snow heap as if he had not noticed it, still calling out, "I say. I say!"

"What is it, Pellinore?" shouted Sir Ector.

"Oh, come quick!" cried the King, and, turning round distracted, he vanished again into the forest.

"Is he all right," inquired Sir Ector, "do you suppose?"

"Excitable character," said Sir Grummore. "Very."

"Better follow up and see what he's doin'."

The procession moved off sedately in King Pellinore's direction, following his erratic course by the fresh tracks in the snow.

The spectacle which they came across was one for which they were not prepared. In the middle of a dead gorse bush King Pellinore was sitting, with the tears streaming down his face. In his lap there was an enormous snake's head, which he was patting. At the other end of the snake's head there was a long, lean, yellow body with spots on it. At the end of the body there were some lion's legs which ended in the slots of a hart.

"There, there," the King was saying. "I did not mean to leave you altogether. It was only because I wanted to sleep in a feather bed, just for a bit. I was coming back, honestly I was. Oh, please don't die, Beast, and leave me without any fewmets!"

When he saw Sir Ector, the King took command of the situation. Desperation had given him authority.

"Now, then, Ector," he exclaimed. "Don't stand there like a ninny. Fetch that barrel of wine along at once."

They brought the barrel and poured out a generous tot for the Questing Beast.

"Poor creature," said King Pellinore indignantly. "It has pined away, positively pined away, just because there was nobody to take an interest in it. How I could have stayed all that while with Sir Grummore and never given my old Beast a thought I really don't know. Look at its ribs, I ask you. Like the hoops of a barrel. And lying out in the snow all by itself, almost without the will to live. Come on, Beast, you see if you can't get down another gulp of this. It will do you good.

"Mollocking about in a feather bed," added the remorseful monarchy, glaring at Sir Grummore, "like a—like a kidney!"

"But how did you—how did you find it?" faltered Sir Grummore.

"I happened on it. And small thanks to you. Running about like a lot of nincompoops and smacking each other with swords. I happened on it in this gorse bush here, with snow all over its poor back and tears in its eyes and no-body to care for it in the wide world. It's what comes of not leading a regular life. Before, it was all right. We got up at the same time, and quested for regular hours, and went to bed at half past ten. Now look at it. It has gone to pieces al-together, and it will be your fault if it dies. You and your bed."

"But, Pellinore!" said Sir Grummore. . . .

"Shut your mouth," replied the King at once. "Don't stand there bleat-ing like a fool, man. Do something. Fetch another pole so that we can carry old Glatisant home. Now, then, Ector, haven't you got any sense? We must just carry him home and put him in front of the kitchen fire. Send somebody on to make some bread and milk. And you, Twyti, or whatever you choose to call yourself, stop fiddling with that trumpet of yours and run ahead to get some blankets warmed.

"When we get home," concluded King Pellinore, "the first thing will be to give it a nourishing meal, and then, if it is all right in the morning, I will give it a couple of hours' start and then hey-ho for the old life once again. What about that, Glatisant, hey? You'll tak' the high road and I'll tak' the low road, what? Come along, Robin Hood, or whoever you are—you may think I don't know, but I do—stop leaning on your bow with that look of negligent woodcraft. Pull yourself together, man, and get that muscle-bound sergeant to help you carry her. Now then, lift her easy. Come along, you chuckle-heads, and mind you don't trip. Feather beds and quarry, indeed; a lot of childish non-sense. Go on, advance, proceed, step forward, march! Feather brains, I call it, that's what I do.

"And as for you, Grummore," added the King, even after he had con-cluded, "you can just roll yourself up in your bed and stifle in it."

The Bear Hunt

BY ABRAHAM LINCOLN

L AWYER, STATESMAN, BACKWOODSMAN . . . Lincoln in all these guises is a familiar figure to every American. But Lincoln as a poet is less well-known. And so it was a real pleasure to come across this little gem—drawing clearly on his own experience, and giving us an early glimpse of that extraordinary, wry sense of humor.

It is interesting to note the similarities between this work and the boar hunt described in an excerpt from T. H. White's *The Sword in the Stone* which appears just previously in this book. About as diverse as two people could be—White an educated and sophisticated Englishman, Lincoln a self-educated, rough-edged frontiersman—they still show a like appreciation for the hunt, the hunter, and the hunted.

★   ★   ★   ★   ★

A WILD-BEAR CHACE, didst never see?
       Then hast thou lived in vain.
Thy richest bump of glorious glee,
       Lies desert in thy brain.

When first my father settled here,
       'Twas then the frontier line:
The panther's scream, filled night with fear
       And bears preyed on the swine.

But wo for Bruin's short lived fun,
       When rose the squealing cry;
Now man and horse, with dog and gun,
       For vengeance, at him fly.

A sound of danger strikes his ear;
       He gives the breeze a snuff:
Away he bounds, with little fear,
       And seeks the tangled *rough*.

On press his foes, and reach the ground,
       Where's left his half munched meal;
The dogs, in circles, scent around,
       And find his fresh made trail.

With instant cry, away they dash,
       And men as fast pursue;
O'er logs they leap, through water splash,
       And shout the brisk halloo.

Now to elude the eager pack,
       Bear shuns the open ground;
Through matted vines, he shapes his track
       And runs it, round and round.

The tall fleet cur, with deep-mouthed voice,
       Now speeds him, as the wind;
While half-grown pup, and short-legged fice,
       Are yelping far behind.

And fresh recruits are dropping in
    To join the merry *corps*;
With yelp and yell,—a mingled din—
    The woods are in a roar.

And round, and round the chace now goes,
    The world's alive with fun;
Nick Carter's horse, his rider throws,
    And more, Hill drops his gun.

Now sorely pressed, bear glances back,
    And lolls his tired tongue;
When as, to force him from his track,
    An ambush on him sprung.

Across the glade he sweeps for flight,
    And fully is in view.
The dogs, new-fired, by the sight,
    Their cry, and speed, renew.

The foremost ones, now reach his rear,
    He turns, they dash away.
And circling now, the wrathful bear,
    They have him full at bay.

At top of speed, the horse-men come,
    All screaming in a row.
"Whoop! Take him Tiger. Seize him Drum."
    Bang,—bang—the rifles go.

And furious now, the dogs he tears,
    And crushes in his ire.
Wheels right and left, and upward rears,
    With eyes of burning fire.

But leaden death is at his heart,
    Vain all the strength he plies.
And, spouting blood from every part,
    He reels, and sinks, and dies.

And now a dinsome clamor rose,
     'Bout who should have his skin;
Who first draws blood, each hunter knows,
     This prize must always win.

But who did this, and how to trace
     What's true from what's a lie,
Like lawyers, in a murder case
     They stoutly *argufy*.

Aforesaid fice, of blustering mood,
     Behind, and quite forgot,
Just now emerging from the wood,
     Arrives upon the spot.

With grinning teeth, and up-turned hair—
     Brim full of spunk and wrath,
He growls, and seizes on dead bear,
     And shakes for life and death.

And swells as if his skin would tear,
     And growls and shakes again;
And swears, as plain as dog can swear,
     That he has won the skin.

Conceited whelp! we laugh at thee—
     Nor mind, that not a few
Of pompous, two-legged dogs there be,
     Conceited quite as you.

Eagle River

From *Winterdance: The Fine Madness of Running the Iditarod*

BY GARY PAULSEN

G ARY PAULSEN IS A purely wonderful writer. His book, *Winterdance: The Fine Madness of Running the Iditarod,* from which this selection was taken, is pretty close to being a masterpiece—it is funny, touching, exciting, and exhausting.

Paulsen adores his dogs . . . *reads* his dogs . . . empathizes and admires and thrills to his dogs. He loves to run with them. Of them he said elsewhere:

> Sweet dogs, sour dogs, dogs that wagged and bit at the same time, dogs that wouldn't be happy unless they had a finger to eat, dogs that just lay down and looked at you when you harnessed them, dogs that loved to run, hated to run, dogs that made war, dogs that gave up and some, rare ones, who never, ever did.
>
> Dogs are like people.

★   ★   ★   ★   ★

THE PROCESS OF BEGINNING the Iditarod in downtown Anchorage is so insane and so completely out of context with what the race really represents that it's almost otherworldly. Then, too, it is all phony—the whole Anchorage start is for television and audiences and sponsors. The truth is, you cannot run a dog team from Anchorage to Nome because outside of Anchorage there is a freeway system that cannot be stopped, even for something as intrinsically Alaskan as the Iditarod. The start is a theatrical event, and is treated as such by everybody.

Except the dogs.

And therein lay the problem of the start. There was much hoopla, television cameras, crowds of people, and nearly fourteen hundred dogs jammed into a short stretch of Fourth Street in the middle of the downtown section. Starting well before the race crowds gathered, loudspeakers began blaring, and dogs started barking as they were harnessed. Barking dogs begot barking dogs and soon the whole street was immersed in a cacophonous roar that made it impossible to hear anything.

Worse, the dogs became excited. And like the barking, excitement breeds on itself until dogs I thought I'd known for years were completely unrecognizable, were almost mad with eagerness. It wasn't just that they wanted to run—there simply wasn't anything else for them. Everything they were, all the ages since their time began, the instincts of countless eons of wolves coursing after herds of bison and caribou were still there, caught in genetic strands, and they came to the fore and the dogs went berserk with it.

And at least as important was that the madness was infectious, carried to the people, the handlers, the mushers—especially the rookies. No matter the plan, no matter the words of caution during briefings, what might start sensibly began to pick up speed and soon everything was imbued with a frantic sense of urgency. People who walked start to trot, then run, with dogs dragging them from trucks to get hooked into the gangline to get them ready to be taken up to the chutes.

By this time I, too, was gone, caught up in the madness of it all, so immersed in the noise and insanity that if somebody had asked my name I would not have known it. I could see only the dogs, lunging on their picket chains, crazed with excitement; feel only that same pull tearing at me, the power of it all sweeping me.

And there was a very real danger in that power, the unleashed power of fifteen dogs in prime, perfect condition suddenly being released in front of a light sled and slick plastic runners. People would be hurt; people would scratch from the race in the first five blocks with broken legs, shoulders, collarbones, concussions. Sleds would be shattered, turned into kindling, and mushers would be dragged for blocks until bystanders could grab the dogs and stop them. The power was enormous and could not be controlled. There was only two inches of snow on the street, trucked in for the start, and the sleds could not be steered or slowed; brakes would not work; snowhooks would bounce off the asphalt.

It was here that I began making rookie mistakes, two of which would prove critical to the beginning of the Iditarod for me.

Caught up in anxiety, not wishing to cause problems with the race, I harnessed my dogs too soon, way too soon, and tied the sled off to the bumper of the truck. The difficulty with this was that I had pulled number thirty-two and with the dogs tied on the side, harnessed, and ready to go, waiting to go, crazy to go—every team going up to the chutes had to be taken past my team—they had to wait. Dogs do not wait well. An old Inuit belief states that dogs and white men stem from the same roots because they cannot wait, have no patience and become frustrated easily, and it showed mightily then.

It took two minutes per team to get them in the chutes, counted down and gone, so there was an hour delay waiting for my team to be called; an hour of slamming into harness, screaming with madness every time a team was taken past us, an hour of frustration and anxiety, an hour that seemed a day, a year.

When finally it was done, or nearly done, and the dogs were completely beyond reason and only three teams were ahead of us, six minutes before chute time, right then I made the second mistake.

I changed leaders. I had Cookie in single lead position. We had worked together for two years and she knew how to lead incredibly well and I trusted her completely. But . . .

The pre-race jim-jams took me and I started thinking of what I perceived to be reality. I had never raced before and Cookie had never raced, had never led a big team in such confusion. I began to worry that since it was all so new she would not know what to do, would not know how to get out of the chutes and line the team out down the street, would be confused about running in a race.

I had a dog that was given to me just before leaving Minnesota. His name was Wilson and I had been told that he had been in races, led in races. (I found out later it was one impromptu race, with a very small team—one dog—and it was only around a yard pulling a child.)

In microseconds the anxiousness about Cookie grew to a mountain and I could easily imagine her being released, stopping in her addled state, getting run over by the team or running into the crowd, heading off in the wrong direction—all I could see was disaster.

With less than three minutes to go I unhooked Cookie and dropped her back to point position (just to the rear of the leader) and put Wilson in the front. This all took moments and before I could think on it, wonder if I'd done the right thing, eleven or twelve volunteers came with a man who was holding a clipboard.

He noted the number on my bib, smiled and nodded. "You're next."

And volunteers took the gangline in back of each set of dogs; I unhooked them from the truck and we surged forward, the dogs nearly dragging the volunteers off their feet as we threaded into the chutes.

People talked to me. A man leaned over and said something and I nodded and smiled but I could not hear a thing over the din from the team. I also had a new sensation. Stark goddamn terror was taking me as I looked down the street over fifteen dogs and realized that this was it, that they were going to take me out hanging like an idiot on the sled.

A man leaned down with a megaphone next to my ear.

"Five!"

"Four!"

"Three!"

"Two!"

"One!"

But the dogs had watched too long, had memorized the count, and when the counter hit three and the volunteers released the team and stood off to the side they lunged, snapped loose from the men holding back the sled and I was, quite literally, gone.

I had started the Iditarod illegally—two seconds too soon.

I do not hold the record for the person coming to disaster soonest in the Iditarod. There have been some mushers who have never left the chutes. Their dogs dove into the spectators or turned back on the team and tried to go out of the chutes backwards. But I rank close.

There is a newspaper photo somewhere showing me leaving the chutes, that shows Wilson with his tongue out the side of his mouth and a wild look in his eye as he snakes the team out and away from the starting line with a great bound. (It also shows me apparently smiling; for the record the smile is not humor but the first stages of rictus caused by something close to terminal fright.)

We made almost two blocks. The distance before the first turn. Wilson ran true down the track left by the previous thirty-one teams. Until the turn.

At the end of two blocks there was a hard turn to the right to head down a side street, then out of town on back trails and alleys and into the trees along the highways away from Anchorage.

I remember watching the turn coming at alarming speed. All the dogs were running wide open and I thought that the only way to make it was to lean well to the right, my weight far out to the side to keep the sled from tumbling and rolling.

I prepared, leaned out and into the turn and would have been fine except that Wilson did not take the turn. He kept going straight, blew on through the crowd and headed off into Anchorage on his own tour of discovery.

I could not stop them. The sled brakes and snowhook merely scraped and bounced off the asphalt and concrete. I tried setting the hook in a car bumper as we passed, tearing it off the car (why in god's name are they all made of plastic?), and for a space of either six blocks or six miles—at our speed time and distance became irrelevant—I just hung on and prayed, screaming *"Whoa!"* every time I caught my breath. Since I had never used the command on the team before it had no effect whatsoever and so I got a Wilson-guided tour of Anchorage.

We went through people's yards, ripped down fences, knocked over garbage cans. At one point I found myself going through a carport and across a backyard with fifteen dogs and a fully loaded Iditarod sled. A woman standing over the kitchen sink looked out with wide eyes as we passed through her yard and I snapped a wave at her before clawing the handlebar again to hang on while we tore down her picket fence when Wilson tried to thread through a hole not much bigger than a housecat. And there is a cocker spaniel who will never come into his backyard again. He heard us coming and turned to bark just as the entire team ran over him; I flipped one of the runners up to just miss his back and we were gone, leaving him standing facing the wrong way barking at whatever it was that had hit him.

I heard later that at the banquet some people had been speaking of me and I was unofficially voted the least likely to get out of Anchorage. Bets were made on how soon I would crash and burn. Two blocks, three. Some said one. It was very nearly true.

Back on the streets I starting hooking signs with the snowhook. They were flimsy and bent when the hook hit them and I despaired of ever stopping, but at last my luck turned and the hook caught on a stop sign just right and hung and held the team while I put Cookie back in the lead and moved

Wilson—still grinning wildly and snorting steam and ready to rip—back into the team.

I now had control but was completely lost and found myself in the dubious position of having to stop along the street and ask gawking bystanders if they knew the way to the Iditarod trail.

"Well, hell, sure I do. You take this street down four blocks, then cross by the small metal culvert and catch the walking path through the park there until you see the gas station with the old Ford parked out front where you hang a kind of oblique right . . ."

It is a miracle that I ever got out of town. Finally I reasoned that I had fallen somehow north of the trail and I headed in a southerly direction and when we had gone a mile or so Cookie put her nose down and suddenly hung a left into some trees, around a sharp turn and I saw sled runner marks and we were back on the trail. (As we moved into this small stand of birch and spruce I saw shattered remnants of a sled in the trees and found later that a man had cracked the whip on the turn and hit the trees and broken his leg and had to scratch. He was not the first one to scratch; there had already been two others who gave it up before getting out of town.)

I was four and a half hours getting to the first official checkpoint at Eagle River—a suburb of Anchorage—where I was met by the handlers and Ruth. We had to unhook the dogs and put them in the truck and drive on the freeway to where the race truly starts, at Knik, on the edge of the bush.

"How's it going?" Ruth asked as I loaded the dogs.

"After this it ought to be all downhill," I said. "Nothing can be as hard as getting out of town . . ."

It was a statement I would come to think of many times during the following weeks.

A Conversation with My Dogs

From *What the Dogs Have Taught Me*

BY MERRILL MARKOE

I N A RADIO INTERVIEW once, the host asked me if I talked to my dog. Upon being assured that indeed, I did, he asked if the dog talked back. Yes, he does. Frequently with some degree of impatience.

Merrill Markoe's dogs talk to her too—and on topics of great familiarity to anyone who owns a dog. Once she wrote her dialogue down, it became clear that many of us have had the same talk with our dogs, up to and including the bad language.

This conversation first appeared in Markoe's book, *What the Dogs Have Taught Me, And Other Amazing Things I've Learned.*

★ ★ ★ ★ ★

IT IS LATE AFTERNOON. Seated at my desk, I call for my dogs to join me in my office. They do.

ME: The reason I've summoned you here today is I really think we should talk about something.

BOB: What's that?

ME: Well, please don't take this the wrong way, but I get the feeling you guys think you *have* to follow me *everywhere* and I just want you both to know that you don't.

STAN: Where would you get a feeling like that?

ME: I get it from the fact that the both of you follow me *everywhere* all day long. Like for instance, this morning. We were all together in the bedroom? Why do you both look blank? Doesn't this ring a bell at all? I was on the bed reading the paper . . .

BOB: Where was I?

ME: On the floor sleeping.

BOB: On the floor sleepi . . . ? Oh, yes. Right. I remember that. Go on.

ME: So, there came a point where I had to get up and go into the next room to get a Kleenex. And you *both* woke up out of a deep sleep to go with me.

STAN: Yes. So? What's the problem?

BOB: We *like* to watch you get Kleenex. We happen to think it's something you do very well.

ME: The point I'm trying to make is why do you both have to get up out of a deep sleep to go *with* me. You sit there staring at me, all excited, like you think something really good is going to happen. I feel a lot of pressure to be more entertaining.

BOB: Would it help if we stood?

STAN: I think what the lady is saying is that where Kleenex retrieval is concerned, she'd just as soon we not make the trip.

BOB: Is that true?

ME: Yes. It is.

BOB *(deeply hurt):* Oh, man.

STAN: Don't let her get to you, buddy.

BOB: I know I shouldn't. But it all comes as such a shock.

ME: I think you may be taking this wrong. It's not that I don't like your company. It's just that I see no reason for you both to follow me every time I get up.

BOB: What if just one of us goes?

STAN: And I don't suppose that "one of us" would be *you*?

ME: *Neither* of you needs to go.

BOB: Okay. Fine. No problem. Get your damn Kleenex alone from now on.

ME: Good.

BOB: I'm just curious. What's your position on pens?

ME: Pens?

BOB: Yes. How many of us can wake up out of a deep sleep to watch you look for a pen?

ME: Why would *either* of you want to wake up out of a deep sleep to follow me around while I'm looking for a pen?

STAN: Is she serious?

BOB: I can't tell. She has such a weird sense of humor.

ME: Let's just level with each other, okay? The *real* reason you both follow me every place I go is that you secretly believe there might be food involved. Isn't that true? Isn't that the real reason for the show of enthusiasm?

STAN: Very nice talk.

BOB: The woman has got some mouth on her.

ME: You mean you *deny* that every time you follow me out of the room it's actually because you think we're stopping for snacks?

BOB: Absolutely false. That is a bald-faced lie. We do it for the life experience. Period.

STAN: And sometimes I think it might work into a game of ball.

BOB: But we certainly don't *expect* anything.

STAN: We're *way* past expecting anything of you. We wouldn't want you to overexert yourself in any way. You have to rest and save up all your strength for all that Kleenex fetching.

BOB: Plus we know it doesn't concern you in the least that we're both *starving to death*.

STAN: We consume on the average about a third of the calories eaten daily by the typical wasted South American street dog.

ME: *One* bowl of food a day is what the *vet* said I should give you. No more.

BOB: One bowl of food is a joke. It's an hors d'oeuvre. It does nothing but whet my appetite.

ME: Last summer, before I cut your food down, you were the size and shape of a hassock.

BOB: Who is she talking to?

STAN: You, pal. You looked like a beanbag chair, buddy.

BOB: But it was not from overeating. In summer, I retain fluids, that's all. I was in very good shape.

STAN: For a hippo. I saw you play ball back then. Nice energy. For a dead guy.

BOB: Don't talk to me about energy. Who singlehandedly ate his way through the back fence. Not just once but on *four separate occasions?*

ME: So *you're* the one who did that?

BOB: One who did what?

ME: Ate through the back fence.

BOB: Is there something wrong with the back fence? I have no idea what happened. Whoever said that is a liar.

STAN: The fact remains that we are starving all day long and you continually torture us by eating right in front of us.

BOB: Very nice manners, by the way.

ME: You have the nerve to discuss my manners? Who drinks out of the toilet and then comes up and kisses me on the face?

BOB: That would be Dave.

ME: No. That would be *you.* And while we're on the subject of manners, who keeps trying to crawl *into* the refrigerator? Who always has *mud* on their tongue?

STAN: Well, that would be Dave.

ME: Okay. That *would* be Dave. But the point I'm trying to make is that where manners are concerned, let's just say that you don't catch me trying to stick my head in *your* dinner.

BOB: Well, that may be more a function of menu than anything else.

ME: Which brings me right back to my original point. The two of you do not have to wake up and offer me fake camaraderie now that you understand that *once* a day is all you're ever going to be fed. Period. Nonnegotiable. For the rest of your natural lives. And if I want to play ball, I'll *say so.* End of sentence.

STAN: Well, I see that the nature of these talks has completely broken down.

BOB: I gotta tell you, it hurts.

ME: There's no reason to have hurt feelings.

STAN: Fine. Whatever you say.

BOB: I just don't give a damn anymore. I'm beyond that, quite frankly. Get your own Kleenex, for all I care.

STAN: I feel the same way. Let her go get all the Kleenex and pens she wants. I couldn't care less.

ME: Excellent. Well, I hope we understand each other now.

BOB: We do. Why'd you get up? Where are you going?

ME: Into the next room.

STAN: Oh. Mm hmm. I see. And why is that?

ME: To get my purse.

STAN: Hey, fatso, out of my way.

BOB: Watch out, asshole, I was first.

STAN: The hell you were. *I* was first.

BOB: Fuck you. We're getting her purse, I go first. I'm *starving*.

STAN: You don't listen at all, do you? Going for *pens* means food. She said she's getting her *purse*. That means *ball*.

Blue and Some Other Dogs

From *From a Limestone Ledge:*
Some Essays and Other Ruminations about Country Life in Texas

BY JOHN GRAVES

J OHN GRAVES IS SOMETIMES characterized as one of Texas's most beloved writers, which seems to me to wrongly confine his craftsmanship. He is another of the thoughtful, caring, and perceptive observers of his surroundings and the characters, both human and canine, that inhabit it. He was nominated for a National Book Award for *Goodbye to a River.*

The story of Blue first appeared in *From a Limestone Ledge: Some Essays and Other Ruminations about Country Life in Texas.* Of him, Graves says, "I waited the better part of a lifetime to own a decent dog, and finally had him, and now don't have him any more." To me, a great epitaph.

★ ★ ★ ★ ★

ONE COOL STILL NIGHT last March, when the bitterest winter in decades was starting to slack its grip and the first few chuck-will's-widows were whistling tentative claims to nest territories, the best dog I ever owned simply disappeared. Dogs do disappear, of course. But not usually dogs like Blue or under conditions like ours here in the cedar hills.

A crossbred sheep dog, he had spent his whole ten years of life on two North Texas country places and had not left the vicinity of the house at either of them without human company since the age of two or less, when his mother was still alive and we also had an aging and lame and anarchic dachshund who liked to tempt the two of them out roaming after armadillos and feral cats and raccoons and other varmints. This happened usually at night when we had neglected to bring the dachshund into the house, or he had tricked his way outside by faking a call of nature or pushing open an unlatched screen door. The dachshund, named Watty (it started as Cacahuate or Peanut), had a very good nose and the two sheep dogs didn't, and having located quarry for them he would scream loud sycophantic applause as they pursued it and attacked, sometimes mustering the courage to run in and bite an exposed hind leg while the deadly mother and son kept the front part occupied.

It was fairly gory at times, nor am I that much at war with varmints except periodically with individual specimens that have developed a taste for chickens or kid goats or garden corn. But the main problem was the roaming itself, which sometimes took them a mile or so from home and onto other property. In the country wandering dogs are an abomination, usually in time shifting their attention from wild prey to poultry and sheep and goats and calves, and nearly always dying sooner or later from a rifle bullet or buckshot or poison bait, well enough deserved. Few people have lived functionally on the land without having to worry sooner or later about such raiders, and the experience makes them jumpy about their own dogs' habits.

To cope, you can chain or pen your dogs when they aren't with you, or you can teach them to stay at home. While I favor the latter approach, with three dogs on hand and one of them a perverse and uncontrollable old house pet too entwined with my own past and with the family to get rid of, it was often hard to make training stick. At least it was until the dachshund perished under the wheels of a pickup truck, his presence beneath it unsuspected by the driver and his cranky senile arrogance too great to let him scuttle out of the way when the engine started.

Blue's mother was a brindle-and-white Basque sheep dog from Idaho— of a breed said to be called Pannish, though you can't prove that by me since I have never seen another specimen. Taut and compact and aggressive, she was quick to learn but also quick to spot ways to nudge rules aside or to get out of work she did not savor. She came to us mature and a bit overdisciplined, and if you tried to teach her a task too roughly she would refuse permanently to have anything to do with it. I ruined her for cow work by whipping her for running a heifer through a net fence for the hell of it, and ever afterward if I started dealing with cattle when she was with me, she would go to heel or disappear. Once while chousing a neighbor's Herefords out of an oat patch toward the spate-ripped fence watergap through which they had invaded it, I looked around for Pan and glimpsed her peeking at me slyly from a shinoak thicket just beyond the field's fringe, hiding there till the risk of being called on for help was past.

Not that she feared cows or anything else that walked—or crawled or flew or swam or for that matter rolled on wheels. She attacked strange dogs like a male and had a contemptuous hatred of snakes that made her bore straight in to grab them and shake them dead, even after she had been bitten twice by rattlers, once badly. After such a bout I have seen her with drops of amber venom rolling down her shoulder, where fangs had struck the thick fine hair but had failed to reach her skin. Occasionally she bit people too—always men, though she was nervous enough around unfamiliar children that we never trusted her alone with them. Women, for her own secret reasons, she liked more or less indiscriminately.

She was a sort of loaded weapon, Pan, and in town there would have been no sense in keeping such a dog around, except maybe to patrol fenced grounds at night. But we were living then on a leased place just beyond the western honkytonk fringe of Fort Worth, where drunken irrationals roved the byways after midnight, and I was often away. There, what might otherwise have been her worst traits were reassuring. She worshipped my wife and slept beside the bed when I was gone, and would I am certain have died in defense of the household with the same driven ferocity she showed in combat with wild things.

A big boar coon nearly got her one January night, before she had Blue to help her out. The old dachshund sicked her on it by the barn, where it had come for a bantam supper, and by the time I had waked to the noise and pulled on pants and located a flashlight, the fight had rolled down to the creek and Pan's chopping yap had suddenly stilled, though Watty was still squalling hard. When I got there and shone the light on a commotion in the water, all that showed was the coon's solemn face and his shoulders. Astraddle Pan's neck with an ear clutched in each hand, he was quite competently holding her head down despite her mightiest struggles. Big bubbles rolled up as I watched the dachshund Watty dancing yet uproarious beside me on good firm land. Grabbing up a stick I waded into the frigid chest-deep pool, whacked the coon out of his saddle, declined his offer to climb me in retaliation, and sent him swimming for the other bank. But by then Pan was unconscious, and on shore I shook and pumped the better part of a gallon of water out of her before she started to wheeze and cough. Which didn't keep her from tearing into the very next coon her brave, small, black friend sniffed out, though I don't recall her ever following another one into the water. She was not too rash to learn what an impossibility was.

We had a plague of feral house cats at that place, strayed outward from the city or dumped along the roads by the kind of people who do that sort of thing, and a huge tom one evening gave the dachshund his comeuppance. After a notable scrap with Pan the tom decided to leave as I arrived, but she grabbed him by the tail as he went. At this point old Watty, thinking in dim light that the customary face-to-face encounter was still in progress and gaining from my arrival some of the courage that the cat had lost, dashed in for a furtive chomp and was received in a loving, tight, clawed embrace with sharp teeth in its middle. His dismay was piercingly loud and he bore those scars all his life. . . . The tomcat got away.

If my less than objective interest in these violent matters is evident, I have the grace to be a bit ashamed of it, but not much. I have friends among the hound-dog men whose main pleasure in life lies in fomenting such pursuits and brawls, and some of them are very gentle people—i.e., I am not of the school that believes hunting per se makes worse brutes of men than they already are, or ever did or ever will. Though I still hunt a little myself, I don't hunt in that way, and these home-ground uproars I seldom encouraged except occasionally much later, when Blue had become our only dog and had constituted himself Protector of Garden and Poultry. The toll of wildlife actually killed over the years was light, reaching a mild peak during the brief period after Blue was full grown and before Pan died, when they hunted and fought as a skillful team. Most chases would end with a treeing and I would go and call the dogs home with no blood having been shed on either side. But Man the Hunter's association with dogs is very very longstanding, and any man who can watch a slashing battle between his own dogs and something wild and tough, when it does occur, without feeling a flow of the old visceral, reckless joy, is either quite skilled at suppressing his emotions or more different from me than I think most men are.

There being of course the additional, perhaps more cogent fact that in the country varmints around the house and barn and chicken yard are bad news, and the best help in keeping them away is aggressive dogs.

Unable to find any males of Pan's breed in this region, we mated her with one of those more numerous sheep dogs, similar in build and coat but colored white and black-speckled gray, known commonly as Australians. Three of the resultant pups had her coloration and the fourth was Blue, marked like his sire but with less speckling and no trace of the blue "glass" or "china" tinge that many, perhaps most Australians have in one or both eyes, sometimes as only a queer pale blaze on an iris. When the time came to choose, we picked him to keep, and as a result he turned out to be a far different sort of grown dog than he would have if we had given him away.

For Pan was an impossibly capricious, domineering mother, neurotic in her protectiveness but punitive toward the pups to the point of drawing blood when they annoyed her, which was often. The others got out from under at six or eight weeks of age, but Blue had to stay and take it, and kept on taking it until Pan died—run over too, while nudging at the rule against chasing cars. Even after he had reached full size—at seventy-five pounds half-again bigger than either Pan or his sire—he had to be always on the watch for her unforeseeable snarling fits of displeasure.

I used to wish he would round on her and whip her hard once and for all, but he never did. Instead he developed the knack of turning clownish at a moment's notice, reverting to ingratiating puppy tricks to deflect the edge of her wrath. He would run around in senseless circles yapping, would roll on his back with his feet wiggling in the air, and above all would grin—crinkle his eyes and turn up the corners of his mouth and loll his tongue out over genially bared teeth. It was a travesty of all mashed-down human beings who have had to clown to survive, like certain black barbershop shoeshine "boys," some of them sixty years old, whom I remember from my youth.

These tricks worked well enough with Pan that they became a permanent part of the way Blue was, and he brought them to his relationship with people, mainly me, where they worked also. It was quite hard to stay angry at a large strong dog, no matter what he had just done, who had his bobtailed butt in the air and his head along his forelegs on the ground and his eyes skewed sidewise at you as he smiled a wide, mad, minstrel-show smile. If I did manage to stay angry despite all, he would most often panic and flee to his hideout beneath the pickup's greasy differential—which may have been another effect of Pan's gentle motherliness or may just have been Australian; they are sensitive dogs, easily cowed, and require light handling. For the most part, all that Blue did require was light handling, for he wanted immensely to please and was the easiest dog to train in standard matters of behavior that I have ever had to deal with. Hating cats, for instance, he listened to one short lecture concerning a kitten just purchased for twenty-five cents at a church benefit sale, and not only let her alone thereafter but became her staunchest friend, except perhaps in the matter of tomcats she might have favored, which he kept on chasing off. And he learned things like heeling in two hours of casual coaching.

Which harks back to my description of him as the best dog I ever owned. He was. But it is needful at this point to confess that that is not really saying much. Nearly all the dogs I owned before Blue and Pan and Watty were pets I had as a boy in Fort Worth, a succession of fox terriers and curs and whatnot that I babied, teased, cajoled, overfed, and generally spoiled in the anthropomorphic manner of kids everywhere. Most perished young, crushed by cars, and were mourned with tears and replaced quite soon by others very much like them in undisciplined worthlessness. In those years I consumed with enthusiasm Jack London's dog books and other less sinewy stuff like the works of Albert Payson Terhune, with their tales of noble and useful canines, but somehow I was never vouchsafed the ownership of anything that faintly resembled Lad or Buck or White Fang.

The best of the lot was a brown-and-white mongrel stray that showed up already old and gray-chopped, with beautiful manners and training, but he liked adults better than children and stayed with my father when he could. The worst but most beloved was an oversized Scotty named Roderick Dhu, or Roddy, who when I was twelve or thirteen or so used to accompany me and a friend on cumbersome hunting and camping expeditions to the Trinity West Fork bottom beyond the edge of town, our wilderness. He had huge negative willpower and when tired or hot would often sit down and refuse to move another inch. Hence from more than one of those forays I came hiking back out of the bottom burdened not only with a Confederate bedroll, an canteen, a twenty-two rifle, a bowie knife, an ax, a frying pan, and other such impedimenta, but with thirty-five dead-weight pounds of warm dog as well.

The friend's dog in contrast was a quick bright feist called Buckshot, destined to survive not only our childhood but our college years and the period when we were away at the war and nearly a decade longer, dying ultimately, my friend swears, at the age of twenty-two. A canine wraith, nearly blind and grayed all over and shrunken, he would lie in corners and dream twitching of old possums and rabbits we had harried through the ferns and poison ivy, thumping his tail on the floor when human movement was near if he chanced to be awake.

With this background, even though I knew about useful dogs from having uncles and friends who kept them for hunting and from having seen good herd dogs during country work in adolescence, as well as from reading, I arrived at my adult years with a fairly intact urban, middle-class, sentimental ideal of the Nice Dog—a clean-cut fellow who obeyed a few selected commands, was loyal and gentle with his masters, and refrained conscientiously from "bad" behavior as delineated by the same said masters. I had never had one and knew it, and the first dog I owned after years of unsettled existence was the dachshund Watty, who was emphatically not one either.

He started out all right, intelligent and affectionate and as willing to learn as dachshunds ever are, and with the nose he had he made a fair retriever, albeit hardmouthed with shot birds and inclined to mangle them a bit before reluctantly giving them up. He was fine company too, afield or in a canoe or a car, and we had some good times together. But his temper started souring when I married and grew vile when children came, and the job was finished by a paralyzing back injury with a long painful recovery, never complete, and by much sympathetic spoiling along the way. As an old lame creature, a stage that lasted at least five years, he snarled, bit, disobeyed, stank more or less constantly and from time to time broke wind to compound it, yowled and barked for his supper in the kitchen for two hours before feeding time, subverted the good sheep dogs' training, and was in general the horrid though small-scale antithesis of a Nice Dog. And yet in replication of my childhood self I loved him, and buried him wrapped in a feed sack beneath a flat piece of limestone with his name scratched deep upon it.

(While for Blue, than whom I will never have a Nicer Dog even if perhaps one more useful, there is no marker at all because there is no grave on which to put one . . .)

I do think Watty knocked out of me most of my residual kid sentimentality about dogs in general—he along with living in the country where realism is forced upon you by things like having to cope with goat-killing packs of canines, and the experience of having the sheep dogs with their strong thrust and potential, never fully attained—to the point that I am certain I will never put up with an unmanageable dog again. I remember one time of sharp realization during the second summer after we had bought this cedar-hill place, long before we lived here any part of the year or even used it for grazing. That spring, after the dachshund had been thrown from the pickup's seat when I jammed the brakes on in traffic, I carried him partly paralyzed to the vet, a friend, who advised me frankly that the smart thing would be to put him away. But he added that he had always wanted to try to cure one of those tricky dachshund spines, and that if I would go along with him he would charge me only his actual costs. Though by that time Watty was already grumpy and snap-pish and very little pleasure to have around, sentimentality of course tri-umphed over smart. The trouble was that with intensive therapy still going strong after several weeks, "actual costs" were mounting to the sky—to the point that even now in far costlier times I can grunt when I think of them.

Engaged that summer in some of the endless construction that has marked our ownership of this place where we now live, I was in and out every day or so with loads of lumber and cement and things, and paused sometimes to talk with a pleasant man who lived on the road I used. He had a heteroge-neous troop of dogs around the yard, some useful and some just there, their ringleader a small white cur with pricked ears and red-rimmed eyes who ran cars and was very noisy, but was prized by the man's children and had the re-deeming trait of being, quote, hell at finding snakes.

One morning as I drove in, this dog was sitting upright under a liveoak fifty yards short of the house, with his head oddly high and askew. He had found one snake too many. His eyes were nearly shut and on the side of his neck was a lump about the size of his head. Nor did he acknowledge my passage with as much as a stifled yap. Thinking perhaps they didn't know, I stopped by the house.

"Yes," said my friend. "He run onto a big one up by the tank yesterday evening and by the time I got there with a hoe it had done popped him good."

"Did you do anything for him?"

"Well, we put some coal oil on it," he said. "I was going to cut it open but there's all those veins and things. You know, they say if a snake hits a dog in the body he's a goner, but if it's the head he'll get all right. You reckon the neck's the head?"

I said I hoped so, and for days as I passed in and out I watched the lit-tle dog under his oak tree, from which he did not stir, and checked with the family about him. They were not at all indifferent; he was a main focus of in-terest and they kept fresh food and water by him. The neck swelled up fatter and broke open, purging terrible fluids. After this happened he seemed to feel better and even ate a little, but then one morning he was dead. Everyone in-cluding me was sad that he had lost his fight to live, and the children held a fu-neral for him, with bouquets of wild prairie pinks.

And such was my changing view that it seemed somehow to make more healthy sense than all that cash I was ramming into a spoiled irascible dachshund's problematic cure. . . .

"Good" country dogs are something else, and are often treated like members of the family and worried over as much when sick. This is not sentimentality but hard realism, because they are worth worrying over in pragmatic terms. There aren't very many of them. As good dogs always have, they come mainly from ruthless culling of promising litters and from close, careful training, and most belong to genuine stockmen with lots of herding work to do. These owners routinely turn down offers of a thousand or more dollars for them, if you believe the stories, as you well may after watching a pair of scroungy border collies, in response to a low whistle or a word, run a half-mile up a brush-thick pasture and bring back seventy-nine Angora wethers and pack them into a fence corner or a pen for shearing, doctoring, or loading into a trailer, all while their master picks his teeth.

Blue wasn't that kind of dog or anywhere near it, nor was there much chance to develop such talent on a place like ours, where the resident cows and goats are fairly placid and few problems emerge in handling them that can't be solved with a little patience and a rattling bucket of feed. For that matter, I don't know nearly enough about the training of such dogs to have helped him become one, though a livestock buyer I know, who has superb dogs himself and handles thousands of sheep and goats each year on their way from one owner to another, did tell me after watching Blue try to help us one morning that if I'd let him have him for six months, he might be able to "make a dog out of him." I was grateful and thought it over but in the end declined, partly because I mistrusted what six months of training by a stranger might do to that queer, one-man, nervous Australian streak in Blue, but mainly because I didn't know what I'd do with such a dog if I had him, in my rather miniature and unstrenuous livestock operations. His skills would rust unused, and the fact I had to face was that I didn't deserve a dog like that.

What Blue amounted to, I guess, was a country Nice Dog, which in terms of utility is a notable cut above the same thing in the city. These dogs stay strictly at home, announce visitors, keep varmints and marauding dogs and unidentified nocturnal boogers away, cope with snakes (Blue, after one bad fanging that nearly killed him, abandoned his mother's tactics of headlong assault and would circle a snake raising hell until I came to kill it, or to call him off if it was harmless), watch over one's younger children, and are middling-to-good help at shoving stock through a loading chute or from one pen to another, though less help in pastures where the aiming point may be a single gate in a long stretch of fence and judgment is required. Some learn simple daily herding tasks like bringing in milk cows at evening, though I have observed that much of the time these tasks involve an illusion on the part of the dog and perhaps his owner that he is making cows or goats or sheep do something, when actually they have full intention of doing it on their own, unforced. Or the whole thing may be for fun, as it was with one old rancher I knew, who had an ancient collie named Babe. When visitors came to sit with the old man on his porch, he would at some point level a puzzled blue glare across the pasture and say in conversational tones, "I declare, Babe, it looks like that old mare has busted out of the corral again. Maybe you better bring her in." And Babe would rise and go do as he was bidden and the visitors would be much impressed, unless they happened to be as aware that that was the one sole thing he could do and that the mare was in on it too.

On the whole, to be honest, Blue was pretty poor at herding even by such lax standards—too eager and exuberant and only occasionally certain of what it was we were trying to do. But he was controllable by single words and gestures and like his mother unafraid, and in his later years when I knew his every tendency, such as nipping goats, I could correct mistakes before he made them, so that he was often of some help. He was even more often comic relief, as when a chuted cow turned fighty and loaded him into the trailer instead of he her, or when a young bull, too closely pressed, kicked him into a thick clump of scrub elm, where he landed upside down and lay stuck with his legs still running in the air. When I went over and saw that he wasn't hurt and started laughing at the way he looked, he started laughing too, at least in his own way.

For a sense of humor and of joy was the other side of that puppyish clowning streak which he always retained but which turned less defensive with time. The nervousness that went with it never left either, but grew separate from the clowning, ritualizing itself most often in a weird habit he had of grinning and slobbering and clicking his teeth together when frustrated or perplexed. He regularly did this, for instance, when friends showed up for visits and brought their own dogs along. Knowing he wasn't supposed to attack these dogs as he did strays, Blue was uncertain what else to do with them. So he would circle them stiff-legged, wagging his stub and usually trying to mount them, male or female, small or large, and after being indignantly rebuffed would walk about popping his jaws and dribbling copious saliva. I expect some of those visiting friends thought him a very strange dog indeed, and maybe in truth he was.

He was a bouncing, bristling, loudmouthed watchdog, bulkily impressive enough that arriving strangers would most often stay in their cars until I came out to call him off. Unlike Pan, he bore them no real hostility and never bit anyone, though I believe that if any person or thing had threatened one of us those big white teeth would have been put to good use. Mainly, unfamiliar people disconcerted him and he wanted nothing to do with them unless I was around and showed myself receptive, at which point he was wont to start nuzzling their legs and hands like a great overgrown pup, demanding caresses. Once when the pickup was ailing I left it at a garage in town and mooched a ride home with a friend whose car Blue did not know. No one in the family was there, and when we drove up to the house there was no sign of Blue, but then I saw him peering furtively around a corner of the porch, much as his mother had eyed me from those shinoak bushes long before.

With his size, clean markings, silky thick coat, broad head, alert eyes, and usual aspect of grave dignity, he was a handsome beast. Having him along was often a social asset with strangers, even if it could turn out to be the opposite if something disturbed him and he went to popping his jaws and grinning that ghastly grin and drooling. One day when he was young and we were still living outside Fort Worth, I was apprehended in that city for running a red light, though I had discerned no light on at all when I drove through the intersection. I explained this to the arresting officer, a decent type, and together we went back and watched the damned thing run through six or eight perfectly sequenced changes from green to yellow to red and back again. Blue watched with us and, attuned to the situation, accepted a pat from the cop with an austere but friendly smile. Against pregnant silence I said with embarrassment that I guessed my eyes were failing faster than I'd thought, accepted the inevitable summons, and went my disgruntled way.

When I got home that afternoon, my wife said the officer had telephoned. More decent even than I had known, he had watched the light for a while longer by himself and had finally caught it malfunctioning, and he told Jane I could get the ticket cancelled.

She thought me off in the cedar hills and believed there was some mistake. "Did he have a sheep dog in the back of the pickup?" she asked.

"No, ma'am," said Blue's till-then secret admirer. "That great big beautiful animal was sitting right up on the front seat with him."

We spent a tremendous lot of time together over the years, Blue and I—around the house and barn and pens, wandering on the place, batting about in a pickup (his pickup more than mine, for he spent much of each day inside it or beneath, even when it was parked by the house), or at farm work in the fields. When young he would follow the tractor around and around as I plowed or harrowed or sowed, but later he learned to sit in the shade and watch the work's progress in comfort, certain I was not escaping from him, though sometimes when he got bored he would bounce out to meet the tractor as it neared him and would try to lead it home. Fond of the whole family and loved by all, he would go along with the girls to swim at the creek or on horseback jaunts across the hills, good protection for them and good company. But he needed a single main focus and I was it, so completely that at times I felt myself under surveillance. No imperfectly latched door missed his notice if I was indoors and he was out, and he could open one either by shoving or by pulling it with his teeth, as permanent marks on some of them still testify. Failing to get in, he would ascertain as best he could, by peeking in windows or otherwise, just where I was located inside and then would lie down by the exterior wall closest to that spot, even if it put him in the full blast of a January norther.

At one friend's house in town that he and I used to visit often, he would if left outside go through the attached garage to a kitchen door at odds with its jamb and seldom completely shut. Easing through it, he would traverse the breakfast room and a hall, putting one foot before another in tense slow motion, would slink behind a sofa into the living room, and using concealment as craftily as any old infantryman, would sometimes be lying beside my chair before I even knew he was in. More usually we would watch his creeping progress while pretending not to notice, and after he got where he was headed I would give him a loud mock scolding and he would roll on his back and clown, knowing he was home free and wouldn't be booted back out as sometimes happened when he was shedding fat ticks or stinking from a recent battle with some polecat.

But there were places he would not go with me, most notable among them the bee yard, his first apicultural experience having been his definite last. It happened one early spring day when I was helping a friend check through a neglected hive someone had given him and Blue had tagged along as usual. The thing was all gummed up with the tree sap bees use for glue and chinking, and the combs in the frames were crooked and connected by bridge wax so that we had to tear them when taking them out, and on that cool day all thirty or forty thousand workers were at home and ready to fight. They got under our veils and into all cracks in our attire, and those that didn't achieve entry just rammed their stings home through two or three layers of cloth. They also found Blue, a prime target for apian rage since they all hate hairy things, probably out of ancestral memory of hive-raiding bears. With maybe a hundred of them hung whining in his hair and stinging when they found skin, he tried to

squeeze between my legs for protection and caused me to drop a frame covered with bees, which augmented the assault. Shortly thereafter, torn between
mirth and pain, we gave up and slapped the hive back together and lit out at a
run, with Blue thirty yards in front and clouds of bees flying escort. And after
that whenever he saw me donning the veil and firing up my smoker, he would
head in the other direction.

He did work out a method of revenge, though, which he used for the
rest of his life despite scoldings and other discouragements. Finding a place
where small numbers of bees were coming for some reason—a spot on the
lawn where something sweet had been spilled, perhaps, or a lime-crusted dripping faucet whose flavor in their queer way they liked—he would stalk it with
his special tiptoeing slink and then loudly snap bees from the air one by one as
they flew, apparently not much minding the occasional stings he got on his lips
and tongue. I suppose I could have broken him of it, but it was a comical thing
to watch and for that matter he didn't get many bees in relation to their huge
numbers—unlike another beekeeper friend's Dalmatian, afflicted with similar
feelings, who used to sit all day directly in front of a hive chomping everything
that emerged, and had to be given away.

Maybe Blue considered bees varmints. He took his guardianship of the
home premises dead seriously and missed few creatures that came around the
yard. Except for the unfortunate armadillos, which he had learned to crunch,
the mortality inflicted on their ranks was low after Pan's death, as I have said,
for most could escape through the net yard fence that momentarily blocked
Blue's pursuit and few of them cared to stay and dispute matters except an occasional big squalling coon. We did have some rousing fine midnight fights
with these, though I suppose I'd better not further sully my humanitarian aura,
if any remains, by going into details. During the time when cantaloupes and
roasting ears were coming ripe and most attractive to coons, I would leave the
garden gate open at dark and Blue would go down during the night on patrol.
There was sometimes a question as to whether a squad of coons given full license could have done half as much damage to garden crops as the ensuing
battles did, but there was no question at all about whether the procedure
worked. After only two or three brawls each year, word would spread around
canny coondom that large hairy danger lurked in the Graves' corn patch and
they would come no more, much to Blue's disappointment.

I talked to him quite a bit, for the most part childishly or joshingly as
one does talk to beasts, and while I am not idiot enough to think he "understood" any of it beyond a few key words and phrases, he knew my voice's in-

flections and tones, and by listening took meaning from them if meaning was there to be had, responding with a grin, a sober stare, melting affection, or some communicative panting, according to what seemed right. Like most dogs that converse with humans he was a thorough yes type, honoring my every point with agreement. Nice Dogs are ego boosters, and have been so since the dim red dawn of things.

I could leave him alone and untied at the place for three or more days at a time, with dry food in a bucket under shelter and water to be had at the cattle troughs. Neighbors half a mile away have told me that sometimes when the wind was right they could hear him crooning softly wolflike, lonely, but he never left. When I came back he would be at the yard gate waiting, and as I walked toward the house he would go beside me leaping five and six feet straight up in the air in pure and utter celebration, whining and grunting maybe but seldom more—he saved loud barks for strangers and snakes and threatening varmints and such.

Last winter I slept inside the house instead of on the screen porch we shared as night quarters during much of he year—unless, as often, he wanted to be outside on guard—and I hadn't moved back out by that March night when he disappeared. He had been sleeping on a horse blanket on a small unscreened side porch facing south, and I had begun to notice that sometimes he would be still abed and pleasantly groggy when I came out at daybreak. He was fattening a bit also, and those eyes were dimmer that once had been able to pick me out of a sidewalk crowd of jostling strangers half a block away in town, and track me as I came toward the car. Because, like mine, his years were piling up. It was a sort of further bond between us.

He ate a full supper that evening and barked back with authority at some coyotes singing across the creek, and in the morning he was gone. I had to drive two counties north that day to pick up some grapevines and had planned to take him along. When he didn't answer my calling I decided he must have a squirrel in the elms and cedars across the house branch, where he would often sit silent and taut for hours staring up at a treed rodent, oblivious to summonings and to everything else. It was a small sin that I permitted him at his age; if I wanted him I could go and search him out and bring him in, for he was never far. But that morning it didn't seem to matter and I took off without him, certain he'd be at the yard gate when I drove in after lunch, as he had invariably been over the years.

Except that he wasn't. Nor did a tour of his usual squirrel ground yield any trace, or careful trudges up and down the branch, or a widening week-long search by myself and my wife and kids (whose spring vacation it used up and thoroughly ruined) that involved every brushpile and crevice we could find within half a mile or more of home, where he might have followed some varmint and gotten stuck or bitten in a vein by a rattler just out of its long winter's doze and full of rage and venom. Or watching for the tight downspiral of feeding buzzards. Or driving every road in the county twice or more and talking with people who, no, had not seen any dogs like that or even any bitches in heat that might have passed through recruiting. Or ads run in the paper and notices taped to the doors of groceries and feed mills, though these did produce some false hopes that led me up to thirty miles away in vain.

Even his friend the two-bit cat, at intervals for weeks, would sit and meow toward the woods in queer and futile lament. . . .

I ended fairly certain of what I had surmised from the first, that Blue lies dead, from whatever cause, beneath some thick heap of bulldozed brush or in one of those deep holes, sometimes almost caves, that groundwater eats out under the limestone ledges of our hills. For in country as brushy and wrinkled and secret as this, we can't have found all of such places roundabout, even close.

Or maybe I want to believe this because it has finality.

And maybe he will still turn up, like those long-lost animals you read about in children's books and sometimes in newspaper stories.

He won't.

And dogs are nothing but dogs and I know it better than most, and all this was for a queer and nervous old crossbreed that couldn't even herd stock right. Nor was there anything humanly unique about the loss, or about the emptiness that came in the searching's wake, which comes sooner or later to all people foolish enough to give an animal space in their lives. But if you are built to be such a fool, you are, and if the animal is to you what Blue was to me the space he leaves empty is big.

It is partly filled for us now by a successor, an Old English pup with much promise—sharp and alert, wildly vigorous but responsive and honest, puppy-clownish but with an underlying gravity that will in time I think prevail. There is nothing nervous about him; he has a sensitivity that could warp in that direction if mishandled, but won't if I can help it. Nor does he show any fear beyond healthy puppy caution, and in the way he looks at cows and goats and listens to people's words I see clearly that he may make a hell of a dog, quite possibly better than Blue. Which is not, as I said, saying much. . . .

But he isn't Blue. In the domed shape of his head under my hand as I sit reading in the evenings I can still feel that broader, silkier head, and through his half-boisterous, half-bashful, glad morning hello I still glimpse Blue's clown grin and crazy leaps. I expect such intimate remembrance will last a good long while, for I waited the better part of a lifetime to own a decent dog, and finally had him, and now don't have him any more. And I resolve that when this new one is grown and more or less shaped in his ways, I am going to get another pup to raise beside him, and later maybe a third. Because I don't believe I want to have to face so big a dose of that sort of emptiness again.

That Spot

BY JACK LONDON

B EST KNOWN FOR HIS BROODING, powerful prose, Jack London is re-membered for *Call of the Wild* and *White Fang* and other tales of des-peration and drama.He brought the untamed North—the gold rush, the fierce Yukon territory, the rock-bottom, down-and-dirty, basic toe-to-toe battle for survival—to millions of readers who had had no idea.

Interestingly enough, it seems London had his moments of lightness. He could tell a joke on himself, and laugh along with us. It wasn't all grim and mean and primeval. So it was a pleasure to discover "That Spot" and the sun-nier side of Jack London.

★　★　★　★　★

I DON'T THINK MUCH of Stephen Mackaye anymore, though I used to swear by him. I know that in those days I loved him more than my own brother. If ever I meet Stephen Mackaye again, I shall not be responsible for my actions. It passes beyond me that a man with whom I shared food and blanket, and with whom I mushed over the Chilcoot Trail, should turn out the way he did. I always sized Steve up as a square man, a kindly comrade, without an iota of anything vindictive or malicious in his nature. I shall never trust my judgment in men again. Why, I nursed that man through typhoid fever; we starved together on the headwaters of the Stewart; and he saved my life on the Little Salmon. And now, after the years we were together, all I can say of Stephen Mackaye is that he is the meanest man I ever knew.

We started for the Klondike in the fall rush of 1897, and we started too late to get over Chilcoot Pass before the freeze-up. We packed our outfit on our backs partway over, when the snow began to fly, and then we had to buy dogs in order to sled it the rest of the way. That was how we came to get that Spot. Dogs were high, and we paid $110 for him. He looked worth it. I say *looked*, because he was one of the finest-appearing dogs I ever saw. He weighed sixty pounds, and he had all the lines of a good sled animal. We never could make out his breed. He wasn't husky, nor malamute, nor Hudson Bay; he looked like all of them and he didn't look like any of them; and on top of it all he had some of the white man's dog in him, for on one side, in the thick of the mixed yellow-brown-red-and-dirty-white that was his prevailing color, there was a spot of coal black as big as a water bucket. That was why we called him Spot.

He was a good looker all right. When he was in condition his muscles stood out in bunches all over him. And he was the strongest-looking brute I ever saw in Alaska, also the most intelligent-looking. To run your eyes over him, you'd think he could outpull three dogs of his own weight. Maybe he could, but I never saw it. His intelligence didn't run that way. He could steal and forage to perfection; he had an instinct that was positively gruesome for divining when work was to be done and for making a sneak accordingly; and for getting lost and not staying lost he was nothing short of inspired. But when it came to work, the way that intelligence dribbled out of him and left him a mere clot of wobbling, stupid jelly would make your heart bleed.

There are times when I think it wasn't stupidity. Maybe, like some men I know, he was too wise to work. I shouldn't wonder if he put it all over us with that intelligence of his.

Maybe he figured it all out and decided that a licking now and again and no work was a whole lot better than work all the time and no licking. He was intelligent enough for such a computation. I tell you, I've sat and looked into that dog's eyes till the shivers ran up and down my spine and the marrow crawled like yeast, what of the intelligence I saw shining out. I can't express myself about that intelligence. It is beyond mere words. I saw it, that's all. At times it was like gazing into a human soul, to look into his eyes; and what I saw there frightened me and started all sorts of ideas in my own mind of reincarnation and all the rest. I tell you I sensed something big in that brute's eyes; there was a message there, but I wasn't big enough myself to catch it. Whatever it was (I know I'm making a fool of myself)—whatever it was, it baffled me. I can't give an inkling of what I saw in that brute's eyes; it wasn't light, it wasn't color; it was something that moved, away back, when the eyes themselves weren't moving. And I guess I didn't see it move, either; I only sensed that it moved. It was an expression, that's what it was, and I got an impression of it. No, it was different from a mere expression; it was more than that. I don't know what it was, but it gave me a feeling of kinship just the same. Oh, no, not sentimental kinship. It was, rather, a kinship of equality. Those eyes never pleaded like a deer's eyes. They challenged. No, it wasn't defiance. It was just a calm assumption of equality. And I don't think it was deliberate. My belief is that it was unconscious on his part. It was there because it was there, and it couldn't help shining out. No, I don't mean shine. It didn't shine; it *moved*. I know I'm talking rot, but if you'd looked into that animal's eyes the way I have, you'd understand. Steve was affected the same way I was. Why, I tried to kill that Spot once—he was no good for anything—and I fell down on it. I led him out into the brush, and he came along slow and unwilling. He knew what was going on. I stopped in a likely place, put my foot on the rope, and pulled my big Colt's. And that dog sat down and looked at me. I tell you he didn't plead. He just looked. And I saw all kinds of incomprehensible things moving, yes, *moving*, in those eyes of his. I didn't really see them move; I thought I saw them, for, as I said before, I guess I only sensed them. And I want to tell you right now that it got beyond me. It was like killing a man, a conscious, brave man who looked calmly into your gun as much as to say, "Who's afraid?" Then, too, the message seemed so near that, instead of pulling the trigger quick, I stopped to see if I could catch the message. There it was, right before me, glimmering all around in those eyes of his. And then it was too late. I got scared. I was trembly all over, and my stomach generated a nervous palpitation that made me seasick. I just sat down and looked at that dog, and he looked at me, till I thought I was going crazy. Do you want to know what I did? I threw down the gun and ran back to camp with the fear of God in my heart. Steve laughed at me. But I noticed that Steve led Spot into the woods, a week later, for the same purpose, and that Steve came back alone, and a little later Spot drifted back, too.

At any rate, Spot wouldn't work. We paid $110 for him from the bottom of our sack, and he wouldn't work. He wouldn't even tighten the traces. Steve spoke to him the first time we put him in harness, and he sort of shivered, that was all. Not an ounce on the traces. He just stood still and wobbled, like so much jelly. Steve touched him with the whip. He yelped, but not an ounce. Steve touched him again, a bit harder, and he howled—the regular long wolf howl. Then Steve got mad and gave him half a dozen, and I came on the run from the tent.

I told Steve he was brutal with the animal, and we had some words—the first we'd ever had. He threw the whip down in the snow and walked away mad. I picked it up and went to it. That Spot trembled and wobbled and cowered before ever I swung the lash, and with the first bite of it he howled like a lost soul. Next he lay down in the snow. I started the rest of the dogs, and they dragged him along while I threw the whip into him. He rolled over on his back and bumped along, his four legs waving in the air, himself howling as though he was going through a sausage machine. Steve came back and laughed at me, and I apologized for what I'd said.

There was no getting any work out of that Spot; and to make up for it, he was the biggest pig-glutton of a dog I ever saw. On top of that, he was the cleverest thief. There was no circumventing him. Many a breakfast we went without our bacon because Spot had been there first. And it was because of him that we nearly starved to death up the Stewart. He figured out the way to break into our meat cache, and what he didn't eat, the rest of the team did. But he was impartial. He stole from everybody. He was a restless dog, always very busy snooping around or going somewhere. And there was never a camp within five miles of us that he didn't raid. The worst of it was that they always came back on us to pay his board bill, which was just, being the law of the land; but it was mighty hard on us, especially that first winter on the Chilcoot, when we were busted, paying for whole hams and sides of bacon that we never ate. He could fight, too, that Spot. He could do everything but work. He never pulled a pound, but he was the boss of the whole team. The way he made those dogs stand around was an education. He bullied them, and there was always one or more of them fresh-marked with his fangs. But he was more than a bully. He wasn't afraid of anything that walked on four legs; and I've seen him march, single-handed, into a strange team, without any provocation whatever, and put the kibosh on the whole outfit. Did I say he could eat? I caught him eating the whip once. That's straight. He started in at the lash, and when I caught him he was down to the handle, and still going.

But he was a good looker. At the end of the first week we sold him for seventy-five dollars to the Mounted Police. They had experienced dog-drivers, and we knew that by the time he'd covered the six hundred miles to Dawson he'd be a good sled dog. I say we *knew*, for we were just getting acquainted with that Spot. A little later we were not brash enough to know anything where he was concerned. A week later we woke up in the morning to the dangdest dogfight we'd ever heard. It was that Spot come back and knocking the team into shape. We ate a pretty depressing breakfast, I can tell you; but cheered up two hours afterward when we sold him to an official courier, bound in to Dawson with government dispatches. That Spot was only three days in coming back, and, as usual, celebrated his arrival with a roughhouse.

We spent the winter and spring, after our own outfit was across the pass, freighting other people's outfits; and we made a fat stake. Also, we made money out of Spot. If we sold him once, we sold him twenty times. He always came back, and no one asked for their money. We didn't want the money. We'd have paid handsomely for anyone to take him off our hands for keeps. We had to get rid of him, and we couldn't give him away, for that would have been suspicious. But he was such a fine looker that we never had any difficulty in selling him. "Unbroke," we'd say, and they'd pay any old price for him. We sold him as low as twenty-five dollars, and once we got 150 for him. That particular party returned him in person, refused to take his money back, and the way he abused us was something awful. He said it was cheap at the price to tell us what he thought of us; and we felt he was so justified that we never talked back. But to this day I've never quite regained all the old self-respect that was mine before that man talked to me.

When the ice cleared out of the lakes and river, we put our outfit in a Lake Bennett boat and started for Dawson. We had a good team of dogs, and of course we piled them on top the outfit. That Spot was along—there was no losing him—and a dozen times, the first day, he knocked one or another of the dogs overboard in the course of fighting with them. It was close quarters, and he didn't like being crowded.

"What that dog needs is space," Steve said the second day. "Let's maroon him."

We did, running the boat in at Caribou Crossing for him to jump ashore. Two of the other dogs, good dogs, followed him; and we lost two whole days trying to find them. We never saw those two dogs again; but the quietness and relief we enjoyed made us decide, like the man who refused his 150, that it was cheap at the price. For the first time in months Steve and I laughed and whistled and sang. We were as happy as clams. The dark days were over. The nightmare had been lifted. That Spot was gone.

Three weeks later, one morning, Steve and I were standing on the riverbank at Dawson. A small boat was just arriving from Lake Bennett. I saw Steve give a start, and heard him say something that was not nice and that was not under his breath. Then I looked; and there, in the bow of the boat, with ears pricked up, sat Spot. Steve and I sneaked immediately, like beaten curs, like cowards, like absconders from justice. It was this last that the lieutenant of police thought when he saw us sneaking. He surmised that there were law officers in the boat who were after us. He didn't wait to find out, but kept us in sight, and in the M. & M. saloon got us in a corner. We had a merry time explaining, for we refused to go back to the boat and meet Spot; and finally he held us under guard of another policeman while he went to the boat. After we got clear of him, we started for the cabin, and when we arrived, there was that Spot sitting on the stoop waiting for us. Now how did he now we lived there? There were forty thousand people in Dawson that summer, and how did he savvy our cabin out of all the cabins? How did he know we were in Dawson, anyway? I leave it to you. But don't forget what I have said about his intelligence and that immortal something I have seen glimmering in his eyes.

There was no getting rid of him anymore. There were too many people in Dawson who had bought him up on Chilcoot, and the story got around. Half a dozen times we put him on board steamboats going down the Yukon; but he merely went ashore at the first landing and trotted back up the bank. We couldn't sell him, we couldn't kill him (both Steve and I had tried), and nobody else was able to kill him. He bore a charmed life. I've seen him go down in a dogfight on the main street with fifty dogs on top of him, and when they were separated, he'd appear on all his four legs, unharmed, while two of the dogs that had been on top of him would be lying dead.

I saw him steal a chunk of moose meat from Major Dinwiddie's cache so heavy that he could just keep one jump ahead of Mrs. Dinwiddie's squaw cook, who was after him with an ax. As he went up the hill, after the squaw gave up, Major Dinwiddie himself came out and pumped his Winchester into the landscape. He emptied his magazine twice, and never touched that Spot. Then a policeman came along and arrested him for discharging firearms inside the city limits. Major Dinwiddie paid his fine, and Steve and I paid him for the moose meat at the rate of a dollar a pound, bones and all. That was what he paid for it. Meat was high that year.

I am only telling what I saw with my own eyes. And now I'll tell you something, also. I saw that Spot fall through a water hole. The ice was three and a half feet thick, and the current sucked him under like a straw. Three hundred yards below was the big water hole used by the hospital. Spot crawled out of the hospital water hole, licked off the water, bit out the ice that had formed between his toes, trotted up the bank, and whipped a big Newfoundland belonging to the Gold Commissioner.

In the fall of 1898, Steve and I poled up the Yukon on the last water, bound for Stewart River. We took the dogs along, all except Spot. We figured we'd been feeding him long enough. He'd cost us more time and trouble and money and grub than we'd got by selling him on the Chilcoot—especially grub. So Steve and I tied him down in the cabin and pulled our freight. We camped that night at the mouth of Indian River, and Steve and I were pretty facetious over having shaken him. Steve was a funny cuss, and I was just sitting up in the blankets and laughing when a tornado hit camp. The way that Spot walked into those dogs and gave them what-for was hair-raising. Now how did he get loose? It's up to you. I haven't any theory. And how did he get across the Klondike River? That's another facer. And anyway, how did he know we had gone up the Yukon? You see, we went by water, and he couldn't smell our tracks. Steve and I began to get superstitious about that dog. He got on our nerves, too; and, between you and me, we were just a mite afraid of him.

The freeze-up came on when we were at the mouth of Henderson Creek, and we traded him off for two sacks of flour to an outfit that was bound up White River after copper. Now that whole outfit was lost. Never trace nor hide nor hair of men, dogs, sleds, or anything was ever found. They dropped clean out of sight. It became one of the mysteries of the country. Steve and I plugged away up the Stewart, and six weeks afterward that Spot crawled into camp. He was a perambulating skeleton, and could just drag along; but he got there. And what I want to know is who told him we were up the Stewart? We could have gone a thousand other places. How did he know? You tell me, and I'll tell you.

No losing him. At the Mayo he started a row with an Indian dog. The buck who owned the dog took a swing at Spot with an ax, missed him, and killed his own dog. Talk about magic and turning bullets aside—I, for one, consider it a blamed sight harder to turn an ax aside with a big buck at the other end of it. And I saw him do it with my own eyes. That buck didn't want to kill his own dog. You've got to show me.

I told you about Spot breaking into our meat cache. It was nearly the death of us. There wasn't any more meat to be killed, and meat was all we had to live on. The moose had gone back several hundred miles and the Indians with them. There we were. Spring was on, and we had to wait for the river to break. We got pretty thin before we decided to eat the dogs, and we decided to eat Spot first. Do you know what that dog did? He sneaked. Now how did he know our minds were made up to eat him? We sat up nights laying for him, but he never came back, and we ate the other dogs. We ate the whole team.

And now for the sequel. You know what it is when a big river breaks up and a few billion tons of ice go out, jamming and milling and grinding. Just in the thick of it, when the Stewart went out, rumbling and roaring, we sighted Spot out in the middle. He'd got caught as he was trying to cross up above somewhere. Steve and I yelled and shouted and ran up and down the bank, tossing our hats in the air. Sometimes we'd stop and hug each other, we were that boisterous, for we saw Spot's finish. He didn't have a chance in a million. He didn't have any chance at all. After the ice run, we got into a canoe and paddled down to the Yukon, and down the Yukon to Dawson, stopping to feed up for a week at the cabins at the mouth of Henderson Creek. And as we came in to the bank at Dawson, there sat that Spot, waiting for us, his ears pricked up, his tail wagging, his mouth smiling, extending a hearty welcome to us. Now how did he get out of that ice? How did he know we were coming to Dawson, to the very hour and minute, to be out there on the bank waiting for us?

The more I think of that Spot, the more I am convinced that there are things in this world that go beyond science. On no scientific grounds can that Spot be explained. It's psychic phenomena, or mysticism, or something of that sort, I guess, with a lot of Theosophy thrown in. The Klondike is a good country. I might have been there yet, and become a millionaire, if it hadn't been for Spot. He got on my nerves. I stood him for two years altogether, and then I guess my stamina broke. It was the summer of 1899 when I pulled out. I didn't say anything to Steve. I just sneaked. But I fixed it up all right. I wrote Steve a note, and enclosed a package of "rough-on-rats," telling him what to do with it. I was worn down to skin and bone by that Spot, and I was that nervous that I'd jump and look around when there wasn't anybody within hailing distance. But it was astonishing the way I recuperated when I got quit of him. I got back twenty pounds before I arrived in San Francisco, and by the time I'd crossed the ferry to Oakland I was my old self again, so that even my wife looked in vain for any change in me.

Steve wrote to me once, and his letter seemed irritated. He took it kind of hard because I'd left him with Spot. Also, he said he'd used the "rough-on-rats," per directions, and that there was nothing doing. A year went by. I was back in the office and prospering in all ways—even getting a bit fat. And then Steve arrived. He didn't look me up. I read his name in the steamer list, and wondered why. But I didn't wonder long. I got up one morning and found that Spot chained to the gatepost and holding up the milkman. Steve went north to Seattle, I learned, that very morning. I didn't put on any more weight. My wife made me buy him a collar and tag, and within an hour he showed his gratitude by killing her pet Persian cat. There is no getting rid of that Spot. He will be with me until I die, for he'll never die. My appetite is not so good since he arrived, and my wife says I am looking peaked. Last night that Spot got into Mr. Harvey's henhouse (Harvey is my next-door neighbor) and killed nineteen of his fancy-bred chickens. I shall have to pay for them. My neighbors on the other side quarreled with my wife and then moved out. Spot was the cause of it. And that is why I am disappointed in Stephen Mackaye. I had no idea he was so mean a man.

Canine Château

BY VERONICA GENG

V ERONICA GENG HAS BEEN CALLED "a humorist's humorist." An editor and writer for the *New Yorker* magazine, she was noted for her incisive satire, puncturing pomposity with an irreverant pen. The shortfalls of Washington were her frequent targets.

I well remember the days when the Pentagon staffers squirmed as huge expenditures were revealed. $700 toilet seats. $400 hammers. Millions of dollars wasted in unsupervised spending. And so Ms. Geng had a perfect target for her brilliant harpooning of Washington excesses. (On the other hand, the French spend 30 billion francs a year—something like 3 billion dollars—on their pets. So who's to say the Canine Château is just a joke?)

★　★　★　★　★

(A DOCUMENT FROM THE PENTAGON'S ONGOING PROBE INTO A DEFENSE CON-
TRACTOR'S $87.25 BILL FOR DOG BOARDING.)

Dear Secretary Weinberger:

    I have received your request for particulars about the "nauseating" and
"preposterous" bill run up at this establishment by Tuffy. I would be more than
happy to supply details—I would be *delighted*. As someone who devotes his life
to the humane treatment of animals, I welcome this opportunity to enlighten
the Department of Defense and the Congress, neither of which seems to have
the faintest idea what a dog requires.

    Before I get into that, however, may I point out that Canine Château
is far from being some little fly-by-night dog dorm with a few bunk beds, a
Small Business Administration loan, and a penchant for padding its bills to
make ends meet. We have been a major and highly profitable concern since
1981. Up until that time, I had been a tool designer at Low-Bid Tool & Die (in
Van Nuys), running a private specialty shop called Jeff's Claw Clipper out of
my office. (And I suppose I'm going to get in trouble for *that* now with the
IRS.) They phased out my job in favor of a computer when Low-Bid won the
contract to produce the "manicure kits" (I think you know what I'm talking
about) that President Reagan sent as small gifts to Saudi Arabia. But I wanted
to remain within the industry, and I realized the potential for expanding Jeff's
Claw Clipper into a full-service kennel targeted specifically to the defense-
contract segment of the pet-boarding market.

    I had heard of a lovely old Spanish Colonial mansion for sale up on
Mulholland Drive, and as soon as I saw it I knew it was absolutely right. At
first I ran into all kinds of opposition—zoning boards, mortgage officers, you
name it—but these people very quickly came around when they found out
who our clientele would be. We are now the largest (and, to my knowledge, the
only) kennel in California catering exclusively to the special needs of defense-
contractor pets. These animals, as you may know, are extremely high-strung,
and are vulnerable to kidnap by agents of foreign powers who might wish to
extort from defense contractors certain classified information (such as details
about the offensive capability of purported "tie clasps" regularly shipped by the
U.S. to El Salvador). This is a particular danger during sensitive arms-
negotiation talks. No kennels could be more relaxing and safe than ours: Canine Château, nestled on a sunny, grass-carpeted five-acre site behind
bougainvillea-twined fencing of 33-mm. molybdenum-reinforced warhead-
quality steel with FX-14 radial vidicon sensors and zinc-carbon detonators;
and, farther south on Mulholland in a newly renovated Art Deco villa, Maison

Meow, similarly secured. (Birds, goldfish, and so on may guest at either location, depending on space availability.) We are constantly upgrading these facilities, thanks to the many satisfied pet owners who generously donate not only their technological expertise but also a good deal of materials and equipment that would otherwise just be thrown away at the end of the defense-contracting workday and carted off to a garbage dump or landfill site (at government expense), where it would serve no conceivable purpose except to pollute the environment.

All things considered, then, perhaps I may be forgiven if I preen myself somewhat on our success and out high standards—aesthetic, hygienic, technological, *and* financial. Canine Chateau operates under my close personal supervision, and I have something of a reputation among the staff as a strict taskmaster. I wear the key to the pantry around my neck on a platinum chain; and not only is the level in the kibble bin measured twice a day but the bin itself is equipped with a state-of-the-art laser lock, which cannot be opened without a microcoded propylene wafer issued to select personnel only after the most rigorous security check of their backgrounds and habits. Waste of any kind is simply not tolerated—let alone fraud.

Now, as to Tuffy's bill. Tuffy's one-week stay at Canine Château was booked under our "No Frills" Plan. We are hardly a dog pound, of course, but I suspect that even you, Secretary Weinberger, with your military-barracks frame of reference, would find Tuffy's accommodations Spartan. We have had dogs here—and I'm not going to say *whose* dogs they were, but I think you know the ones I mean—who have run up astronomical bills on shopping sprees at our accessories bar. I'm not criticizing them; most of our dogs are accustomed to a California standard of living, and we can't just suddenly alter a dog's lifestyle, because the dog won't understand and will become morose. Nor am I suggesting that you, Secretary Weinberger, would seek favorable publicity at the expense of the innocent animals whose taste for luxuries was created by profits in the very same industries that you depend upon for the perpetuation of your own livelihood and the good of the country. However, I question the Pentagon's decision to pay without a peep such previous bills as $3,000 for one golden retriever's ion-drive-propulsion duck decoy with optional remote aerial-guidance system and quartz-fiber splashdown shield, and then to quibble over Tuffy's, which was relatively modest.

But enough. As you requested, I am enclosing an annotated itemization of Tuffy's bill, which I trust will carry my point.

Very truly yours,
Jeff Chateau
President, Canine Château

————————TUFFY 2/11/85–2/18/85————————
Catalina Suite . . . . @ $40 = $280

[All "No Frills" accommodations are suites, and this is our cheapest rate. If it seems a bit steep, consider that each suite is actually an individual bunker, deployed with gyroscopic mounts on an elliptical underground track and activated to a speed of 35 m.p.h. by random changes in the earth's magnetic field. This is a security precaution, and, we feel, an essential one.]

Variety Menu (mature Dog Cycle), plus tips . . $340

[I suppose that you, Secretary Weinberger, when *your* family goes away, would be just thrilled to have a neighbor shove a bowl of something through the door once a day. Well, an animal is no different. Our gracious waiters and waitresses are trained to make each animal's regular mealtimes as relaxed, enjoyable, and *safe* as possible. They carry conventional Geiger counters at all times, and constantly monitor food, water, and serving utensils with a combat-type bacterial scanner.]

Valet $15

[Dry-cleaning of hand-knitted dog sweater. This was February, remember, and winter in the Hollywood Hills can be cruel.]

3 Cases of Marinated Mouse Knuckles $156

[Obviously a computer billing error, as this item is served only at Maison Meow. We will be pleased to delete the charge from the original invoice.]

Contribution $100

[A tax-deductible voluntary charge to support our lobbying efforts in Congress for continuation of the tax-deductible status for this charge.]

Insurance $10

[Indemnifies us against layoffs, work stoppages, and rises in the wholesale-price index.]

Cost Overrun $245
                                    Subtotal $1,146.00
Discounts

[We then applied our discount schedule, which allows us to maintain a high volume of business while welcoming guests from a wide range of economic brackets: not just executive animals but those at entry level in the defense-contracting and subcontracting industries, whose owners may be privy to compromising information about seemingly innocuous items manufactured for the U.S. government. The discounts were offered at our discretion and may be revoked at any time (for instance, if government-required paperwork increases our operating costs).]

Discount for booking 30 days in advance $400
Special discount for off-peak arrival
and departure $275
Reduction for booking through a state-
certified pet-kennel reservations agent $149.75
Quantity refund for four or more stays
per annum when the prime interest rate
is at or below 15% $200.00
Rebate for using Teamsters-approved
pet-carrier $34

	DISCOUNTS:	$1,058.75
	SUBTOTAL:	$1,146.00
	LESS DISCOUNTS:	$1,058.75
		————
	TOTAL:	$87.25

[Our billing is calculated by the same model of computer used to regulate the range finder on a Polaris submarine. We have every confidence in its conclusion that $87.25 is neither too low nor too high a price to pay for peace of mind.]

The Cover Artist

From *The Cover Artist*

BY PAUL MICOU

S USPEND YOUR DISBELIEF for a while and join with Paul Micou and
Elizabeth, who *is* The Cover Artist—a painter of great talent and repute. Her canvases are sought after, purchased for high prices, analyzed
and dissected. A Labrador of rather simple tastes, she becomes the toast
of the town—in this instance a small but sophisticated spot in the south of
France.

This selection is a chapter from *The Cover Artist,* in which Elizabeth's
tale of fame and fortune is told.

★ ★ ★ ★ ★

OSCAR LIMPED HOME from the high-diving party. . . . He returned to his house to find Elizabeth asleep on the floor next to a finished painting, exhausted by her labors. She dragged herself to her paws and wagged her tail in greeting, but wore the downcast expression of an art student whose work was about to be appraised by a professional. Oscar picked up the stretched canvas and held it at arm's length. Elizabeth had always done her best work in acrylics, and in this case she had outdone herself. True to her exhaustive training, there wasn't a pawmark on the canvas, and even the floor near where she had been working was clean. The painting itself was another example of Canine Expressionism, a school of art that held cleanliness in the workplace above all other considerations, but otherwise had much in common with most of the Abstract Expressionist works dating back fifty years. The painting in Oscar's hands, which he decided to call *High Dive,* employed Elizabeth's two favorite colors—black (the color of her coat), and pink (the color of her tongue)—an approximately twenty brushstrokes. Elizabeth had been trained to execute her works starting at the top of the canvas and moving steadily to the bottom, to avoid stepping in her own paint. She had started *High Dive* with a broad black stroke, a broad pink one next to but not touching it, like two-tone eyebrows. In her impatience to finish—she no longer had the endurance of a young artist—she had repeated the same strokes all the way to the bottom of the canvas where they began to mix in a noisome confluence that was, Oscar thought, particularly appropriate to her age. Because such paintings amount to nothing in the absence of someone who makes a living talking about them, Oscar imagined a learned voice speaking of Elizabeth's deep preoccupation with good and evil, and the stunning simplicity with which she elicited a feeling of straddling polarized moral choices that finally blended into the dismal lot of man and dog.

"Give me your paw, Elizabeth," said Oscar. "You haven't signed your beautiful painting."

Still Is the Land

From *West with the Night*

BY BERYL MARKHAM

ERNEST HEMINGWAY CHARACTERIZED *West With the Night,* the autobiography from which this excerpt is taken, as "really a bloody wonderful book." Beryl Markham led an extraordinary life, growing up in Africa in the 1920s. She was the daughter of a horseman, farmer, and mill-owner who apparently let her run around pretty much unchecked. When the farm went bankrupt, seventeen-year-old Beryl saddled up and rode across Africa, alone, to take a job as a horse-trainer. She subsequently became a bush pilot and record-holding aeronaut.

This piece is a fascinating glimpse of life in colonial Africa, its people, and Beryl and her dog, Buller, in particular.

★ ★ ★ ★ ★

WAININA, THE HEAD SYCE, tolled the stable bell each morning and its rusty voice brought wakefulness to the farm. The Dutchmen inspanned their oxen, syces reached for their saddles, the engines at the mills got up steam. Milkers, herdsmen, poultry boys, swineherds, gardeners, and house boys rubbed their eyes, smelled the weather, and trotted to their jobs.

On ordinary days Buller and I were a part of this, but on hunting days we escaped before the bell had struck a note and before the cocks had stretched their wings on the fences. I had lessons to do, and therefore lessons to avoid.

I remember one such day.

It began with the stirring of Buller asleep, as always, at the foot of my reimpie bed in the mud and daub hut we shared together—and with the hustle and hum of a million small insects.

I moved, I stretched, I opened my eyes on the far tableland of the Liakipia Escarpment outlined in the frame of my unglazed window, and I stepped on the earthen floor.

The water in the stable bucket was cold on my face, because nights in the East African Highlands are cold. The rawhide thong I tied around my waist was stiff and the blade of my 'bushman's friend' was unfriendly. Even the shaft of my Masai spear, which surely had life of its own, was rigid and unyielding, and its steel point, sunk in a sheath of black ostrich feather, emerged from it like a dull stone. The morning was still part of the night and its color was gray.

I patted Buller and he wagged his lump of a tail to say he understood the need for silence. Buller was my accomplice in everything. He was a past-master at stealth and at more other things than any dog I ever owned or knew.

His loyalty to me was undeviating, but I could never think of him as being a sentimental dog, a dog fit for a pretty story of the kind that tears the heartstrings off their pegs; he was too rough, too tough, and too aggressive.

He was bull terrier and English sheep dog, thoroughly mixed, and turned out to look not very much like either. His jaw protruded, though, and his muscles were hard and ropy like the ones on the fantastic coursing dogs in the stone friezes of ancient Persia.

He was cynical toward life, and his black-and-white hide bore, in a cryptology of long, short, and semicircular scars, the history of his fighting career. He fought anything that needed to be fought, and when there was nothing immediately available in this category, he killed cats.

It was my father's complaint that when Buller was beaten for this, as he often was, he considered the punishment only as part of the inevitable hazard that went with cat-killing; and when the corrective treatment had been administered, it was always my father who looked chastened, and never Buller.

One night, a leopard, no doubt the chosen avenger of his species, crept through the open door of my hut and abducted Buller from the foot of my bed. Buller weighed something over sixty-five pounds and most of it was nicely coordinated offensive equipment. The sound and the fury of the first round of that battle sometimes still ring in my ears. But the advantage was with the attacker. Before I could do much more than scramble out of bed, dog and leopard disappeared in the moonless night.

My father and I followed a trail of blood through the bush, by the light of a hurricane lamp, until the trail dwindled and led to nothing. But at dawn I set out again and found Buller, barely breathing, his hard skull and his lower jaw pierced as if they had been skewered. I ran for help and carried him back on a stretcher made of sacking. He recovered, after ten months' tedious nursing, and became the same Buller again—except that his head had lost what little symmetry it ever had and cat-killing developed from a sport to a vocation.

As for the leopard, we caught him the next night in a trap, but he was beyond all caring anyway. He had no ears, only part of a throat, and great disillusionment in his handsome eyes. To my knowledge, and I think to his, it was the first time any dog of any size had been caught by a leopard and lived to dream about it.

Together, Buller and I slipped out into the little yard that separated my hut from the dining quarters. There was still no real dawn, but the sun was awake and the sky was changing color.

Peering round the corner of my father's hut, which was close to my own, I could see that one or two of the more conscientious syces were already opening their stable doors.

Gay Warrior's box had even got a heap of manure outside it. That meant his syce had been there for some time. It also meant that my father would be out any minute to send his first string of race-horses to their morning work. If he were to see me with my spear, my dog, and the 'bushman's friend' strapped to my waist, he would hardly conclude that my mind was wrapped in ardent thoughts of 'The Fundamentals of English Grammar' or 'Exercises in Practical Arithmetic.' He would conclude, and rightly, that Buller and I were on our way to the nearest Nandi singiri to hunt with the Murani.

But we were adepts at our game. We scampered quickly through the cluster of domestic buildings, got behind the foaling boxes, and, when the moment was ripe, we hurried along the twisted path that, except to ourselves and the Natives whose feet had made it, was completely hidden by the high dry weather grass. It was wet grass so early in the day, heavy with morning dew, and the wetness clung to my bare legs and soaked into Buller's wiry coat.

I swung into the hop-and-carry-one gait—a kind of bounding lope used by the Nandi and Masai Murani—and approached the singiri.

It was surrounded by a lattice and thorn boma, high as the withers of a cow. Inside the fence, the low thatched huts, looking as if they had grown from the earth and not been built upon it, extended in a haphazard circle. Their walls were made of logs cut from the forests, placed upright and caulked with mud. Each hut had a single door, a low door that could only be entered by crouching, and there were no windows. Smoke curled upward through the leaves of the thatch and on a still day made the singiri seem, from a distance, like a patch in the prairie wreathed in the last wisps of a burned-out fire.

The ground in front of the doors and all that encircling the boma was flat and beaten hard with the feet of men, cattle, and goats.

A pack of dogs, half-bred, fawning, some of them snarling, rushed at Buller and me the moment we entered the boma. Buller greeted them as he always did—with arrogant indifference. He knew them too well. In packs they were good hunters; individually they were as cowardly as the hyena. I spoke to them by name to silence their foolish yapping.

We were at the door of the hut of the head Murani, and the beginning of a Nandi hunt, even so small as this would be, did not take place in the midst of noise or too much levity.

I drove the blunt end of my spear into the ground and stood beside it, waiting for the door to open.

Praise God for the Blood of the Bull

Arab Maina clasped the gourd of blood and curdled milk in both hands and looked toward the sun. He chanted in a low voice:

"Praise God for the blood of the bull which brings strength to our loins, and for the milk of the cow which gives warmth to the breasts of our lovers."

He drank deeply of the gourd then, let his belch roll upward from his belly and resound against the morning silence. It was a silence that we who stood there preserved until Arab Maina had finished, because this was religion; it was the ritual that came before the hunt. It was the Nandi custom.

"Praise God for the blood of the bull," we said, and stood before the singiri, and waited.

Jebbta had brought the gourds for Arab Maina, for Arab Kosky, and for me. But she looked only at me.

"The heart of a Murani is like unto stone," she whispered, "and his limbs have the speed of an antelope. Where do you find the strength and the daring to hunt with them, my sister?"

We were as young as each other, Jebbta and I, but she was a Nandi, and if the men of the Nandi were like unto stone, their women were like unto leaves of grass. They were shy and they were feminine and they did the things that women are meant to do, and they never hunted.

I looked down at the ankle-length skins Jebbta wore, which rustled like taffeta when she moved, and she looked at my khaki shorts and lanky, naked legs.

"Your body is like mine," she said; "it is the same and it is no stronger." She turned, avoiding the men with her eyes, because that too was law, and went quickly away tittering like a small bird.

"The blood of the bull . . ." said Arab Maina.

"We are ready." Arab Kosky drew his sword from its scabbard and tested its blade. The scabbard was of leather, dyed red, and it hung on a beaded belt that encircled narrow and supple hips. He tested the blade and put it back into the red scabbard.

"By the sacred womb of my mother, we will kill the wild boar today!"

He moved forward behind Arab Maina with his broad shield and his straight spear, and I followed Arab Kosky with my own spear that was still new and very clean, and lighter than theirs. Behind me came Buller with no spear and no shield, but with the heart of a hunter and jaws that were weapons enough. There were the other dogs, but there was no dog like Buller.

We left the singiri with the first light of the sun warming the roofs of the huts, with cattle, goats, and sheep moving along the trails that led to open pastures—fat cattle, pampered cattle, attended as always by the young, uncircumcised boys.

There were cows, steers, and heifers—liquid brown eyes, wet, friendly nostrils, slobbery mouths that covered our legs with sticky fluid as Arab Maina pushed the stupid heads aside with his shield.

There were the pungent stench of goat's urine and a hot, comforting odor seeping through the hides of the cattle, and light on the long muscles of Arab Maina and Arab Kosky.

There was the whole of the day ahead—and the world to hunt in.

His little ritual forgotten now, Arab Maina was no longer stern. He laughed when Arab Kosky or I slipped in the cattle dung that littered our path, and shook his spear at a big black bull busy tearing up the earth with his hooves. "Take care of your people and dare not insult me with a barren cow this year!"

But, for the most part, we ran silently in single file skirting the edge of the dense Mau Forest, wheeling north to descend into the Rongai Valley, its bottom a thousand feet below us.

Eight weeks had passed since the end of the heavy rains and the grass in the valley had already reached the height of a man's knee. The ears had begun to ripen in patches. Looking down upon it, the whole was like a broad counterpane dyed in rust and yellow and golden brown.

We filed along our path, almost invisible now, through the fresh-smelling leleshwa bush, avoiding with quick turns and careful leaps the sting-ing nettle and the shrubs that were armed with thorns. Buller ran at my heels with the native dogs spread fanwise behind.

Halfway down the slope of the valley a bevy of partridges rose from the grass and wheeled noisily into the sky. Arab Maina lifted his spear almost imperceptibly; Arab Kosky's long muscles were suddenly rigid. Watching him, I froze in my tracks and held my breath. It was the natural reaction of all hunters—that moment of listening after any alarm.

But there was nothing. The spear of Arab Maina dipped gently, the long muscles of Arab Kosky sprang again to life, Buller flicked his stubby tail, and we were off again, one behind another, with the warm sunlight weaving a pattern of our shadows in the thicket.

The heat of the valley rose to meet us. Singing cicadas, butterflies like flowers before a wind fluttered against our bodies or hovered over the low bush. Only small things that were safe in the daylight moved.

We had run another mile before the cold nose of Buller nudged against my leg and the dog slipped quickly past me, past the two Murani, to plant himself, alert and motionless, in the center of our path.

"Stop." I whispered the word, putting my hand on Arab Kosky's shoul-der. "Buller has scented something."

"I believe you are right, Lakweit!" With a wave of his hand Arab Kosky ordered the pack of native dogs to crouch. In that they were well trained. They pressed their lean bellies on the ground, cocked their ears, but scarcely seemed to breathe.

Arab Maina, sensing the need for free action, began laying down his shield. The fingers of his left hand still touched the worn leather of its handle, his legs were still bent at the knee, when a male reed-buck bounded high into the air more than fifty yards away.

I saw Arab Kosky's body bend like a bow and watched his spear fly to his shoulder, but he was too late. The spear of Arab Maina flashed in a quick arc of silver light and the reed-buck fell with the hard point sunk deep under his heart. Not even his first frantic bound had been completed before Arab Maina's arm had brought him down.

"Karara-ni! The hand of our leader is swifter than the flight of an arrow and stronger than the stroke of a leopard." Heaping praise on Arab Maina, Arab Kosky ran toward the fallen reed-buck, the sword from his red leather sheath drawn for the kill.

I looked at Arab Maina's slender arms with their even, flat muscles and saw no visible sign of such immense strength. Arab Maina, like Arab Kosky, was tall and lithe as a young bamboo, and his skin glowed like an ember under a whisper of wind. His face was young and hard, but there was soft humor in it. There was love of life in it—love for the hunt, love for the sureness of his strength, love for the beauty and usefulness of his spear.

The spear was made of pliant steel tempered and forged by the metallist of his own tribe. But it was also more than that.

To each Murani his spear is a symbol of his manhood, and as much a part of himself as the sinews of his body. His spear is a manifestation of his faith; without it he can achieve nothing—no land, no cattle, no wives. Not even honor can be his until that day comes, after his circumcision, when he stands before the gathered members of his tribe—men and women of all ages, from manyattas as scattered as the seeds of wild grass—and swears allegiance to them and to their common heritage.

He takes the spear from the hands of the ol-oiboni and holds it, as he will always hold it while there is strength in his arms and no cloud of age before his eyes. It is the emblem of his blood and his breeding, and possessing it, he is suddenly a man.

Possessing it, it is never afterward beyond his reach.

Arab Maina placed his left foot on the reed-buck and carefully drew out his spear.

"I do not know, it may have struck a bone," he said.

He ran bloody fingers along the sharp edges of the weapon and let a little smile twist his lips. "By the will of God, the metal is not chipped! My spear is unhurt." He stooped to pluck a handful of grass and wiped the blood from the bright, warm steel.

Arab Kosky and I had already begun to skin the animal, using our "bushman's friends." There was not much time to waste, because our real hunt for the wild boar had not yet begun. But still the meat of the reed-buck would provide food for the dogs.

"The sun has hit the valley," said Arab Maina; "if we do not hurry the pigs will have gone in all directions like rolling weeds in a wind."

Arab Kosky buried his fingers along the walls of the reed-buck's stomach, tearing it from the animal's frame.

"Hold this, Lakwani," he said, "and help me separate the intestines for the dogs."

I took the slippery, jelly-like stomach in my hands and held it while I kneeled over the reed-buck.

"Maina, I still don't know how you managed to throw in time from the position you were in!"

Arab Kosky smiled.

"He is a Murani, Lakwani—and a Murani must always throw in time. Otherwise, some day a dangerous animal might charge swifter than the spear. Then, instead of mourning his death, our girls would laugh and say he should have stayed at home with the old men!"

Arab Maina leaned down and cut a chunk of meat from the cleanly skinned buck. He handed it to me for Buller. The rest, he and Arab Kosky left to the native mongrels.

Buller trotted a short distance away from the kill, dropped his reward in a little pool of shade, and regarded his snarling cousins with exquisite disdain. In the language that he spoke, and only I understood, he said quite clearly (with just a tinge of Swahili accent), "By the noble ancestry of my bull terrier father, those animals behave like the wild dog!"

"And now," said Arab Maina, moving away from the carnage, "we must make ready for the hunt."

The two Murani wore ochre-colored shukas, each falling loosely from a single knot on the left shoulder, and each looking somewhat like a scanty Roman toga. They untied the knots now, wrapped the shukas prudently around their waists, and stood in the sun, the muscles in their backs rippling under their oiled skins like fretted water over a stony bed.

"Who can move freely with clothes on his body?" Arab Kosky said as he helped Arab Maina with the leather thong that bound his braided headdress in place. "Who has seen the antelope run with rags upon his back to hinder his speed!"

"Who indeed?" said Arab Maina, smiling. "I think sometimes you babble like a demented goat, Kosky. The sun is high and the valley still lies below us—and you speak to Lakwani of antelope wearing shukas! Take up your spears, my friends, and let us go."

Single file again, with Arab Maina in the lead, then Arab Kosky, then myself, and Buller just behind, we ran on down into the valley.

There were no clouds and the sun stared down on the plain making heat waves rise from it like flames without color.

The Equator runs close to the Rongai Valley, and, even at so high an altitude as this we hunted in, the belly of the earth was hot as live ash under our feet. Except for an occasional gust of fretful wind that flattened the high, corn-like grass, nothing uttered—nothing in the valley stirred. The chirrup-like drone of grasshoppers was dead, birds left the sky unmarked. The sun reigned and there were no aspirants to his place.

We stopped by the red salt-lick that cropped out of the ground in the path of our trail. I did not remember a time when the salt-lick was as deserted as this. Always before it had been crowded with grantii, impala, kongoni, eland, water-buck, and a dozen kinds of smaller animals. But it was empty today. It was like a marketplace whose flow and bustle of life you had witnessed ninety-nine times, but, on your hundredth visit, was vacant and still without even an urchin to tell you why.

I put my hand on Arab Maina's arm. "What are you thinking, Maina? Why is there no game today?"

"Be quiet, Lakweit, and do not move."

I dropped the butt of my spear on the earth and watched the two Murani stand still as trees, their nostrils distended, their ears alert to all things. Arab Kosky's hand was tight on his spear like the claw of an eagle clasping a branch.

"It is an odd sign," murmured Arab Maina, "when the salt-lick is without company!"

I had forgotten Buller, but the dog had not forgotten us. He had not forgotten that, with all the knowledge of the two Murani, he still knew better about such things. He thrust his body roughly between Arab Maina and myself, holding his black wet nose close to the ground. And the hairs along his spine stiffened. His hackles rose and he trembled.

We might have spoken, but we didn't. In his way Buller was more eloquent. Without a sound, he said, as clearly as it could be said—"Lion."

"Do not move, Lakweit." Arab Kosky stepped closer to me.

"Steady, Buller," I whispered to the dog, trying to soothe his rising belligerence.

Our eyes followed the direction of Arab Maina's eyes. He was staring into a small grass-curtained donga a few yards from the edge of the salt-lick.

The lion that stood in the donga was not intimidated by Arab Maina's stare. He was not concerned with our number. He swung his tail in easy arcs, stared back through the wispy grass, and his manner said, "I am within my rights. If you seek a battle, what are we waiting for?"

He moved slowly forward, increasing the momentum of his tail, flaunting his thick black mane.

"Ach! This is bad! He is angry—he wants to attack!" Arab Maina spoke in an undertone.

No animal, however fast, has greater speed than a charging lion over a distance of a few yards. It is a speed faster than thought—faster always than escape.

Under my restraining hand I felt the muscles of Buller knot and relax, in a surging flow of mounting fury. Buller's mind had reached its blind spot. Uncontrolled, he would throw himself in gallant suicide straight at the lion. I dug my fingers into the dog's coat and held tight.

Arab Maina's appearance was transformed. His face had taken on a sullen, arrogant expression, his square, bold jaw jutted forward. His eyes dimmed almost dreamily and sank behind high, shiny cheekbones. I watched the muscles on his neck swell like those on the neck of an angry snake, and saw flecks of white froth appear in the corners of his mouth. Passive and rigid he stared back at the lion.

He raised his shield at last, as if to make sure it was still in his hand, and let his spear arm drop to his side to preserve all of its power for whatever might come.

He knew that if the lion attacked, his own skill and Arab Kosky's would, in the end, prove sufficient—but not before at least one of us had been killed or badly mauled. Arab Maina was more than a Murani; he was a leader of Murani, and as such he must be able to think as well as to fight. He must be capable of strategy.

Watching him still, as he in turn watched the lion, I knew that he had a plan of action.

"Observe his eyes," he said; "he thinks very hard of many things. He believes that we also think of those same things. We must show him that we are fearless as he himself is fearless, but that his desires are not our desires. We must walk straight past him firmly and with courage, and we must shame his anger by laughter and loud talk."

Arab Kosky's brow was dotted with small bubbles of sweat. A slight flicker of a smile crept over his face.

"Yes, true enough! The lion thinks of many things. I too think of many things, and so does Lakweit. But your plan is a good one. We will try it."

Arab Maina lifted his head a little higher, turning it only enough to keep the lion within the scope of his vision. He placed one sinewy leg in front of the other, and stiffly, like a man walking the trunk of a tree that bridges a chasm, he began to move. One after another, we followed. My hand still lay upon Buller's neck, but Arab Kosky let the dog and me slip past him to walk between the two Murani.

"Stay close to me, Lakweit"—Arab Maina's voice was anxious. "I fear for you when it is not possible to see you."

Arab Kosky burst suddenly into forced laughter.

"There is a tale about a rhino who needed a needle to do her husband's sewing . . ." he began.

"So she borrowed one from the porcupine . . ." said Arab Kosky.

"And swallowed it," I contributed. "I have heard that tale before, Kosky!"

The Murani laughed louder. "But perhaps our friend the lion has not. Look at him. He is listening!"

"But not laughing," said Arab Maina. "He moves as we move. He comes closer!"

The lion had stalked out of the donga. Now, as we walked, we could see that he guarded the slain body of a large kongoni. Smears of blood were fresh on his forelegs, his jowls, and his chest. He was a lone hunter—an individualist—a solitary marauder. His tail had stopped swinging. His great head turned exactly in ratio to the speed of our stride. The full force of the lion-smell, meaty, pungent, almost indescribable, struck against our nostrils.

"Having swallowed the needle . . ." said Arab Kosky.

"Silence—he attacks!"

I do not know who moved with greater speed—Arab Maina or the lion. I believe it must have been Arab Maina. I think the Murani anticipated the charge even before the lion moved, and because of that, it was a battle of wills instead of weapons.

The lion rushed from the fringe of the donga like a rock from a catapult. He stopped like the same rock striking the walls of a battlement.

Arab Maina was down on his left knee. Beside him was Arab Kosky. Each man, with his shield, his spear, and his body, was a fighting machine no longer human, but only motionless and precise and coldly ready. Buller and I crouched behind them, my own spear as ready as I could make it in hands that were less hot from the sun than from excitement and the pounding of my heart.

"Steady, Buller."

"Do not move, Lakweit."

The lion had stopped. He stood a few strides from Arab Maina's buffalo-hide shield, stared into Arab Maina's eyes challenging him over the top of it, and swung his tail like the weight of a clock. At that moment I think the ants in the grass paused in their work.

And then Arab Maina stood up.

I do not know how he knew that that particular instant was the right instant or how he knew that the lion would accept a truce. It may have been accomplished by the sheer arrogance of Arab Maina's decision to lower his shield, even if slightly, and to rise, no longer warlike, and to beckon us on with superb and sudden indifference. But however it was, the lion never moved.

We left him slicing the tall grass with his heavy tail, the blood of the kongoni drying on his coat. He was thinking many things.

And I was disappointed. Long after we had continued our trot toward the place where we knew there would be warthog, I thought how wonderful it would have been if the lion had attacked and I had been able to use my spear on him while he clawed at the shields of the two Murani, and how later they might have said, "If it hadn't been for you, Lakweit . . . !"

But then, I was very young.

We ran until we reached the Molo River.

The river took its life from the Mau Escarpment and twisted down into the valley and gave life, in turn, to mimosa trees with crowns as broad as clouds, and long creepers and liana that strangled the sunlight and left the riverbank soothing and dark.

The earth on the bank was damp and pitted with footprints of the game that followed a web-work of thin trails to drink at dawn, leaving the racy smell of their droppings and their bodies in the air. The river forest was narrow and cool and vibrant with the songs of multi-colored birds, and clotted with bright flowers that scorned the sun.

We laid down our weapons and rested under the trees and drank the chilled water, making cups with our hands.

Arab Maina lifted his face from the edge of the river and smiled gently. "My mouth was like unto ashes, Lakweit," he said, "but truly this water is even sweeter than Jebbta's carefully brewed tembo!"

"It is sweeter," said Arab Kosky, "and at this moment it is more welcome. I promise you, my stomach had turned almost sour with thirst!"

Looking at me, Arab Maina laughed.

"Sour with thirst, he says, Lakweit! Sour, I think, with the sight of the lion at the salt-lick. Courage lives in a man's stomach, but there are times when it is not at home—and then the stomach is sour!"

Arab Kosky stretched his lithe, straight limbs on the tangled grass and smiled, showing teeth white as sun-cured bone. "Talk lives in a man's head," he answered, "but sometimes it is very lonely because in the heads of some men there is nothing to keep it company—and so talk goes out through the lips."

I laughed with both of them and pressed my shoulders comfortably against the tree I leaned upon and looked through a chink in the ceiling of the forest at a vulture flying low.

"Maina, you know, I hate those birds. Their wings are separated like a lot of small snakes."

"As you say, Lakwani, they are creatures of evil omen—messengers of the dead. Too cowardly to slay for themselves, they are satisfied with the stinking flesh from another man's kill." Arab Maina spat, as if to clean his mouth after talking of unpleasant things.

Buller and the native dogs had gone into the river and wallowed in the cool black muck along its banks. Buller returned now, sleek with slime, dripping and happy. He waited until he had the two Murani and me easily within range and then shook himself with a kind of devilish impudence and stood wagging his stump tail as we wiped water and mud from our faces.

"It is his way of making a joke," said Arab Kosky, looking at his spattered shuka.

"It is also his way of telling us to move," said Arab Maina. "The hunter who lies on his back in the forest has little food and no sport. We have spent much time today at other things, but the warthog still waits."

"What you say is true." Arab Kosky rose from the grass. "The warthog still waits, and who is so without manners as to keep another waiting? Surely Buller is not. We must take his advice and go."

We went up the riverbank, falling into single file again, and threaded our way through a labyrinth of silver-gray boulders and rust-red anthills, shaped variously like witches caps or like the figures of kneeling giants or like trees without branches. Some of the anthills were enormous, higher than the huts we lived in, and some were no higher than our knees. They were scattered everywhere.

"Seek 'em out, Buller!"

But the dog needed no urging from me. He knew warthog country when he saw it and he knew what to do about it. He rushed on ahead followed by the native mongrels running in a little storm of their own dust.

I know animals more gallant than the African warthog, but none more courageous. He is the peasant of the plains—the drab and dowdy digger in the earth. He is the uncomely but intrepid defender of family, home, and bourgeois convention, and he will fight anything of any size that intrudes upon his smug existence. Even his weapons are plebeian—curved tusks, sharp, deadly, but not beautiful, used inelegantly for rooting as well as for fighting.

He stands higher than a domestic pig when he is full grown, and his hide is dust-colored and tough and clothed in bristles. His eyes are small and lightless and capable of but one expression—suspicion. What he does not understand, he suspects, and what he suspects, he fights. He can leap into the air and gut a horse while its rider still ponders a strategy of attack, and his speed in emerging from his hole to demonstrate the advantage of surprise is almost phenomenal.

He is not lacking in guile. He enters his snug little den (which is borrowed, not to say commandeered, from its builder, the ant-bear) tail foremost so that he is never caught off guard. While he lies thus in wait for the curiosity or indiscretion of his enemy to bring him within range, he uses his snout to pile a heap of fine dust inside the hole. The dust serves as a smoke screen, bursting into a great, enshrouding billow the moment the warthog emerges to battle. He understands the tactical retreat, but is incapable of surrender, and if a dog is less than a veteran, or a man no more than an intrepid novice, not the only blood spilled will be the warthog's.

These facts were always in my mind when Buller hunted with us, as he always did. But there was never any question of leaving him. It would have been like preventing a born soldier from marching with his regiment or like denying a champion fighter the right to compete in the ring on the grounds that he might be hurt. So Buller always came, and often I worried.

He ran ahead now, flanked by native dogs. The two Murani and I spread out fanwise, running behind.

Our first sign of warthog was the squeal of a baby surprised in a patch of grass by one of the mongrels. The squeal was followed by what seemed to be the squeals of all the baby warthogs in Africa, blended, magnified, and ear-splitting. Panic-stricken, the little pigs ran in all directions, like mice in the dream of a tabby cat. Their tails, held straight and erect, whisked through the grass as if so many bulrushes had come to life to join in a frantic dance—a mad and somewhat gay dance, but hardly as abandoned as it appeared, because the squeals were not without intent or meaning. They were meant for the small, alert ears of their father, who, when he came, would come with murder aforethought.

And come he did. None of us quite knew from where, but in the midst of the bedlam the grass in front of Arab Maina parted as if cleaved by a scythe, and a large boar, blind with rage, plunged from it straight at the Murani.

If Buller had not run ahead after his own quarry, things might have happened differently. As it was, there was more amusement than tragedy in what did happen.

The boar was larger than average, and the bigger they are the tougher they are. Their hides are tough as boot-leather and nothing less than a spear thrust in a vital part will stop them.

Arab Maina was ready and waiting. The boar lunged, the Murani side-stepped, the spear flashed—and the boar was gone. But not alone. Behind him, spitting the flying dust, swearing in Nandi and in Swahili, ran Arab Maina assisted by two of his mongrels—all of them following, with their eyes and their legs, the drunkenly swaying shaft of Arab Maina's spear, its point lodged fast and solid between the shoulders of the boar.

Arab Kosky and I began to follow, but we couldn't laugh and run at the same time, so we stopped running and watched. In less than a minute the dogs, the man, and the warthog had found the horizon and disappeared behind it like four fabulous characters in search of Æsop.

We turned and trotted in the direction Buller had taken, listening to his deep, excited barks which came at regular intervals. After covering about three miles, we found him at the side of a large hole where he had run his warthog to ground.

Buller stood gazing at the dusty opening in silence, as if hoping the warthog would be such a fool as to think that since there were no more barks, there was no more dog. But the warthog was not taken in. He would emerge in his own good time, and he knew as well as Buller did that no dog would enter an occupied pig-hole and expect to come out alive.

"That's a good boy, Buller!" As usual, I was relieved to find him still unhurt, but the moment I spoke, he broke his strategic silence and demanded, with much tail-wagging and a series of whining barks, that the warthog be roused from his den and be brought to battle.

More than once every inch of Buller's body had been ripped open in deep, ugly gashes on such pig-hunts, but at least he had lately learned not to go for the boar's head which, in the end, is fatal for any dog. Until now I had always managed to reach the scene of conflict in time to spear the warthog. But I might not always be so lucky.

I moved carefully to the back of the opening while Arab Kosky stood far to one side.

"If only we had some paper to rustle down the hole, Kosky . . ."

The Murani shrugged. "We will have to try other tricks, Lakweit."

It seems silly, and perhaps it is, but very often, after every other method had failed, we had enticed warthogs into the open, long before they were quite ready to attack, simply by rustling a scrap of paper over the entrance of their holes. It was not always easy to get so limited an article as paper in East Africa at that time, but when we had it, it always worked. I haven't any idea of why it worked. Poking a stick through the hole never did, nor shouting into it, nor even using smoke. To the warthog, I think, the paper made a sound that was clearly insulting—comparable perhaps to what is known here and there nowadays as a Bronx cheer.

But we had no paper. We tried everything else without the least success, and decided finally, in the face of Buller's contempt, to give it up and find out what had happened to Arab Maina on his quest for the vanished spear.

We were leaving the scene of our mutual discouragement when Arab Kosky's curiosity overcame his natural caution. He bent down in front of the dark hole and the warthog came out.

It was more like an explosion than an attack by a wild pig. I could see nothing through the thick burst of dust except extremities—the tail of the boar, the feet of Arab Kosky, the ears of Buller, and the end of a spear.

My own spear was useless in my hands. I might thrust at the warthog only to strike the dog or the Murani. It was an unholy tangle with no end, no beginning, and no opening. It lasted five seconds. Then the warthog shot from the tumbling mass like a clod from a whirlwind and disappeared through a corridor of anthills with Buller just behind slashing at the fleeing gray rump.

I turned to Arab Kosky. He sat on the ground in a puddle of his own blood, his right thigh cut through as if it had been hacked with a sword. He pressed a fold of his shuka against the wound and stood up. Buller's bark grew fainter, echoing through the forest of anthills. The boar had won the first battle—and might win the second, unless I hurried.

"Can you walk, Kosky? I must follow Buller. He may get killed."

The Murani smiled without mirth. "Of course, Lakweit! This is nothing—except reward for my foolishness. I will go back to the singiri slowly and have it attended to. It is best that you lose no time and follow Buller. Already the sun is sinking. Go now, and run quickly!"

I clasped the round shaft of the spear tight in my hand and ran with all my strength. For me—because I was still a child—this was a heart-sinking experience. So many thoughts flashed through my mind. Would my strength hold out long enough to save Buller from the tusks of the boar? What had become of Arab Maina, and why had I ever left him? How would poor Kosky get home? Would he bleed too badly on the way?

I ran on and on, following the barely audible bark of Buller, and the few drops of blood clinging at intervals to the stalks of grass or soaking into the absorbent earth. It was either Buller's blood or the warthog's. Most likely it was both.

"Ah-yey, if I could only run a little faster!"

I must not stop for a minute. My muscles begin to ache, my legs bleed from the "wait-a-bit" thorns and the blades of elephant grass. My hand, wet with perspiration, slips on the handle of my spear. I stumble, recover, and run on as the sound of Buller's bark grows louder, closer, then fades again.

The sun is going and shadows lay like broad hurdles across my path. Nothing is of any importance to me except my dog. The boar is not retreating; he is leading Buller away from me, away from my help.

The blood spoor grows thicker and there is more of it. Buller's bark is weak and irregular, but a little nearer. There are trees now jutting from the plain, large, solitary, and silent.

The barking stops and there is nothing but the blood to follow. How can there be so much blood? Breathless and running still, I peer ahead into the changing light and see something move in a patch of turf under a flat-topped thorn tree.

I stop and wait. It moves again and takes color—black and white and splattered with red. It is silent, but it moves. It is Buller.

I need neither breath nor muscles to cover the few hundred yards to the thorn tree. I am suddenly there, under its branches, standing in a welter of blood. The warthog, as large as any I have ever seen, six times as large as Buller, sits exhausted on his haunches while the dog rips at its belly.

The old boar sees me, another enemy, and charges once more with magnificent courage, and I sidestep and plunge my spear to his heart. He falls forward, scraping the earth with his great tusks, and lies still. I leave the spear in his body, turn to Buller, and feel tears starting to my eyes.

The dog is torn open like a slaughtered sheep. His right side is a valley of exposed flesh from the root of his tail to his head, and his ribs show almost white, like the fingers of a hand smeared with blood. He looks at the warthog, then at me beside him on my knees, and lets his head fall into my arms. He needs water, but there is no water anywhere, not within miles.

"Ah-yey! Buller, my poor, foolish Buller!"

He licks my hand, and I think he knows I can do nothing, but forgives me for it. I cannot leave him because the light is almost gone now and there are leopards that prowl at night, and hyenas that attack only the wounded and helpless.

"If only he lives through the night! If only he lives through the night!"

There is a hyena on a near hill who laughs at that, but it is a coward's laugh. I sit with Buller and the dead boar under the thorn tree and watch the dark come closer.

The world grows bigger as the light leaves it. There are no boundaries and no landmarks. The trees and the rocks and the anthills begin to disappear, one by one, whisked away under the magical cloak of evening, I stroke the dog's head and try to close my eyes, but of course I cannot. Something moves in the tall grass, making a sound like the swish of a woman's skirt. The dog stirs feebly and the hyena on the hill laughs again.

I let Buller's head rest on the turf, stand up, and pull my spear from the body of the boar. Somewhere to the left there is a sound, but I do not recognize it and I can see only dim shapes that are motionless.

I lean for a moment on my spear peering outward at what is nothing, and then turn toward my thorn tree.

"Are you here, Lakwani?"

Arab Maina's voice is cool as water on shaded rocks.

"I am here, Maina."

He is tall and naked and very dark beside me. His shuka is tied around his left forearm to allow his body freedom to run.

"You are alone, and you have suffered, my child."

"I am all right, Maina, but I fear for Buller. I think he may die."

Arab Maina kneels on the earth and runs his hands over Buller's body. "He is badly hurt, Lakwani—very badly hurt—but do not grieve too much. I think your spear has saved him from death, and God will reward you for that. When the moon shines at midnight, we will carry him home."

"I am so happy that you have come, Maina."

"How is it Kosky dared to leave you alone? He has betrayed the trust I had in him!"

"Do not be angry with Kosky. He is badly hurt. His thigh was ripped by the warthog."

"He is no child, Lakweit. He is a Murani, and he should have been more careful, knowing I was not there. After I recovered my spear, I turned back to find you. I followed the blood on the grass for miles—and then I followed Buller's barking. If the direction of the wind had been wrong, you would still be alone. Kosky has the brains of the one-eyed hare!"

"Ah-yey! What does it matter now, Maina? You are here, and I am not alone. But I am very cold."

"Lakwani, lie down and rest. I will keep watch until it is light enough for us to go. You are very tired. Your face has become thin."

He cuts handfuls of grass with his sword and makes a pillow, and I lie down, clasping Buller in my arms. The dog is unconscious now and bleeding badly. His blood trickles over my khaki shorts and my thighs.

The distant roar of a waking lion rolls against the stillness of the night, and we listen. It is the voice of Africa bringing memories that do not exist in our minds or in our hearts—perhaps not even in our blood. It is out of time, but it is there, and it spans a chasm whose other side we cannot see.

A ripple of lightning plays across the horizon.

"I think there will be a storm tonight, Maina."

Arab Maina reaches out in the darkness and puts his hand on my forehead. "Relax, Lakwani, and I will tell you an amusing fable about the cunning little Hare."

He begins very slowly and softly, "The Hare was a thief . . . In the night he came to the manyatta . . . He lied to the Cow, and told her that her Calf would die if she moved . . . Then he stood up on his hind legs and began sucking the milk from the Cow's milk bag . . . The other . . ."

But I am asleep.

Country Matters

BY VANCE BOURJAILY

VANCE BOURJAILY HAS SOME strong opinions—how to raise a dog, how to hunt a dog, how to house a dog. In short, the best way to bring up and train a good bird dog. In this story he shows us what happens when it's done wrong—how to sour a dog.

It does my heart good to read strong words, firmly given, on a subject of importance, like dogs. And it's even more satisfying when the author of those words has the prestige and authority of Vance Bourjaily.

★ ★ ★ ★ ★

ONE OF THE STRONGEST of the several minority hunting opinions I hold is that a bird dog's place is in the home. Perhaps the most depressing thing related to this opinion is precisely that it should be a minority one, nor will I pretend to be anything but self-righteous about the matter; since I admit no possibility that I am wrong, it must follow that in my view the majority of American sporting men are about as sorry a collection of dog handlers as could readily be imagined.

The basic tenet of this majority, and it is always advanced as if it were a fact, is that hunting dogs are ruined if they are allowed to become pets. Advocates of this fact are apt to know for sure such other facts as that dogs must be penned or tied outdoors, regardless of how hot or cold it is; that dogs benefit from being hauled to and from the hunting field in airless car trunks; that the more harshly they are spoken to or punished, the more eagerly they respond; and that, in a general way, any impulse of consideration, let alone affection, for the animal must be stoutly fought down. This indicator of the handler's infinite virility is for the dog's own good.

The basic tenet of the minority is one I shall advance as a fact, without any expectation of provoking much agreement: every really good hunting dog I've ever known has been the pet of the man he hunted with. The rest are an army of lost dogs.

Let me cite the revolting case of Eddie-Joe X., whose dialogue in the following should be read in a mean, midsouthern accent:

A mutual, nonhunting friend whom I am visiting has arranged for Eddie-Joe to take me out for quail; we are driving in Eddie-Joe's car. His dogs, two wan pointers called Jake and Birdie, are, of course, in the trunk; my dog, thank heavens, is five hundred miles away. I have protested, as we got in, that there's no need to shut the dogs away on my account, hell, I don't mind them climbing on me. Eddie-Joe's reply has been a sour look, which conveyed considerable doubt that he and I were going to get along.

Now, as we drive, perhaps considering his obligation to the friend who arranged this hunt, Eddie-Joe decides to be ingratiating:

"That son-of-a-bitching Jake dog, back there. I got him right at the end of last season. He's a real dog, but he's a stubborn bastard if you let him get by with it. He'll chase fur, and there's only one cure for that."

"This looks like bird country all right," I say, hoping to be spared the particulars of Eddie-Joe's prescription.

"Let him get on a rabbit in the brush, maybe forty, fifty yards out and shoot him in the ass with birdshot."

"You've done that?" I ask. I have heard other rabid pharmacists prescribe corrective shooting, but never met one who'd say he'd actually administered the dose.

"Hell, yes, I let go a blast at him," Eddie-Joe says. "We were hunting through the woods, hunting singles, and I don't think any of the shot got to him. But he came back in right now."

"How was he afterwards?" I ask.

"You won't see him chase fur," Eddie-Joe says.

He is absolutely right. No one will ever see old Jake chase anything again. He slinks along, not always in front of us, tail down, looking over at us from time to time, not so much (I fancy) in the shy hope of being approved of as simply to keep the fount of correction located at all times.

Yet there is something of the bird dog he once was left in Jake. When he scents quail in the air, he does quicken, and his tail comes up. He leads us into a rather steep draw, false points, moves forward stiff-legged, points, moves—this is the behavior, if I am any judge, of a dog working an unalarmed covey which is strung out, feeding, walking along. Birdie, the other dog, who has less experience but more training, stiffens into a point, backing Jake.

As I am about to observe that these must be moving birds, two of them rise, whir away; then another; then half a dozen from various points in the draw. Eddie-Joe and I both fire, late and disconcerted, missing what seem easy enough shots but are actually the most unlikely kind—the shots one takes without being quite set for them. In the serene, philosophical moment which follows such a display of skill, Eddie-Joe screams:

"Did you see him blink that point?" And runs at Jake with the intention of kicking him. Jake, who has been kicked before, apparently, and has some curious objection to it, crawls under a bush, and Birdie, the other dog, gets knocked off balance as surrogate, by Eddie-Joe swiping side-footed.

Eddie-Joe has had Birdie just two weeks, he tells me, and right now's the time to stop her from picking up any bad habits. She's a young dog, and quite well trained; she makes the next point for us, half an hour later, and this time the birds are properly coveyed up. Old Jake, I notice, doesn't back her. He just lies down, panting, while Eddie-Joe and I walk in. The covey goes up and this time Eddie-Joe shows me how to shoot, dropping two birds neatly. I make my customary covey rise score, a hit and a miss, so we have three quail in front of us now, lying out in the grass.

Birdie, steady to wing and shot, is still holding her point, and is praised for the achievement with the soothing words, "Hunt dead, goddamnit!"—as if her waiting for the command were a fault rather than a virtue some trainer has spent many weeks of patience (and, perhaps, love) to develop. By now Jake has slipped by, is out hunting dead, and retrieves one of the birds for us. He brings it to me instead of Eddie-Joe, and I risk patting him for it. He goes out to resume searching; Birdie has found a quail, and holds it in her mouth, looking over at us, a bit uncertain just what's wanted.

Eddie-Joe informs her: "FETCH!" loud enough to make *me* jump. "What the hell's the matter with you? FEH-ETCH!"

When I jumped, Jake scurried away. As for Birdie, she sees Eddie-Joe running at her, and a good bit before he arrives she puts the bird down and backs away from it.

He picks it up. "Hunt dead," he commands. "Come on, you dogs, there's another bird out here."

I hand him the one Jake brought me. "Here's your other one," I say.

"Didn't you get a bird?"

"No. No, I missed."

"Could've sworn you got one," Eddie-Joe says, and we move towards the next field, where the singles are scattered. The dogs seem happy to be leaving.

By the time we have shot a single or two, and chanced onto another covey while looking for more, the hunt has gone on for just over an hour, covering about a two-mile circle around the car. Birdie, who is still eager, has probably run six or eight miles as Eddie-Joe and I walked the two, and Jake, in spite of his moping, must have covered four. Birdie, eager though she may feel, is beginning to look exhausted, and Jake is pretty much dragging himself along. I understand that their thinness is from underfeeding, not exercise. These dogs don't get out of the pen from the end of one hunting season till the beginning of the next.

"Dogs are starting to settle down and work careful now," Eddie-Joe says, throwing a clod of dirt at Jake to get him moving.

"I wish I could say the same," I say, angling us towards the car. "Guess I'm out of condition."

"The hell you are."

Actually, I feel great. I love this country and I love these birds. It's the first real quail shoot for me in a long while, and I've carefully arranged to keep the whole day clear for it.

"Want to rest a while?" Eddie-Joe says.

"I'm sorry, Eddie-Joe," I say. "Guess I just can't take it. I'd like to go back to town."

"Well, I'll be go-to-hell," Eddie-Joe says, and tries to cajole me, but I insist I've had enough.

In the disgruntled silence on the way back to town, I ask the one question which could induce Eddie-Joe ever to speak a civil word to me again. It's not that I feel any great civility towards him, but I want to confirm a hunch.

"What'll you take for Birdie?"

"Hell, you want a dog you better buy Jake. You can't keep up with her."

"That's my business. Is she for sale?"

"Any dog's for sale," Eddie-Joe says. "Last week it would've cost you five hundred for her, but you saw how she was about retrieving. I don't know. What'll you give? See, I know a man's got some year-old setters. . . ."

I can't really buy the two exhausted dogs in the trunk, though I wish I could. Well, it'll protect one of those setter pups from what happens when an Eddie-Joe ventures into trying an untrained dog—the pup's allowed to hunt once, makes a few zealous mistakes and after that is tied in the yard where he learns to bark. But I've learned what I wanted to now, which is that Eddie-Joe's a shopper and swapper, who will go through several dogs a season, ruining each in turn. Eddie-Joe is a composite, too, of course, of some number of men that I've encountered—but every characteristic and attitude with which I've endowed my composite is prevalent, and often stoutly defended as correct.

There is all too much resemblance to all too many people, living and dead, in my composite, and that is really why I can't buy poor old Jake and young Birdie—if we rescued them all, at a dollar a dog, it would still run up around a million.

One can err, I guess, in the other direction, and I suppose I have. I've hunted the same dog for ten years now. He is my old Weimaraner, Moon, of indifferent conformation and average breeding. He is a house dog, and because of it he knows me well enough to know precisely what he can get away with as far as obedience goes.

On the other hand, he has never been out of condition; a dog whining in the kennel can be ignored, but one living in the house, bugging you to exercise him, cannot. You find that you are making time, somehow (or your wife is), to give the dog his daily run, and I cannot see that the daily walk you must take after him does you anything but good.

Though Moon was beautifully trained at one time by Chet Cummings, an absolutely first-rate professional up in Litchfield, Connecticut, I have been too soft-headed to keep him properly in hand. He is still reasonably steady to wing, but at the sound of a shot he charges off like a berserk locomotive, and I no longer try to control this. Instead of a pattern of precise control, what Moon and I have worked out is a high degree of compatibility, based on our mutual pleasure in what we are doing—he knows his part of it, rough though it may be around the edges. And it can be said that very few of the men who have hunted with Moon and me more than a time or two have failed to inquire if there weren't some way to get one of Moon's pups. Since this can't come from admiration for a polished performance, it must come from seeing how much Moon and I are enjoying one another—and this enjoyment, I am convinced, comes from nothing more than the fact that Moon has been a pet, played with and catered to, since the time he was a pup.

Admittedly, this can get to be a bother. Moon sleeps on beds, is often reluctant to yield a favorite sofa corner to a guest and must be figured on like two extra persons when we are calculating the seating capacity of the car. He is, in his resting behavior at home, particularly fond of goose down; we own four goose-down pillows, and Moon can generally manage to pre-empt one, particularly if forestalled from settling onto the goose-down comforter with which my wife keeps warm; I have often speculated on whether, if I should sometime manage to shoot a goose while hunting with Moon, he would try to retrieve it or run over and lie down on it.

Let me acknowledge that there are occasional private dog owners who operate like professional trainers and handlers—that is, they provide well-kept, thermally sound kennels, feed intelligently and keep their dogs in training and in condition in hunting season and out. Such a hobbyist, assuming him to be a reasonably gifted trainer with time to work at it, would certainly produce a more finished hunting field performance than I get from Moon. Whether this perfectionist would get as much pleasure out of hunting his dogs may well be a matter of temperament—some prefer hunting with a close friend, some with an absolutely efficient guide.

Same say, "I love to watch the dogs work"; others like to go hunting with their dogs.

The sort of devoted and successful amateur I've described—a briefer and more abstract composite—may argue that good hunting dogs are ruined if allowed to become pets, then, but he and I will be talking about different things. As for all the others, who support his view without following his practices, I can only say that it seems to me that we have the whole licensing thing backwards. It isn't dogs who need licenses, it's owners, and if I were your commissioner, there'd be damned few issued.

The Dog That Bit People

From *My Life and Hard Times*

BY JAMES THURBER

I DON'T SUPPOSE THERE'S a person alive who needs an introduction to James Thurber—cartoonist, essayist, comic writer. A mainstay of the old *New Yorker* magazine, whose brilliant cartoons and often unnerving stories speared the plight of mankind in odd and bizarre ways.

He and E. B. White, who appears elsewhere in this book, were colleagues at *The New Yorker,* and a side-splitting combination they must have been.

Thurber was a dog fancier, having owned, as he says, "fifty-four or -five" of them over his lifetime. But even he admits the most extraordinary of them was Muggs, the dog who bit people.

★ ★ ★ ★ ★

PROBABLY NO ONE MAN should have as many dogs in his life as I have had, but there was more pleasure than distress in them for me except in the case of an Airedale named Muggs. He gave me more trouble than all the other fifty-four or five put together, although my moment of keenest embarrassment was the time a Scotch terrier named Jeannie, who had just had six puppies in the clothes closet of a fourth floor apartment in New York, had the unexpected seventh and last at the corner of Eleventh Street and Fifth Avenue during a walk she had insisted on taking. Then, too, there was the prize-winning French poodle, a great big black poodle—none of your little, untroublesome white miniatures—who got sick riding in the rumble seat of a car with me on her way to the Greenwich Dog Show. She had a red rubber bib tucked around her throat and, since a rain storm came up when we were half way through the Bronx, I had to hold over her a small green umbrella, really more of a parasol. The rain beat down fearfully and suddenly the driver of the car drove into a big garage, filled with mechanics. It happened so quickly that I forgot to put the umbrella down and I will always remember, with sickening distress, the look of incredulity mixed with hatred that came over the face of the particular hardened garage man that come over to see what we wanted, when he took a look at me and the poodle. All garage men, and people of that intolerant stripe, hate poodles with their curious hair cut, especially the pom-poms that you have got to leave on their hips if you expect the dogs to win a prize.

But the Airedale, as I have said, was the worst of all my dogs. He really wasn't my dog, as a matter of fact: I came home from a vacation one summer to find that my brother Roy had bought him while I was away. A big, burly, choleric dog, he always acted as if he thought I wasn't one of the family. There was a slight advantage in being one of the family, for he didn't bite the family as often as he bit strangers. Still, in the years that we had him he bit everybody but mother, and he made a pass at her once but missed. That was during the month when we suddenly had mice, and Muggs refused to do anything about them. Nobody ever had mice exactly like the mice we had that month. They acted like pet mice, almost like mice somebody had trained. They were so friendly that one night when mother entertained at dinner the Friraliras, a club she and my father had belonged to for twenty years, she put down a lot of little dishes with food in them on the pantry floor so that the mice would be satisfied with that and wouldn't come into the dining room. Muggs stayed out in the pantry with the mice, lying on the floor, growling to himself—not at the mice, but about all the people in the next room that he would have liked to get at. Mother slipped out into the pantry once to see how everything was going.

Everything was going fine. It made her so mad to see Muggs lying there, oblivious of the mice—they came running up to her—that she slapped him and he slashed at her, but didn't make it. He was sorry immediately, mother said. He was always sorry, she said, after he bit someone, but we could not understand how she figured this out. He didn't act sorry.

Mother used to send a box of candy every Christmas to the people the Airedale bit. The list finally contained forty or more names. Nobody could understand why we didn't get rid of the dog. I didn't understand it very well myself, but we didn't get rid of him. I think that one or two people tried to poison Muggs—he acted poisoned once in a while—and old Major Moberly fired at him once with his service revolver near the Seneca Hotel in East Broad Street—but Muggs lived to be almost eleven years old and even when he could hardly get around he bit a Congressman who had called to see my father on business. My mother had never liked the Congressman—she said the signs of his horoscope showed he couldn't be trusted (he was Saturn with the moon in Virgo)—but she sent him a box of candy that Christmas. He sent it right back, probably because he suspected it was trick candy. Mother persuaded herself it was all for the best that the dog had bitten him, even though father lost an important business association because of it. "I wouldn't be associated with such a man," mother said. "Muggs could read him like a book."

We used to take turns feeding Muggs to be on his good side, but that didn't always work. He was never in a very good humor, even after a meal. Nobody knew exactly what was the matter with him, but whatever it was it made him irascible, especially in the mornings. Roy never felt very well in the morning, either, especially before breakfast, and once when he came downstairs and found that Muggs had moodily chewed up the morning paper he hit him in the face with a grapefruit and then jumped up on the dining room table, scattering dishes and silverware and spilling the coffee. Muggs' first free leap carried him all the way across the table and into a brass fire screen in front of the gas grate but he was back on his feet in a moment and in the end he got Roy and gave him a pretty vicious bite in the leg. Then he was all over it; he never bit anyone more than once at a time. Mother always mentioned that as an argument in his favor; she said he had a quick temper but that he didn't hold a grudge. She was forever defending him. I think she liked him because he wasn't well. "He's not strong," she would say pityingly, but that was inaccurate; he may not have been well but he was terribly strong.

One time my mother went to the Chittenden Hotel to call on a woman mental healer who was lecturing in Columbus on the subject of "Harmonious Vibrations." She wanted to find out if it was possible to get harmonious vibrations into a dog. "He's a large tan-colored Airedale," mother explained. The woman said that she never treated a dog but she advised my mother to hold the thought that he did not bite and would not bite. Mother was holding the thought the very next morning when Muggs got the iceman but she blamed that slip-up on the iceman. "If you didn't think he would bite you, he wouldn't," mother told him. He stomped out of the house in a terrible jangle of vibrations.

One morning when Muggs bit me slightly, more or less in passing, I reached down and grabbed his short stumpy tail and hoisted him into the air. It was a foolhardy thing to do and the last time I saw my mother, about six months ago, she said she didn't know what possessed me. I don't either, except that I was pretty mad. As long as I held the dog off the floor by his tail he couldn't get at me, but he twisted and jerked so, snarling all the time, that I realized I couldn't hold him that way very long. I carried him to the kitchen and flung him onto the floor and shut the door on him just as he crashed against it. But I forgot about the backstairs. Muggs went up the backstairs and down the frontstairs and had me cornered in the living room. I managed to get up onto the mantelpiece above the fireplace, but it gave way and came down with a tremendous crash throwing a large marble clock, several vases, and myself heavily to the floor. Muggs was so alarmed by the racket that when I picked myself up he had disappeared. We couldn't find him anywhere, although we whistled and shouted, until old Mrs. Detweiler called after dinner that night. Muggs had bitten her once, in the leg, and she came into the living room only after we assured her that Muggs had run away. She had just seated herself when, with a great growling and scratching of claws, Muggs emerged from under a davenport where he had been quietly hiding all the time, and bit her again. Mother examined the bite and put arnica on it and told Mrs. Detweiler that it was only a bruise. "He just bumped you," she said. But Mrs. Detweiler left the house in a nasty state of mind.

Lots of people reported our Airedale to the police but my father held a municipal office at the time and was on friendly terms with the police. Even so, the cops had been out a couple of times—once when Muggs bit Mrs. Rufus Sturtevant and again when he bit Lieutenant-Governor Malloy—but mother told them that it hadn't been Muggs' fault but the fault of the people who were bitten. "When he starts for them, they scream," she explained, "and that excites him." The cops suggested that it might be a good idea to tie the dog up, but mother said that it mortified him to be tied up and that he wouldn't eat when he was tied up.

Muggs at his meals was an unusual sight. Because of the fact that if you reached toward the floor he would bite you, we usually put his food plate on top of an old kitchen table with a bench alongside the table. Muggs would stand on the bench and eat. I remember that my mother's Uncle Horatio, who boasted that he was the third man up Missionary Ridge, was splutteringly indignant when he found out that we fed the dog on a table because we were afraid to put his plate on the floor. He said he wasn't afraid of any dog that ever lived and that he would put the dog's plate on the floor if we would give it to him. Roy said that if Uncle Horatio had fed Muggs on the ground just before the battle he would have been the first man up Missionary Ridge. Uncle Horatio was furious. "Bring him in! Bring him in now!" he shouted. "I'll feed the — on the floor!" Roy was all for giving him a chance, but my father wouldn't hear of it. He said that Muggs had already been fed. "I'll feed him again!" bawled Uncle Horatio. We had quite a time quieting him.

In his last year Muggs used to spend practically all of his time outdoors. He didn't like to stay in the house for some reason or other—perhaps it held too many unpleasant memories for him. Anyway, it was hard to get him to come in and as a result the garbage man, the iceman, and the laundryman couldn't come near the house. We had to haul the garbage down to the corner, take the laundry out and bring it back, and meet the iceman a block from home. After this had gone on for some time we hit on an ingenious arrangement for getting the dog in the house so that we could lock him up while the gas meter was read, and so on. Muggs was afraid on only one thing, an electrical storm. Thunder and lightning frightened him out of his senses (I think he thought a storm had broken the day the mantelpiece fell). He would rush into the house and hide under a bed or in a clothes closet. So we fixed up a thunder machine out of a long narrow piece of sheet iron with a wooden handle on one end. Mother would shake this vigorously when she wanted to get Muggs into the house. It made an excellent imitation of thunder, but I suppose it was the most roundabout system for running a household that was ever devised. It took a lot out of mother.

A few months before Muggs died, he got to "seeing things." He would rise slowly from the floor, growling low, and stalk stiff-legged and menacing toward nothing at all. Sometimes the Thing would be just a little to the right or left of a visitor. Once a Fuller Brush salesman got hysterics. Muggs came wandering into the room like Hamlet following his father's ghost. His eyes were fixed on a spot just to the left of the Fuller Brush man, who stood it until Muggs was about three slow, creeping paces from him. Then he shouted. Muggs wavered on past him into the hallway grumbling to himself but the

Fuller man went on shouting. I think mother had to throw a pan of cold water on him before he stopped. That was the way she used to stop us boys when we got into fights.

Muggs died quite suddenly one night. Mother wanted to bury him in the family lot under a marble stone with some such inscription as "Flights of angels sing thee to thy rest" but we persuaded her it was against the law. In the end we just put up a smooth board above his grave along a lonely road. On the board I wrote with an indelible pencil "Cave Canem." Mother was quite pleased with the simple classic dignity of the old Latin epitaph.

The Emissary

BY RAY BRADBURY

YOU WILL NOT EASILY forget "The Emissary"—it's a haunting tale told by a master of the weird.

As a science fiction writer, Ray Bradbury chilled his readers with novels and short stories like *Fahrenheit 451* and *Dandelion Wine*. A prolific writer, he also produced poetry, film scripts, and plays. It's always a real pleasure to discover short stories by writers we admire—as it is to find that classic Bradbury touch of off-center eeriness in this tale of a dying boy. It starts off sweet and tender . . . and rapidly becomes bizarre.

★   ★   ★   ★   ★

MARTIN KNEW IT WAS autumn again, for Dog ran into the house bringing wind and frost and a smell of apples turned to cider under trees. In dark clocksprings of hair, Dog fetched goldenrod, dust of farewell-summer, acorn-husk, hair of squirrel, feather of departed robin, sawdust from fresh-cut cordwood, and leaves like charcoals shaken from a blaze of maple trees. Dog jumped. Showers of brittle fern, blackberry vine, marsh grass sprang over the bed where Martin shouted. No doubt, no doubt of it at all, this incredible beast was October!

"Here, boy, here!"

And Dog settled to warm Martin's body with all the bonfires and subtle burnings of the season, to fill the room with soft or heavy, wet or dry odors of far-traveling. In spring, he smelled of lilac, iris, lawn-mowered grass; in summer, ice-cream-mustached, he came pungent with firecracker, Roman candle, pinwheel, baked by the sun. But autumn! Autumn!

"Dog, what's it like outside?"

And lying there, Dog told as he always told. Lying there, Martin found autumn as in the old days before sickness bleached him white on his bed. Here was his contact, his carryall, the quick-moving part of himself he sent with a yell to run and return, circle and scent, collect and deliver the time and texture of worlds in town, country, by creek, river, lake, down-cellar, up-attic, in closet or coalbin. Ten dozen times a day he was gifted with sunflower seed, cinder-path, milkweed, horse chestnut, or full flame smell of pumpkin. Through the looming of the universe Dog shuttled; the design was hid in his pelt. Put out your hand, it was there. . . .

"And where did you go this morning?"

But he knew without hearing where Dog had rattled down hills where autumn lay in cereal crispness, where children lay in funeral pyres, in rustling heaps, the leaf-buried but watchful dead, as Dog and the world blew by. Martin trembled his fingers, searched the thick fur, read the long journey. Through stubbled fields, over glitters of ravine creek, down marbled spread of cemetery yard, into woods. In the great season of spices and rare incense, now Martin ran through his emissary, around, about, and home!

The bedroom door opened.

"That dog of yours is in trouble again."

Mother brought in a tray of fruit salad, cocoa, and toast, her blue eyes snapping.

"Mother . . ."

"Always digging places. Dug a hole in Miss Tarkins's garden this morning. She's spittin' mad. That's the fourth hole he's dug there this week."

"Maybe he's looking for something."

"Fiddlesticks, he's too darned curious. If he doesn't behave he'll be locked up."

Martin looked at this woman as if she were a stranger.

"Oh, you wouldn't do that! How would I learn anything? How would I find things out if Dog didn't tell me?"

Mom's voice was quieter. "Is that what he does—tell you things?"

"There's nothing I don't know when he goes out and around and back, *nothing* I can't find out from him!"

They both sat looking at Dog and the dry strewings of mold and seed over the quilt.

"Well, if he'll just stop digging where he shouldn't, he can run all he wants," said Mother.

"Here, boy, here!"

And Martin snapped a tin note to the dog's collar:

MY OWNER IS MARTIN SMITH

TEN YEARS OLD

SICK IN BED

VISITORS WELCOME.

Dog barked. Mother opened the downstairs door and let him out.

Martin sat listening.

Far off and away you could hear Dog run in the quiet autumn rain that was falling now. You could hear the barking-jingling fade, rise, fade again as he cut down alley, over lawn, to fetch back Mr. Holloway and the oiled metallic smell of the delicate snowflake-interiored watches he repaired in his home shop. Or maybe he would bring Mr. Jacobs, the grocer, whose clothes were rich with lettuce, celery, tomatoes, and the secret tinned and hidden smell of the red demons stamped on cans of deviled ham. Mr. Jacobs and his unseen pink-meat devils waved often from the yard below. Or Dog brought Mr. Jackson, Mrs. Gillespie, Mr. Smith, Mrs. Holmes, *any* friend or near-friend, encountered, cornered, begged, worried, and at last shepherded home for lunch, or tea and biscuits.

Now, listening, Martin heard Dog below, with footsteps moving in a light rain behind him. The downstairs bell rang, Mom opened the door, light voices murmured. Martin sat forward, face shining. The stair treads creaked. A young woman's voice laughed quietly. Miss Haight, of course, his teacher from school!

The bedroom door sprang open.

Martin had company.

Morning, afternoon, evening, dawn and dusk, sun and moon circled with Dog, who faithfully reported temperatures of turf and air, color of earth and tree, consistency of mist or rain, but—most important of all—brought back again and again and again—Miss Haight.

On Saturday, Sunday, and Monday she baked Martin orange-iced cupcakes, brought him library books about dinosaurs and cavemen. On Tuesday, Wednesday, and Thursday somehow he beat her at dominoes, somehow she lost at checkers, and soon, she cried, he'd defeat her handsomely at chess. On Friday, Saturday, and Sunday they talked and never stopped talking, and she was so young and laughing and handsome and her hair was a soft, shining brown like the season outside the window, and she walked clear, clean, and quick, a heartbeat warm in the bitter afternoon when he heard it. Above all, she had the secret of signs, and could read and interpret Dog and the symbols she searched out and plucked forth from his coat with her miraculous fingers. Eyes shut, softly laughing, in a gypsy's voice, she divined the world from the treasure in her hands.

And on Monday afternoon, Miss Haight was dead.

Martin sat up in bed, slowly.

"Dead?" he whispered.

Dead, said his mother, yes, dead, killed in an auto accident a mile out of town. Dead, yes, dead, which meant cold to Martin, which meant silence and whiteness and winter come long before its time. Dead, silent, cold, white. The thoughts circled round, blew down, and settled in whispers.

Martin held Dog, thinking; turned to the wall. The lady with the autumn-colored hair. The lady with the laughter that was very gentle and never made fun and the eyes that watched your mouth to see everything you ever said. The-other-half-of-autumn-lady, who told what was left untold by Dog, about the world. The heartbeat at the still center of gray afternoon. The heartbeat fading . . .

"Mom? What do they do in the graveyard, Mom, under the ground? Just lay there?"

"*Lie* there."

"Lie there? Is that *all* they do? It doesn't sound like much fun."

"For goodness' sake, it's not made out to be fun."

"Why don't they jump up and run around once in a while if they get tired of lying there? God's pretty silly—"

"Martin!"

"Well, you'd think He'd treat people better than to tell them to lie still for keeps. That's impossible. Nobody can do it! I tried once. Dog tries. I tell him, 'Dead Dog!' He plays dead awhile, then gets sick and tired and wags his tail or opens one eye and looks at me, bored. Boy, I bet sometimes those graveyard people do the same, huh, Dog?"

Dog barked.

"Be still with that kind of talk!" said Mother.

Martin looked off into space.

"Bet that's exactly what they do," he said.

Autumn burned the trees bare and ran Dog still farther around, fording creek, prowling graveyard as was his custom, and back in the dusk to fire off volleys of barking that shook windows wherever he turned.

In the late last days of October, Dog began to act as if the wind had changed and blew from a strange country. He stood quivering on the porch below. He whined, his eyes fixed at the empty land beyond town. He brought no visitors for Martin. He stood for hours each day, as if leashed, trembling, then shot away straight, as if someone had called. Each night he returned later, with no one following. Each night, Martin sank deeper and deeper in his pillow.

"Well, people are busy," said Mother. "They haven't time to notice the tag Dog carries. Or they mean to come visit, but forget."

But there was more to it than that. There was the fevered shining in Dog's eyes, and his whimpering tic late at night, in some private dream. His shivering in the dark, under the bed. The way he sometimes stood half the night, looking at Martin as if some great and impossible secret was his and he knew no way to tell it save by savagely thumping his tail, or turning in endless circles, never to lie down, spinning and spinning again.

On October 30, Dog ran out and didn't come back at all, even when after supper Martin heard his parents call and call. The hour grew late, the streets and sidewalks stood empty, the air moved cold about the house, and there was nothing, nothing.

Long after midnight, Martin lay watching the world beyond the cool, clear glass windows. Now there was not even autumn, for there was no Dog to fetch it in. There would be no winter, for who could bring the snow to melt in your hands? Father, Mother? No, not the same. They couldn't play the game with its special secrets and rules, its sounds and pantomimes. No more seasons. No more time. The go-between, the emissary, was lost to the wild throngings of civilization, poisoned, stolen, hit by a car, left somewhere in a culvert. . . .

Sobbing, Martin turned his face to his pillow. The world was a picture under glass, untouchable. The world was dead.

Martin twisted in bed and in three days the last Halloween pumpkins were rotting in trash cans, papier-mâché skulls and witches were burnt on bonfires, and ghosts were stacked on shelves with other linens until next year.

To Martin, Halloween had been nothing more than one evening when tin horns cried off in the cold autumn stars, children blew like goblin leaves along the flinty walks, flinging their heads, or cabbages, at porches, soap-writing names or similar magic symbols on icy windows. All of it as distant, unfathomable, and nightmarish as a puppet show seen from so many miles away that there is no sound or meaning.

For three days in November, Martin watched alternate light and shadow sift across his ceiling. The fire pageant was over forever; autumn lay in cold ashes. Martin sank deeper, yet deeper in white marble layers of bed, motionless, listening, always listening. . . .

Friday evening, his parents kissed him good night and walked out of the house into the hushed cathedral weather toward a motion-picture show. Miss Tarkins from next door stayed on in the parlor below until Martin called down he was sleepy, then took her knitting off home.

In silence, Martin lay following the great move of stars down a clear and moonlit sky, remembering nights such as this when he'd spanned the town with Dog ahead, behind, around about, tracking the green-plush ravine, lapping slumbrous streams gone milky with the fullness of the moon, leaping cemetery tombstones while whispering the marble names; on, quickly on, through shaved meadows where the only motion was the off-on quivering of stars, to streets where shadows would not stand aside for you but crowded all the sidewalks for mile on mile. Run, now, run! Chasing, being chased by bitter smoke, fog, mist, wind, ghost of mind, fright of memory; home, safe, sound, snug-warm, asleep. . . .

Nine o'clock.

Chime. The drowsy clock in the deep stairwell below. Chime.

Dog, come home, and run the world with you. Dog, bring a thistle with frost on it, or bring nothing else but the wind. Dog, where *are* you? Oh, listen now, I'll call.

Martin held his breath.

Way off somewhere—a sound.

Martin rose up, trembling.

There, again—the sound.

So small a sound, like a sharp needle-point brushing the sky long miles and many miles away.

The dreamy echo of a dog—barking.

The sounds of a dog crossing fields and farms, dirt roads and rabbit paths, running, running, letting out great barks of steam, cracking the night. The sound of a circling dog which came and went, lifted and faded, opened up, shut in, moved forward, went back, as if the animal were kept by some-one on a fantastically long chain. As if the dog were running and someone whistled under the chestnut trees, in mold-shadow, tar-shadow, moon-shadow, walking, and the dog circled back and sprang out again toward home.

Dog! Martin thought. Oh, Dog, come home, boy! Listen, oh, listen, where have you *been*? Come on, boy, make tracks!

Five, ten, fifteen minutes; near, very near, the bark, the sound. Martin cried out, thrust his feet from the bed, leaned to the window. Dog! Listen, boy! Dog! Dog! He said it over and over. Dog! Dog! Wicked Dog, run off and gone all these days! Bad Dog, good Dog, home, boy, hurry, and bring what you can!

Near now, near, up the street, barking, to knock clapboard housefronts with sound, whirl iron cocks on rooftops in the moon, firing of volleys—Dog! now at the door below. . . .

Martin shivered.

Should he run—let Dog in, or wait for Mom and Dad? Wait? Oh, God, wait? But what if Dog ran off again? No, he'd go down, snatch the door wide, yell, grab Dog in, and run upstairs so fast, laughing, crying, holding tight, that . . .

Dog stopped barking.

Hey! Martin almost broke the window, jerking to it.

Silence. As if someone had told Dog to hush now, hush, hush.

A full minute passed. Martin clenched his fists.

Below, a faint whimpering.

Then, slowly, the downstairs front door opened. Someone was kind enough to have opened the door for Dog. Of course! Dog had brought Mr. Jacobs or Mr. Gillespie or Miss Tarkins, or . . .

The downstairs door shut.

Dog raced upstairs, whining, flung himself on the bed.

"Dog, Dog, where've you *been*, what've you *done*! Dog, Dog!"

And he crushed Dog hard and long to himself, weeping. Dog, Dog. He laughed and shouted. Dog! But after a moment he stopped laughing and crying, suddenly.

He pulled back away. He held the animal and looked at him, eyes widening.

The odor coming from Dog was different.

It was a smell of strange earth. It was a smell of night within night, the smell of digging down deep in shadow through earth that had lain cheek by jowl with things that were long hidden and decayed. A stinking and rancid soil fell away in clods of dissolution from Dog's muzzle and paws. He had dug deep. He had dug very deep indeed. That *was* it, wasn't it? Wasn't it? *Wasn't* it?

What kind of message was this from Dog? What could such a message mean? The stench—the ripe and awful cemetery earth.

Dog was a very bad dog, digging where he shouldn't. Dog was a good dog, always making friends. Dog loved people. Dog brought them home.

And now, moving up the dark hall stairs, at intervals, came the sound of feet, one foot dragged after the other, painfully, slowly, slowly, slowly.

Dog shivered. A rain of strange night earth fell seething on the bed.

Dog turned.

The bedroom door whispered in.

Martin had company.

The Joy of Balls

From *A Dog's Life*

BY PETER MAYLE

P ETER MAYLE FIRST CAME to prominence with his hilarious books on life in France, starting with *A Year in Provence,* which was (more or less) factual. *A Dog's Life,* from which this selection is taken, is (more or less) fictional. For myself, I find I'm pretty sure my dogs have had those same kinds of thoughts . . . I just couldn't interpret them as well.

Being a dog in an expatriate household in the south of France has some real compensations: special tennis balls straight from Wimbledon, paté and wine, and human foibles for entertainment.

★ ★ ★ ★ ★

A FRIEND OF THE FAMILY who descends on us from time to time is one of the few people I know who shares my habit of relaxing under the dining table. Not for him the stiff formality of the chair and polite social intercourse. On occasion, once he has eaten, he has been known to slide gently down to join me, and we bond. You may find this hard to believe, but there are photographs in existence to prove it. He maintains that it helps his digestion, although I feel it has more to do with a longing for quiet and serene company after all the conversational cut-and-thrust that takes place on the top deck. In any event, he is a kindred spirit.

It happens that he is also some kind of eminence in the world of British tennis—head ball boy at the Queen's Club, it may be, or possibly a senior catering executive, I'm not sure. Whatever it is, his position gives him access to the highest levels of the annual Queen's Tournament. He rubs shoulders with players and royalty and is permitted to use the VIP toilet facilities, which apparently is an honor reserved for the fortunate few. All this, I learned in the course of a long session under the table after lunch one day.

As I may have mentioned, I do like to have something to chew when the mood takes me, live preferably, but that involves catching it first, and for some reason it's not too popular with the management. And so, faute de mieux, I usually have to make do with an inanimate object such as a stick, the Labrador's blanket, or a guest's shoe. Dull pickings, for the most part, although I did manage to get hold of a child's teddy bear once. It didn't put up much of a fight, I have to say, and there were tearful recriminations over the remains, much wailing and gnashing of teeth, followed by solitary confinement for the winner. The stuffing gave me a bilious attack, too. Everything these days are man-made fibers, which I can tell you are highly indigestible. If you've ever eaten squid in a cheap Italian restaurant, you'll know what I mean.

It was shortly after the teddy bear incident that I was given my first tennis ball, and I took to it immediately. Round, springy, and small enough to carry in one side of the mouth while barking from the other, it was my constant companion for weeks. You can imagine my hurt feelings, therefore, when the refugee from Queen's arrived one day, took a look at my ball, and sneered. "Not up to championship standards," he said. "Furthermore, it's bald, soiled, and out of shape." Well, you could say the same about quite a few of the guests who I've seen come and go, but I'm not one for the gratuitous insult. Goodwill to all men is my rule in life as long as they make themselves useful with the biscuits.

I had more or less recovered from the disparaging remarks about my recreational equipment when what should arrive at the house but a large box,

addressed to me. This was unusual enough for the postman to come in and deliver it by hand, together with some facetious and quite unnecessary comments
about my inability to sign for it. While he was congratulating himself on his
feeble witticism, I took the opportunity to go and lift my leg on a sackful of
undelivered mail that he'd left outside the door. Revenge is damp.

I came back to find the box open and the management studying a letter that described the pedigree of the contents. These were tennis balls, dozens
of them, barely marked and with full heads of bright yellow fur. But they were
not just everyday balls. According to the letter, they were balls of tremendous
importance and fame, having appeared on television. They had been used in
the men's finals of the Queen's Tournament and collected, still warm from
their exertions, by our man on the spot and sent over for my personal use.

To begin with, I just sat and looked at them, and gloated. After being rationed to a single ball, a whole box of them gave me a delightful feeling of sudden
wealth. French politicians must have a similar sensation when elected to high office and permitted to dip into the châteaux and limousines and government-issue
caviar. No wonder they cling to power long after they should be tucked away in
an old folks' home. I'd do the same.

I was sorting through the balls before selecting my playmate for the
day when I was struck by an interesting difference in the messages they were
sending to the nose. If you've ever watched tennis—I'm sure some people do
when they have nothing better to amuse themselves—you will have noticed
that the contestants always keep a couple of spare balls in the pocket of their
shorts. In this dark, overheated space, some kind of osmosis occurs, and the
balls take on the character of the athletic and perspiring thigh. And if you happen to possess, as I do, a sensitive and highly tuned sense of smell, it's possible to
identify the thigh's owner—not by name, of course, but by place of origin.

I applied the deductive faculties and was able to divide the balls into
two groups. On the left was the Old World—complex, mature, with a long
Teutonic finish and a hint of alcohol-free beer. On the right, a clear signal from
the Dark Continent, hot and dusty, with a refreshing tang of the high veldt.
Now, as I said, I can't give you names, but if you go back over the records, I
think you'll find the finalists for that year were German and South African.
Advantage, *moi*. Fascinating, isn't it?

And that, in my considered opinion, is one of the few interesting as-
pects of tennis. As in much of what passes for sport, a basic principle has been
misunderstood. The essence of any game, it seems to me, is to gain possession
of the ball and find a quiet corner where one can destroy it in peace. But what
do we see these highly paid and luridly dressed people doing with the ball?

They hit it, kick it, throw it, bounce it, put it in a net, put it in a hole, and generally play the fool with it. Then they either kiss each other and slap hands or have a tantrum and go and mope in the corner. Adult men and women they are, too, although you'd never guess it. I've know five-year-olds with a better grip on themselves.

But I wouldn't want you to think that I'm completely devoid of sporting instincts. My own version of fetch the ball, for example, provides me with hours of harmless enjoyment and keeps participating adults away from the bar and out of mischief. I always win, too, which is as it should be.

First, I choose an elevated spot. It could be the top of a flight of stairs, a wall, the raised edge of the swimming pool—anywhere that gives me a height advantage. Stairs are best, because of the added cardiovascular benefits, but I shall come to that in a minute.

I take up my position, ball in mouth, and lurk with lowered head in the manner of the vulture contemplating the imminent death of his breakfast. Sooner or later, this motionless and rather extraordinary pose attracts attention. "What is Boy doing?" they say. Or, "Is he going to be sick?" With the eyes of the assembled spectators upon me, I slowly open my mouth and let the ball bounce free. Down the steps, off the wall, or into the deep end it goes. I remain completely still, the unblinking eye fixed on the ball below me. It is a tense and focused moment.

The tension lasts until someone has the common sense to gasp the purpose of the game, which is to retrieve the ball and return it to me. If the spectators are particularly dense—and I've known a few, believe me, who didn't seem to know whether it was lunchtime or Tuesday—I might have to give a short bark to indicate start of play. The ball is fetched, brought back, and presented to me. I give the players a minute or two to settle down and get over the excitement, and then I repeat the process.

I mentioned stairs earlier. These have the double attraction of noise and healthy physical exertion, in contrast to the visitors' usual program of elbow bending and free-weight training with knife and fork. The falling ball provides multiple bouncing sounds, and the retriever has to climb up the stairs to give it back to me. As any doctor will tell you, this is very beneficial for the legs and lungs.

I'll admit, though, that there have been days when I've been off form with the long game. Balls take unlucky bounces, as we all know, and sometimes get lost in the rough. Or, more often, the spectators have been too preoccupied with refreshments to pay attention. And here, I think, is an inspirational example of dedication and the will to win coming through against all odds.

It was one of those evenings when nothing I could do impinged on the happy hour. I lurked, I dropped, I barked, and still the merriment continued. I even suffered the ignominy of having to fetch the ball myself—which, as any of those tennis people will tell you, is a fate worse than having to pay for your own rackets. But instead of bursting into tears and calling for the manager, as most of *them* do, I brought out my short game.

The assembled guests—there must have been eight or ten of them in varying stages of incoherence—were all seated around a low table, bleating away about the hardships of life as they punished the hors d'oeuvres and held out their empty glasses for more of the same. None of them noticed me as I slipped, wraith-like, through the forest of legs and arms to the table.

Then—overhead smash!—I dropped the ball into a bowl of tapenade, which, as you may know, is a dark, oily dip made from olives. It splatters in a most satisfying way, and those in the immediate vicinity came out in a black rash.

You could have heard a jaw drop. It was well worth the retribution that followed, and to this day, whenever I pick up my ball of choice, I am regarded with the wary respect befitting a champion. Incidentally, if you've never tried tapenade-flavored tennis ball, I can recommend it. Recipe on request.

Garm, a Hostage

BY RUDYARD KIPLING

I T WAS AS A CHILD that I first read "Garm"; some perceptive adult gave me a book of dog stories that I read and re-read. "Garm" made such an impression on me that the first dog I bought when I grew up was a bull-terrier. Kipling caught the essence of all bull-terriers—the way they move and smile and fight. I think he must have owned one at some time.

Written during Kipling's period as a newspaperman in India, this story is a fascinating look at a world long since gone, with all the flavor of the Raj. Even more, it is a moving tale of the interdependency between a man and his dog.

★ ★ ★ ★ ★

ONE NIGHT, A VERY long time ago, I drove to an Indian military encampment called Mian Mir to see amateur theatricals. At the back of the Infantry barracks a soldier, his cap over one eye, rushed in front of the horses and shouted that he was a dangerous highway robber. As a matter of fact, he was a friend of mine, so I told him to go home before any one caught him; but he fell under the pole, and I heard voices of a military guard in search of some one.

The driver and I coaxed him into the carriage, drove home swiftly, undressed him and put him to bed, where he waked next morning with a sore headache, very much ashamed. When his uniform was cleaned and dried, and he had been shaved and washed and made neat, I drove him back to barracks with his arm in a fine white sling, and reported that I had accidentally run over him. I did not tell this story to my friend's sergeant, who was a hostile and unbelieving person, but to his lieutenant, who did not know us quite so well.

Three days later my friend came to call, and at his heels slobbered and fawned one of the finest bull-terriers—of the old-fashioned breed, two parts bull and one terrier—that I had ever set eyes on. He was pure white, with a fawn-colored saddle just behind his neck, and a fawn diamond at the root of his thin whippy tail. I had admired him distantly for more than a year; and Vixen, my own fox-terrier, knew him too, but did not approve.

"'E's for you," said my friend; but he did not look as though he liked parting with him.

"Nonsense! That dog's worth more than most men, Stanley," I said.

"'E's that and more. 'Tention!"

The dog rose on his hind legs, and stood upright for a full minute.

"Eyes right!"

He sat on his haunches and turned his head sharp to the right. At a sign he rose and barked twice. Then he shook hands with his right paw and bounded lightly to my shoulder. Here he made himself into a necktie, limp and lifeless, hanging down on either side of my neck. I was told to pick him up and throw him in the air. He fell with a howl and held up one leg.

"Part o' the trick," said his owner. "You're going to die now. Dig yourself your little grave an' shut your little eye."

Still limping, the dog hobbled to the garden edge, dug a hole and lay down in it. When told that he was cured, he jumped out, wagging his tail, and whining for applause. He was put through half a dozen other tricks, such as showing how he would hold a man safe (I was that man, and he sat down before me, his teeth bared, ready to spring), and how he would stop eating at the word of command. I had no more than finished praising him when my friend made a gesture that stopped the dog as though he had been shot, took a piece of blue-ruled canteen-paper from his helmet, handed it to me and ran away, while the dog looked after him and howled. I read:

> *Sir—I give you the dog because of what you got me out of. He is the best I know, for I made him myself, and he is as good as a man. Please do not give him too much to eat, and please do not give him back to me, for I'm not going to take him, if you will keep him. So please do not try to give him back any more. I have kept his name back, so you can call him anything and he will answer, but please do not give him back. He can kill a man as easy as anything, but please do not give him too much meat. He knows more than a man.*

Vixen sympathetically joined her shrill little yap to the bull-terrier's despairing cry, and I was annoyed, for I knew that a man who cares for dogs is one thing, but a man who loves one dog is quite another. Dogs are at the best no more than verminous vagrants, self-scratchers, foul feeders, and unclean by the law of Moses and Mohammed; but a dog with whom one lives alone for at least six months in the year; a free thing, tied to you so strictly by love that without you he will not stir or exercise; a patient, temperate, humorous, wise soul, who knows your moods before you know them yourself, is not a dog under any ruling.

I had Vixen, who was all my dog to me; and I felt what my friend must have felt, at tearing out his heart in this style and leaving it in my garden.

However, the dog understood clearly enough that I was his master, and did not follow the soldier. As soon as he drew breath I made much of him, and Vixen, yelling with jealousy, flew at him. Had she been of his own sex, he might have cheered himself with a fight, but he only looked worriedly when she nipped his deep iron sides, laid his heavy head on my knee, and howled anew. I meant to dine at the Club that night, but as darkness drew in, and the dog snuffled through the empty house like a child trying to recover from a fit of sobbing, I felt that I could not leave him to suffer his first evening alone. So we fed at home, Vixen on one side, and the stranger-dog on the other; she watching his every mouthful, and saying explicitly what she thought of his table manners, which were much better than hers.

It was Vixen's custom, till the weather grew hot, to sleep in my bed, her head on the pillow like a Christian; and when morning came I would always find that the little thing had braced her feet against the wall and pushed me to the very edge of the cot. This night she hurried to bed purposefully, every hair up, one eye on the stranger, who had dropped on a mat in a helpless, hopeless sort of way, all four feet spread out, sighing heavily. She settled her head on the pillow several times, to show her little airs and graces, and struck up her usual whiney sing-song before slumber. The stranger-dog softly edged towards me. I put out my hand and he licked it. Instantly my wrist was between Vixen's teeth, and her warning *aaarh!* said as plainly as speech, that if I took any further notice of the stranger she would bite.

I caught her behind her fat neck with my left hand, shook her severely, and said:

"Vixen, if you do that again you'll be put into the veranda. Now, remember!"

She understood perfectly, but the minute I released her she mouthed my right wrist once more, and waited with her ears back and all her body flattened, ready to bite. The big dog's tail thumped the floor in a humble and peace-making way.

I grabbed Vixen a second time, lifted her out of bed like a rabbit (she hated that and yelled), and, as I had promised, set her out in the veranda with the bats and the moonlight. At this she howled. Then she used coarse language—not to me, but to the bull-terrier—till she coughed with exhaustion. Then she ran around the house trying every door. Then she went off to the stables and barked as though some one were stealing the horses, which was an old trick of hers. Last she returned, and her snuffing yelp said, "I'll be good! Let me in and I'll be good!"

She was admitted and flew to her pillow. When she was quieted I whispered to the other dog, "You can lie on the foot of the bed." The bull jumped up at once, and though I felt Vixen quiver with rage, she knew better than to protest. So we slept till the morning, and they had early breakfast with me, bite for bite, till the horse came round and we went for a ride. I don't think the bull had ever followed a horse before. He was wild with excitement, and Vixen, as usual, squealed and scuttered and scooted, and took charge of the procession.

There was one corner of a village near by, which we generally pass with caution, because all the yellow pariah-dogs of the place gathered about it. They were half-wild, starving beasts, and though utter cowards, yet where nine or ten of them get together they will mob and kill and eat an English dog. I kept a whip with a long lash for them. That morning they attacked Vixen, who, perhaps of design, had moved from beyond my horse's shadow.

The bull was ploughing along in the dust, fifty yards behind, rolling in his run, and smiling as bull-terriers will. I heard Vixen squeal; half a dozen of the curs closed in on her; a white streak came up behind me; a cloud of dust rose near Vixen, and, when it cleared, I saw one tall pariah with his back broken, and the bull wrenching another to earth. Vixen retreated to the protection of my whip, and the bull padded back smiling more than ever, covered with the blood of his enemies. That decided me to call him "Garm of the Bloody Breast," who was a great person in his time, or "Garm" for short; so, leaning forward, I told him what his temporary name would be. He looked up while I repeated it, and then away. I shouted "Garm!" He stopped, raced back, and came up to ask my will.

Then I saw that my soldier friend was right, and that that dog knew and was worth more than a man. At the end of the ridge I gave an order which Vixen knew and hated: "Go away and get washed!" I said. Garm understood some part of it, and Vixen interpreted the rest, and the two trotted off together soberly. When I went to the back veranda Vixen had been washed snowy-white, and was very proud of herself, but the dog-boy would not touch Garm on any account unless I stood by. So I waited while he was being scrubbed, and Garm, with the soap creaming on the top of his broad head, looked at me to make sure that this was what I expected him to endure. He knew perfectly that the dog-boy was only obeying orders.

"Another time," I said to the dog-boy, "you will wash the great dog with Vixen when I send them home."

"Does *he* know?" said the dog-boy, who understood the ways of dogs.

"Garm," I said, "another time you will be washed with Vixen."

I knew that Garm understood. Indeed, next washing-day, when Vixen as usual fled under my bed, Garm stared at the doubtful dog-boy in the veranda, stalked to the place where he had been washed last time, and stood rigid in the tub.

But the long days in my office tried him sorely. We three would drive off in the morning at half-past eight and come home at six or later. Vixen, knowing the routine of it, went to sleep under my table; but the confinement ate into Garm's soul. He generally sat on the veranda looking out on the Mall; and well I knew what he expected.

Sometimes a company of soldiers would move along on their way to the Fort, and Garm rolled forth to inspect them; or an officer in uniform entered into the office, and it was pitiful to see poor Garm's welcome to the cloth—not the man. He would leap at him, and sniff and bark joyously, then run to the door and back again. One afternoon I heard him bay with a full throat—a thing I had never heard before—and he disappeared. When I drove into my garden at the end of the day a soldier in white uniform scrambled over the wall at the far end, and the Garm that met me was a joyous dog. This happened twice or thrice a week for a month.

I pretended not to notice, but Garm knew and Vixen knew. He would glide homewards from the office about four o'clock, as though he were only going to look at the scenery, and this he did so quietly that but for Vixen I should not have noticed him. The jealous little dog under the table would give a sniff and a snort, just loud enough to call my attention to the flight. Garm might go out forty times in the day and Vixen would never stir, but when he slunk off to see his true master in my garden she told me in her own tongue. That was the one sign she made to prove that Garm did not altogether belong to the family. They were the best of friends at all times, *but*, Vixen explained that I was never to forget Garm did not love me as she loved me.

I never expected it. The dog was not my dog—could never be my dog—and I knew he was as miserable as his master who tramped eight miles a day to see him. So it seemed to me that the sooner the two were reunited the better for all. One afternoon I sent Vixen home alone in the dog-cart (Garm had gone before), and rode over to cantonments to find another friend of mine, who was an Irish soldier and a great friend of the dog's master.

I explained the whole case, and wound up with:

"And now Stanley's in my garden crying over his dog. Why doesn't he take it back? They're both unhappy."

"Unhappy! There's no sense in the little man anymore. But 'tis his fit."

"What *is* his fit? He travels fifty miles a week to see the brute, and he pretends not to notice me when he sees me on the road; and I'm as unhappy as he is. Make him take the dog back."

"It's his penance he's set himself. I told him by way of a joke, after you'd run over him so convenient that night, when he was drunk—I said if he was a Catholic he'd do penance. Off he went wid that fit in his head *an'* a dose of fever, an' nothin' would suit but givin' you the dog as a hostage."

"Hostage for what? I don't want hostages from Stanley."

"For his good behavior. He's keepin' straight now, the way it's no pleasure to associate wid him."

"Has he taken the pledge?"

"If 'twas only that I need not care. Ye can take the pledge for three months on an' off. He sez he'll never see the dog again, an' *so* mark you, he'll keep straight for evermore. Ye know his fits? Well, this is wan of them. How's the dog takin' it?"

"Like a man. He's the best dog in India. Can't you make Stanley take him back?"

"I can do no more than I have done. But ye know his fits. He's just doin' his penance. What will he do when he goes to the Hills? The docthor's put him on the list."

It is the custom in India to send a certain number of invalids from each regiment up to stations in the Himalayas for the hot weather; and though the men ought to enjoy the cool and the comfort, they miss the society of the barracks down below, and do their best to come back or to avoid going. I felt that this move would bring matters to a head, so I left Terrence hopefully, though he called after me:

"He won't take the dog, sorr. You can lay your month's pay on that. Ye know his fits."

I never pretended to understand Private Ortheris; and so I did the next best thing—I left him alone.

That summer the invalids of the regiment to which my friend belonged were ordered off to the Hills early, because the doctors thought marching in the cool of the day would do them good. Their route lay south to a place called Umballa, a hundred and twenty miles or more. Then they would turn east and march up into the Hills to Kasauli or Dugshai or Subathoo. I dined with the officers the night before they left—they were marching at five in the morning. It was midnight when I drove into my garden, and surprised a white figure flying over the wall.

"That man," said my butler, "has been here since nine, making talk to that dog. He is quite mad. I did not tell him to go away because he has been here many times before, and because the dog-boy told me that if I told him to go away, that great dog would immediately slay me. He did not wish to speak to the Protector of the Poor, and he did not ask for anything to eat or drink."

"Kadir Buksh," said I, "that was well done, for the dog would surely have killed thee. But I do not think the white soldier will come any more."

Garm slept ill that night and whimpered in his dreams. Once he sprang up with a clear, ringing bark, and I heard him wag his tail till it waked him and the bark died out in a howl. He had dreamed he was with his master again, and I nearly cried. It was all Stanley's silly fault.

The first halt which the detachment of invalids made was some miles from their barracks, on the Amritsar road, and ten miles distant from my house. By a mere chance one of the officers drove back for another good dinner at the Club (cooking on the line of march is always bad), and there we met. He was a particular friend of mine, and I knew that he knew how to love a dog properly. His pet was a big retriever who was going up to the Hills for his health, and, though it was still April, the round, brown brute puffed and panted in the Club veranda as though he would burst.

"It's amazing," said the officer, "what excuses these invalids of mine make to get back to the barracks. There's a man in my company now asked me for leave to go back to cantonments to pay a debt he'd forgotten. I was so taken by the idea I let him go, and he jingled off in an *ekka* as pleased as Punch. Ten miles to pay a debt! Wonder what it was really?"

"If you'll drive me home I think I can show you," I said.

So he went over to my house in his dog-cart with the retriever; and on the way I told him the story of Garm.

"I was wondering where that brute had gone to. He's the best dog in the regiment," said my friend. "I offered the little fellow twenty rupees for him a month ago. But he's a hostage, you say, for Stanley's good conduct. Stanley's one of the best men I have—when he chooses."

"That's the reason why," I said. "A second-rate man wouldn't have taken things to heart as he has done."

We drove in quietly at the far end of the garden, and crept round the house. There was a place close to the wall all grown about with tamarisk trees, where I know Garm kept his bones. Even Vixen was not allowed to sit near it. In the full Indian moonlight I could see a white uniform bending over the dog.

"Good-bye, old man," we could not help hearing Stanley's voice. "For 'Eving's sake don't get bit and go mad by any measly pi-dog. But you can look after yourself, old man. *You* don't get drunk an' run about 'ittin' your friends. You takes your bones an' eats your biscuit, an' kills your enemy like a gentleman. I'm goin' away—don't 'owl—I'm goin' off to Kasauli, where I won't see you no more."

I could hear him holding Garm's nose as the dog drew it up to the stars.

"You'll stay here an' be'ave, an'—an' I'll go away an' try to be'ave, an' I don't know 'ow to leave you. I don' think—"

"I think this is damn silly," said the officer, patting his foolish fubsy old retriever. He called to the private who leaped to his feet, marched forward, and saluted.

"You here?" said the officer, turning away his head.

"Yes, sir, but I'm just goin' back."

"I shall be leaving here at eleven in my cart. You come with me. I can't have sick men running about all over the place. Report yourself at eleven, *here*."

We did not say much when we went indoors, but the officer muttered and pulled his retriever's ears.

He was a disgraceful, overfed format of a dog; and when he waddled off to my cookhouse to be fed, I had a brilliant idea.

At eleven o'clock that officer's dog was nowhere to be found, and you never heard such a fuss as his owner made. He called and shouted and grew angry, and hunted through my garden for half an hour.

Then I said:

"He's sure to turn up in the morning. Send a man in by rail, and I'll find the beast and return him."

"Beast?" said the officer. "I value that dog considerably more than I value any man I know. It's all very fine for you to talk—your dog's here."

So she was—under my feet—and, had she been missing, food and wages would have stopped in my house till her return. But some people grow fond of dogs not worth a cut of the whip. My friend had to drive away at last with Stanley in the backseat; and then the dog-boy said to me:

"What kind of animal is Bullen Sahib's dog? Look at him!"

I went to the boy's hut, and the fat old reprobate was lying on a mat carefully chained up. He must have heard his master calling for twenty minutes, but had not even attempted to join him.

"He has no face," said the dog-boy scornfully. "He is a *punniarkooter* [a spaniel]. He never tried to get that cloth off his jaws when his master called. Now Vixen-baba would have jumped through the window, and that Great Dog would have slain me with his muzzled mouth. It is true that there are many kinds of dogs."

Next evening who should turn up but Stanley. The officer had sent him back fourteen miles by rail with a note begging me to return the retriever if I had found him, and, if I had not, to offer huge rewards. The last train to camp left at half-past ten, and Stanley stayed till ten talking to Garm. I argued and entreated, and even threatened to shoot the bull-terrier, but the little man was firm as a rock, though I gave him a good dinner and talked to him most severely. Garm knew as well as I that this was the last time he could hope to see his man, and followed Stanley like a shadow. The retriever said nothing, but licked his lips after his meal and waddled off without so much as saying "Thank you" to the disgusted dog-boy.

So that last meeting was over, and I felt as wretched as Garm, who moaned in his sleep all night. When we went to the office he found a place under the table close to Vixen, and dropped flat till it was time to go home. There was no more running out into the verandas, no slinking away for stolen talks with Stanley. As the weather grew warmer the dogs were forbidden to run beside the cart, but sat at my side on the seat. Vixen with her head under the crook of my left elbow, and Garm hugging the left handrail.

Here Vixen was ever in great form. She had to attend to all the moving traffic, such as bullock-carts that blocked the way, and camels, and led ponies; as well as to keep up her dignity when she passed low friends running in the dust. She never yapped for yapping's sake, but her shrill, high bark was known all along the Mall, and other men's terriers ki-yied in reply, and bullock-drivers looked over their shoulders and gave us the road with a grin.

But Garm cared for none of these things. His big eyes were on the horizon and his terrible mouth was shut. There was another dog in the office who belonged to my chief. We called him "Bob the Librarian," because he always imagined vain rats behind the bookshelves, and in hunting for them would drag out half the old newspaper-files. Bob was a well-meaning idiot, but Garm did not encourage him. He would slide his head round the door panting, "Rats! Come along, Garm!" and Garm would shift one forepaw over the other, and curl himself round, leaving Bob to whine at a most uninterested back. The office was nearly as cheerful as a tomb in those days.

Once, and only once, did I see Garm at all contented with his surroundings. He had gone for an unauthorized walk with Vixen early one Sunday morning, and a very young and foolish artilleryman (his battery had just moved to that part of the world) tried to steal both. Vixen, of course, knew better than to take food from soldiers, and, besides, she had just finished her breakfast. So she trotted back with a large piece of the mutton that they issue to our troops, laid it down on my veranda, and looked up to see what I thought. I asked her where Garm was, and she ran in front of the house to show me the way.

About a mile up the road we came across our artilleryman sitting very stiffly on the edge of a culvert with a greasy handkerchief on his knees. Garm was in front of him, looking rather pleased. When the man moved leg or hand, Garm bared his teeth in silence. A broken string hung from his collar, and the other half of it lay, all warm, in the artilleryman's still hand. He explained to me, keeping his eye straight in front of him, that he had met this dog (he called him awful names) walking alone, and was going to take him to the Fort to be killed for a masterless pariah.

I said that Garm did not seem to me much of a pariah, but that he had better take him to the Fort if he thought best. He said he did not care to do so. I told him to go to the Fort alone. He said he did not want to go at that hour, but would follow my advice as soon as I had called off the dog. I instructed Garm to take him to the Fort, and Garm marched him solemnly up to the gate, one mile and a half under a hot sun, and I told the quarter-guard what had happened; but the young artilleryman was more angry than was at all necessary when they began to laugh. Several regiments, he was told, had tried to steal Garm in their time.

That month the hot weather shut down in earnest, and the dogs slept in the bathroom on the cool wet bricks where the bath is placed. Every morning, as soon as the man filled my bath, the two jumped in, and every morning the man filled the bath a second time. I said to him that he might as well fill a small tub especially for the dogs. "Nay," said he smiling, "it is not their custom. They would not understand. Besides, the big bath gives them more space."

The punkah-coolies who pull the punkahs day and night came to know Garm intimately. He noticed that when the swaying fan stopped I would call out to the coolie and bid him pull with a long stroke. If the man still slept I would wake him up. He discovered, too, that it was a good thing to lie in the wave of air under the punkah. Maybe Stanley had taught him all about this in barracks. At any rate, when the punkah stopped, Garm would first growl and cock his eye at the rope, and if that did not wake the man—it nearly always did—he would tiptoe forth and talk in the sleeper's ear. Vixen was a clever little dog, but she could never connect the punkah and the coolie; so Garm gave me grateful hours of cool sleep. But he was utterly wretched—as miserable as a human being; and in his misery he clung so close to me that other men noticed it, and were envious. If I moved from one room to another Garm followed; if my pen stopped scratching, Garm's head was thrust into my hand; if I turned, half awake, on the pillow, Garm was up at my side, for he knew that I was his only link with his master, and day and night, and night and day, his eyes asked one question—"When is this going to end?"

Living with the dog as I did, I never noticed that he was more than ordinarily upset by the hot weather, till one day at the Club a man said: "That dog of yours will die in a week or two. He's a shadow." Then I dosed Garm with iron and quinine, which he hated; and I felt very anxious. He lost his appetite, and Vixen was allowed to eat his dinner under his eyes. Even that did not make him swallow, and we held a consultation on him, of the best man-doctor in the place; a lady-doctor, who had cured the sick wives of kings; and the Deputy Inspector-General of the veterinary service of all India. They pronounced upon his symptoms, and I told them his story, and Garm lay on a sofa licking my hand.

"He's dying of a broken heart," said the lady-doctor suddenly.

" 'Pon my word," said the Deputy Inspector-General, "I believe Mrs. Macrae is perfectly right—as usual."

The best man-doctor in the place wrote a prescription, and the veterinary Deputy Inspector-General went over it afterwards to be sure that the drugs were in the proper dog-proportions; and that was the first time in his life that our doctor ever allowed his prescriptions to be edited. It was a strong tonic, and it put the dear boy on his feet for a week or two; then he lost flesh again. I asked a man I knew to take him up to the Hills with him when he went, and the man came to the door with his kit packed on the top of the carriage. Garm took in the situation at one red glance. The hair rose along his back; he sat down in front of me, and delivered the most awful growl I have ever heard in the jaws of a dog. I shouted to my friend to get away at once, and as soon as the carriage was out of the garden Garm laid his head on my knee and whined. So I knew his answer, and devoted myself to getting Stanley's address in the Hills.

My turn to go to the cool came late in August. We were allowed thirty-days' holiday in a year, if no one fell sick, and we took it as we could be spared. My chief and Bob the Librarian had their holiday first, and when they were gone I made a calendar, as I always did, and hung it up at the head of my cot, tearing off one day at a time till they returned. Vixen had gone up to the Hills with me five times before; and she appreciated the cold and the damp and the beautiful wood fires there as much as I did.

"Garm," I said, "we are going back to Stanley at Kasauli. Kasauli—Stanley; Stanley—Kasauli." And I repeated it twenty times. It was not Kasauli really, but another place. Still I remembered what Stanley had said in my garden on the last night, and I dared not change the name. Then Garm began to tremble; then he barked; and then he leaped up at me, frisking and wagging his tail.

"Not now," I said, holding up my hand. "When I say 'Go,' we'll go, Garm." I pulled out the little blanket coat and spiked collar that Vixen always wore up in the Hills to protect her against sudden chills and thieving leopards, and I let the two smell them and talk it over. What they said of course I do not know, but it made a new dog of Garm. His eyes were bright; and he barked joyfully when I spoke to him. He ate his food, and he killed his rats for the next three weeks, and when he began to whine I had only to say "Stanley—Kasauli; Kasauli—Stanley," to wake him up. I wish I had thought of it before.

My chief came back, all brown with living in the open air, and very angry at finding it so hot in the Plains. That same afternoon we three and Kadir Buksh began to pack for our month's holiday, Vixen rolling in and out of the bullock-trunk twenty times a minute, and Garm grinning all over and thumping on the floor with his tail. Vixen knew the routine of traveling as well as she knew my office-work. She went to the station, singing songs, on the front seat of the carriage, while Garm sat with me. She hurried into the railway carriage, saw Kadir Buksh make up my bed for the night, got her drink of water, and curled up with her black-patch eye on the tumult of the platform. Garm followed her (the crowd gave him a lane all to himself) and sat down on the pillow with his eyes blazing, and his tail a haze behind him.

We came to Umballa in the hot misty dawn, four or five men, who had been working hard for eleven months, shouting for our dâks—the two-horse traveling carriages that were to take us up to Kalka at the foot of the Hills. It was all new to Garm. He did not understand carriages where you lay at full length on your bedding, but Vixen knew and hopped into her place at once; Garm following. The Kalka road, before the railway was built, was about forty-seven miles long, and the horses were changed every eight miles. Most of them jibbed, and kicked, and plunged, but they had to go, and they went rather better than usual for Garm's deep bay in their rear.

There was a river to be forded, and four bullocks pulled the carriage, and Vixen stuck her head out of the sliding-door and nearly fell into the water while she gave directions. Garm was silent and curious, and rather needed reassuring about Stanley and Kasauli. So we rolled, barking and yelping, into Kalka for lunch, and Garm ate enough for two.

After Kalka the road wound among the Hills, and we took a curricle with half-broken ponies, which were changed every six miles. No one dreamed of a railroad to Simla in those days, for it was seven thousand feet up in the air. The road was more than fifty miles long, and the regulation pace was just as fast as the ponies could go. Here, again, Vixen led Garm from one carriage to the other; jumped into the backseat and shouted. A cool breath from the snows met us about five miles out of Kalka, and she whined for her coat, wisely fearing a chill on the liver. I had had one made for Garm too, and, as we climbed to the fresh breezes, I put it on, and Garm chewed it uncomprehendingly, but I think he was grateful.

"Hi-yi-yi-yi!" sang Vixen as we shot around the curves; "Toot-toot-toot!" went the driver's bugle at the dangerous places, and "Yow! Yow! Yow! Yow!" bayed Garm. Kadir Buksh sat on the front seat and smiled. Even he was glad to get away from the heat of the Plains that stewed in the haze behind us. Now and then we would meet a man we knew going down to his work again, and he would say: "What's it like below?" and I would shout: "Hotter than cinders. What's it like above?" and he would shout back: "Just perfect!" and away we would go.

Suddenly Kadir Buksh said, over his shoulder: "Here is Solon;" and Garm snored where he lay with his head on my knee. Solon is an unpleasant little cantonment, but it has the advantage of being cool and healthy. It is all bare and windy, and one generally stops at a rest-house near by for something to eat. I got out and took both dogs with me, while Kadir Buksh made tea. A soldier told us we should find Stanley "out there," nodding his head towards a bare, bleak hill.

When we climbed to the top we spied that very Stanley, who had given me all this trouble, sitting on a rock with his face in his hands, and his overcoat hanging loose about him. I never saw anything so lonely and dejected in my life as this one little man, crumpled up and thinking, on the great gray hillside.

Here Garm left me.

He departed without a word, and, so far as I could see, without moving his legs. He flew through the air bodily, and I heard the whack of him as he flung himself at Stanley, knocking the little man clean over. They rolled on the ground together, shouting, and yelping, and hugging. I could not see which was dog and which was man, till Stanley got up and whimpered.

He told me that he had been suffering from fever at intervals, and was very weak. He looked all he said, but even while I watched, both man and dog plumped out to their natural sizes, precisely as dried apples swell in water. Garm was on his shoulder, and his breast and feet all at the same time, so that Stanley spoke all through a cloud of Garm—gulping, sobbing, slavering Garm. He did not say anything that I could understand, except that he had fancied he was going to die, but that now he was quite well, and that he was not going to give up Garm any more to anybody under the rank of Beelzebub.

Then he said he felt hungry, thirsty, and happy.

We went down to tea at the rest-house, where Stanley stuffed himself with sardines and raspberry jam, and beer, and cold mutton and pickles, when Garm wasn't climbing over him; and then Vixen and I went on.

Garm saw how it was at once. He said good-bye to me three times, giving me both paws one after another, and leaping onto my shoulder. He further escorted us, singing Hosannas at the top of his voice, a mile down the road. Then he raced back to his own master.

Vixen never opened her mouth, but when the cold twilight came, and we could see the lights of Simla across the hills, she snuffled with her nose at the breast of my ulster. I unbuttoned it, and tucked her inside. Then she gave a contented little sniff, and fell fast asleep, her head on my breast, till we bundled out of Simla, two of the four happiest people in all the world that night.

The Dog Who Paid Cash

BY WILL ROGERS

A DOG STORY by America's cowboy humorist is a rare find. People were more often the butt of Rogers's gentle joking than animals. Rogers wrote, appeared in movies, did lecture tours around the country—swinging his lariat 'round in circles he delivered monologues that poked fun at human foibles and made a world laugh when there wasn't always much to laugh at.

The dog who paid for what he wanted was just one of the characters Rogers met on his travels . . . one who gave good measure whether buying food or being the subject of a tongue-in-cheek short story.

★　★　★　★　★

WHILE I DIDN'T HAVE anything else to do, I got to watching an old spotted dog. He was just an ordinary dog, but when I looked at him close, he was alert and friendly with everyone. Got to inquiring around and found out he'd been bumped off a freight train and seemed to have no owner. He made himself at home and started right in business. When a crowd of cowboys would go into a saloon, he would follow 'em in and begin entertaining. He could do all kinds of tricks—turn somersaults, lay down and roll over, sit up on his hind feet, and such like.

He would always rush to the door and shake hands with all the new-comers. The boys would lay a coin on his nose, and he'd toss it high in the air and catch it in his mouth and pretend to swallow it. But you could bet your life he didn't swallow it—he stuck it in one side of his lip and when he got a lip full of money, he'd dash out the back door and disappear for a few minutes. What he had really done was hide his money. As soon as he worked one saloon, he would pull out and go to another place.

I got to thinking while watching this old dog, how much smarter he is than me. Here I am out of a job five hundred miles from home and setting around and can't find a thing to do, and this old dog hops off a train and starts right in making money, hand over fist.

Me and some boys around town tried to locate his hidden treasure but this old dog was too slick for us. He never fooled away no time on three or four of us boys that was looking for work. He seemed to know we was broke, but he was very friendly. As he was passing along by me, he'd wag his tail and kinda wink. I musta looked hungry and forlorn. I think he wanted to buy me a meal.

When times was dull and he got hungry, he would mysteriously disap-pear. Pretty soon he'd show up at a butcher shop with a dime in his mouth and lay it on the counter and the butcher would give him a piece of steak or a bone. He always paid for what he got in the line of grub. Pretty soon he seemed to get tired of the town, and one morning he was gone. A railroad man told us later that he seen the same dog in Trinidad, Colorado.

"That'll Do!"

From *Of Sheep and Men*

BY R. B. ROBERTSON

I WAS INTRODUCED to R. B. Robertson by a friend who runs a bunch of sheep and some Highland cattle with the aid of his border collies; when it comes to assessing descriptions of working dogs, he knows whereof he speaks.

Robertson's book *Of Sheep and Men,* from which this excerpt is taken, is a rare find—he writes smoothly and with grace and humor about a truly pastoral time spent on the Scottish borders.

To make interpretation easier: a "tup" is a male sheep, and is referred to as a "ram" only in poetry and government pamphlets on sheep husbandry. A "yowe" is a female sheep and was a female sheep for centuries before the English began to mispronounce it.

★　★　★　★　★

"A purebred and registered Working Collie shall be considered as of PROVEN WORK-ING ABILITY when: Said dog, under command, is capable of GATHERING a group of sheep, making not less than a 200-yard outrun, a cautious approach, a careful lift, and a straight fetch. Said dog, under command, is also capable of DRIVING a designated group of sheep a specified direction, to a designated point, and for a distance of not less than fifty yards from the handler. Said dog, under command, is also capable of PEN-NING a group of sheep; all the above work to be accomplished in true, quiet Working Collie style, using 'eye' for effective control and free of vicious gripping."

BYLAWS OF THE NORTH AMERICAN SHEEPDOG SOCIETY

THE COURSE OF LIFE ran smoothly on the three glens during the month or so following the autumn Dippin'. The sun had slipped off down around the South Pole somewhere, leaving us with no light but that of oil lamps for eighteen hours out of the twenty-four; but our little cottages had stone walls four feet thick, our larders and tattie bins were full, and the village coal man had conveniently forgotten that his commodity was still rationed and controlled by the government. Mrs. Tam, in her capacity as Wisewoman, had got our households and our lives all organized to her satisfaction, as also the lives of the dozen or so dogs and several thousand sheep of the glens.

And then there was a catastrophe, the full gravity of which we did not appreciate until we saw Mrs. Tam herself, with Tam three paces behind her, striding up the glen to cope with the situation in person. It was, we were made to understand, entirely our fault. The Blackface tup had been reported missing from the next glen over a week ago, and all that time it had been "jumpin'" among the Cheviot yowes on the hill right at the back of our house, and we had hadn't even noticed it! God alone knew how many crossbred lambs there would be on the hill next year, and it would take many years to work the damage done out of the stock. Had we "nae eyes in oor heeds?" Had we "nae seen it workin' and jumpin' all day long? It must have put five or six score o' the finest Cheviot yowes in Scotland in lamb," right under our very noses!

Mrs. Tam was very cross with us indeed, and when the great horned black-faced brute—dyed bright yellow to make it more conspicuous, and with a large blue "P" on its rump instead of our local "G"—was pointed out to us, we had to confess that we *had* been somewhat unobservant. But Tam, if he was cross with us, did not show it, but quietly announced that he would come back in the afternoon "wi' a dug," and would rectify the situation before further damage was done.

So, about two o'clock, he came back up the glen, accompanied by Gyp, the oldest and most experienced collie bitch in the three glens.

Like most great sheepdogs, Gyp is nothing much to look at, but no shepherd ever chose a dog for its looks. In fact, it is safe to say that, were any Border herd offered a dog like the handsome and immortal Lassie, of Hollywood, he would not consider it worth the price of its feed. And there is certainly nothing Lassie-like about Gyp. Gyp would have as much chance of getting employment as an extra in Hollywood as Lassie would have of "shedding" the Blackface tup from the flock of Cheviot yowes; and the only compliment ever paid to Gyp in her life was by a lady visitor to the glen who remarked: "What strange spooky eyes that scraggy little brute has got!" But that spooky eye is the first point the shepherd looks for when choosing his dog.

I think it was Clifton Fadiman who told the story of the psychologist who shut the chimp in a room to observe its behavior, and, tiptoeing to the keyhole and peeping through to see what the ape was up to, found, gazing back at him—one beady eye.

That, if not actually what one experiences when observing and reporting on the conduct of sheepdogs, is certainly the feeling these strange little black-and-white workers convey to their human superiors, and Gyp has the beadiest eye of all, with which she can fix and overawe the largest flock of yowes or the heftiest tup.

Under this disconcerting scrutiny, I would not dare to say that practically everything that ever has been written or told or believed about the sheepdog and its touching relationship with its master is a lot of sentimental bunk. I would, however, risk saying that a great deal of what is told and believed about the collie is decidedly shaggy, to say the least.

Every year, for example, we get from some part of the world (usually from Scotland, I will allow!) the tear-jerking tale of the shepherd overwhelmed by the blizzard, and found days later lifeless and stiff, but with his faithful dog, starving and nearly dead itself, refusing to leave the corpse of its beloved master.

Well . . . I do not doubt the veracity of the reporters of such incidents, and facts as stated are probably true; but, as so is often the case with animal stories, the interpretation put upon the dog's behavior is over-flattering and erroneous. The answer, of course, really is that, outside Pavlov's laboratories, the well-trained sheepdog is the nearest thing to a vital automaton that man has yet succeeded in conditioning. So if—as happens when the shepherd lies down in the snow and doesn't get up again, and the dog is faced with a new and unrehearsed situation, all the stimuli to which it is accustomed removed—it is incapable of doing anything but sitting down to wait, this is not because it wants to, and not because any emotion or sense of loyalty prompts it to do so, but because, I repeat, it is incapable of doing anything else.

There are a thousand stories of cases where sheepdogs appear to act intelligently and by deductive reasoning, and certainly when one sees them working on the hill, gathering, driving, or shedding sheep, one cannot fail to be impressed by what seems to be their prompt decision and their quick adjustment to changing circumstances. But—alas! the prompt decision is no more than a response to the herd's whistle or other signal, and the circumstances, which may seem novel to the untutored observer, are the same with which the dog has been faced a thousand times before during its training and working life.

Let us be honest about the sheepdog, and our admiration for it need not be the less because of our honesty. The evolutions which a good, well-trained dog can perform are eight in number: to lie motionless; to go out away from the shepherd; to come in toward him; to go right; to go left; to go uphill; to go downhill; and—but the eighth and most dramatic performance of the dog is illegal, and will ensure its immediate disqualification if it employs it during a sheepdog trial, so we shall leave a description of it until later.

And for each of these few movements the shepherd has a different signal or command (or both) which the dog comes to understand and obey, to the astonishment of the gaping but unenlightened observer, who has not seen the endless practice and heartbreaking repetition which has gone into the dog's training in each movement. The vocabulary understood by the sheepdog consists of no more than about ten words, of which at least three are unprintable cuss-words. The brain behind the apparently marvelous maneuvers the dog executes upon the hill is the brain of the shepherd, and, at the risk of bringing the Canine Defense League down on my head, I must put it on the record that the intelligence quotient of the dog, if assessed on the human scale, would be well down in the imbecile grade, very near the idiot border.

I would like to accept and believe all dog stories at their face value. I would like to believe, for example, that Auld Kenneth's dogs, Tim and Meg, are really intelligent and that it is their love for him that makes them come racing back to the village pub at night to seek our assistance if Auld Kenneth falls flat on his face on the way home. Maybe it *is* intelligence and love that brings them back to yap at the bar door to warn us of Kenneth's plight, and not just that they want to be re-admitted into the warmth of the firelit taproom. And maybe it is not true that Kenneth has spent a considerable amount of time training them for this particular duty. I would like to think so, just as I would

like to believe (and don't mind the Shepherdess's believing) that our own collie growls and barks when anybody speaks sharply to us, because our collie
loves us and would protect us with her life; rather than the more likely explanation that she loves a good fight, and will join in one anywhere, no matter
whom it is between and what it is about. And similarly, courage being a trait
we all respect, I would like to admire the Minister's little terrier more than I
did when it faced up to a vixen twice its size with her cubs; only I rather suspected that the little brute just wanted to make a meal of the newborn cubs,
and it sensed anyway that a soft-fanged vixen, debilitated by parturition and
heavy with milk, does not stand a chance against a healthy Border terrier.

The Shepherdess immediately took issue with me when I expressed
these heresies. Unlike myself, she had survived a course of experimental psychology still believing that the dog she owned at the time and loved very
dearly was a sensate intelligent being. And since she has come to live among
and own real sheepdogs, her admiration and respect for every lesser breed with
paws has daily been enhanced. She is not, I should quickly explain, foolishly
sentimental about animals, and has never to my knowledge been a member of
the Tail-Waggers Club or the Bow-Wow League, but she is the only person I
know who pays her dog-license fees and subscriptions to the International
Sheepdog Society on time and without demur. And since she believes that
sheep, too, have their separate and recognizable individual personalities, and
even loves modern mass-produced men and women, her regard for the dog is
not by comparison excessive.

"You try training a small boy to obey even simple instructions and use
his common sense in the way Gyp does, and your respect for the sheepdog will
rise mightily!" she challenged me. I started to explain that, given the help of an
electronics engineer, I would undertake to produce a dog-shaped machine
which would work at twice the speed of Gyp on half the signals, and would win
the challenge cup at every sheepdog trial in the country at the first attempt.

She growled scornfully, and I must admit the little pup at her heels
growled at me too, but I was saved from attack by an interruption.

"Come on!" yelled Mrs. Tam. Since it was all our fault anyway, would
we at least come and lend a hand with the catching of this tup, and not stand
there blethering about dogs all afternoon. The black brute had worked another
three yowes while we had been maligning Gyp, who at least had brains enough
to ken that the black-and-yellow bastard had no right on this hirsel!

We came on, up the hill toward the adulterous interloper, not quite
sure what was expected of us. The huge harem of yowes was already streaming

off up the hillside, with the ugly tup making a pretense of protecting them from the rear, but ensuring that if an attack were to be made on the flock, he would not be the first available victim. And then:

"Up now, Gyp! Go by! Go by!" A small black-and-white bundle of potential murder streaked away from us at Tam's command and in a few seconds was nearly atop the hill and ahead of the sheep, cutting off their escape. The sheep turned and charged back down the hill toward us, their Lord Protector not exactly heading the rush, but not now making any pretense of fighting a rearguard action.

An ear-splitting "wheeeep!" issued from Tam's practiced teeth and lips, and the dog rushed directly down toward us, right into the middle of the flock, scattering them in panic in all directions. The tup dashed off up the glen to our right, with now only about ten of his ladies still trusting to his flagging protection. A whistle of a different note from Tam sent the dog too off to the right, and the tup's dwindling group was halted, while the yowes that had abandoned his dubious guardianship were scattered in all directions.

The wolf-on-the-fold technique was repeated on the tup's group, leaving him this time with but four female companions, who were now surrounding him, perhaps to protect him, for a change, perhaps to prevent his making a getaway. Another charge of the black-and-white fury at Tam's whistled command, and this time but two faithful adherents remained beside the black-and-yellow master. And then the ram made the mistake that cost him his freedom. Perhaps dimly calculating his chances and reckoning that the dog might prefer to make a meal of the last succulent yowes rather than himself, he basely deserted them and made a dash up the glen. As soon as he did so, Tam rapped out to his dog the illegal command, which every shepherd uses, though as seldom as possible, and only in cases of emergency such as this, when his whole stock is in danger:

"That yin, Gyp! Grip him!" and with a snarl which would have scared a bull, the little collie made a wolflike spring on the tup. At first its fangs found only wool, which tore away in its jaws, and the ram, prepared now to defend its own life with greater courage than it had shown in the defense of its mates, turned to face up to the dog. It stamped its forefoot, lowered its huge and ugly curved horns, and switched around with an agility almost equal to the dog's, as that little animal raced snarling and yapping around it, looking for another chance to give vent to its strongest and deadliest instinct. What happened then was as difficult to follow as a swift rally between expert fencers, and what mistakes the tup made I could not see at the distance, but suddenly there was another snarling bound, and the tup was this time caught in a grip at the shoulder which sank deeper than the wool, and which it could not break, toss and turn as it might.

This apparently was where our help was needed, for, led by Mrs. Tam, we all leaped up the hillside and threw ourselves on the struggling pair.

"Coup it! Coup it!" yelled Tam, as we all laid hands on various parts of the ram, and grabbing the back legs himself, he pulled them from under the beast and turned it over on its back. Only now did Gyp relax her grip, but still stood by expectantly, her beady eye flicking from the tup to Tam, then back again, and certainly giving every appearance of taking an intelligent interest in the situation, and anxious, it seemed, to be of any further assistance that she could.

But Tam gave her the final command—that strange grudging admission with which the shepherd informs his dog that it has completed a job to his satisfaction, and all that it ever gets by way of thanks: "That'll do! Gyp!" and Gyp went mooning and sniffing off a few yards away.

I know of only one other profession which uses this cursory expression in approval of a job well done, and only one other occasion when such reluctant thanks are given for hard work completed. When a ship ties up in her home port after a voyage, the master takes her in alongside the wharf, but it is the responsibility of the mate to ensure that the ship is securely made fast alongside. When the master has left the bridge and gone below for his glass of sherry and to receive thanks of the owners, the mate goes around the ship, inspecting every hawser and rope between ship and shore, having this one tightened and that one slacked, a fender adjusted here and a gangway or a light raised or lowered slightly. Only when he is satisfied that every last detail is in order and that the ship is safe from all hazards does he dismiss the crew. And he does so with the same curt phrase: "That'll do!"—then turns his back and goes below to join the master.

There is no speech of thanks or congratulations to the men, however long and arduous the voyage has been and however hard they may have worked. Just: "That'll do!" and the voyage is over. And the men, released at last from their allegiance to the ship, heave their sea-bags on their shoulders and go silently ashore.

It may seem a far cry from a ship in a great port, returned from the ends of the earth, to a herd and his dog on the Border moors, but there are other resemblances between the lives of those who work ships on the high seas and those who work sheep on the hills. I have never seen a collie dog afloat, but I would commend the breed to pet-loving seamen, for I feel sure that, though at present it is the most landlocked of lubbers, it would soon adjust itself to the strange environment and would very quickly fit into shipboard routine and even perhaps find some way of making itself a useful and invaluable member of the crew—especially on passenger ships.

But to return to the glen again, where we had by now hobbled the big blackface tup and heaved it into the back of the Land-Rover, to be returned to its own *apartheid* hunting and breeding ground ten miles away, and to return to the story of Gyp.

The little dog did not seem the least bit tired after her hectic chase of the big tup, though it must have taken her in all about three miles' hard running, and during the chase she must have ascended and descended a thousand feet three times. For though I seem to detract from the popular conception of the sheepdog's intelligence, I can do nothing but confirm and add to everything that ever has been said of its physical prowess and powers of endurance. It has been estimated that for every mile a hill shepherd covers in a normal day's working with his sheep on the hill, his dog covers no less than *fourteen*. With Gyp, at least, I can believe that this is not only true, but an underestimate. When I asked Tam, he said he "wouldna' be surprised if it was richt," which in Border language means that he would stake his life it is true. And since Tam reckons that during an ordinary working day on the hill he, the herd, covers at least six miles, that means, fantastic though it seems, that his little black brute cover eighty-four miles during *its* working day. Another estimate, backed by pedometer readings and quoted in an official British Government publication on sheepdogs, goes higher, and claims that during the lambing season a hill collie covers up to or over one hundred miles a day, every day for nearly six weeks.

And its reward for this immense labor—at the end of the day when it is given its final "That'll do!"—is to be taken home, fed its first meal of the day, consisting of two handfuls of crushed corn in hot water, and then put to bed in a dry and comfortable, but totally dark and cheerless box, where it will remain until needed again the next day on the hill. For Tam belongs to the old school, comprising half of the herds I know, who believe that diversion, amusement, or any interest or distraction other that the working of sheep, is bad for the collie during its training or working life.

Mrs. Tam belongs to the opposite school of thought. Her dogs are brought up in the house. From earliest puppyhood they eat when the family eats, romp and play with the children, and (to Tam's oft-expressed disgust) sleep on armchairs before the cottage fire instead of in a black box in the cowshed. Yet they, too, work the hill and seem to my inexperienced eye to do so as willingly and energetically and efficiently as Tam's strictly disciplined dogs. But, Tam tells me, the snag is that Mrs. Tam's dogs will "run"—work sheep, that is— for Mrs. Tam and for nobody else. If he borrows them, they will quickly "get in a pet," and have been known to "leave him on the hill," the greatest sin a sheepdog can commit other than sheep-killing.

It must not be thought that Tam, and the other herds who believe in the stricter discipline and segregation, as it were, of their dogs from the human race, are thereby unkind to them, and that there is no bond (call it affection if you will) between the Spartan dog and its master. Tam has never in his life lifted a hand or stick to his dogs, and seldom does he even raise his voice when they fail to understand or obey. "Come in, ye wee whore, you!" spoken in a quiet but firm voice, is the worst in the way of reproof or punishment I have ever known Gyp to receive from her master. And Gyp came in, more quickly and cheerfully that do Mrs. Tam's dogs, even though Mrs. Tam, following her principle of treating dogs "like one o' the family, til they ken every word ye say to them," also believes, as she does with children, that a "guid cuffin' now an' again does them nae harm."

Similarly, though Tam's dogs are fed but once a day, and then only with handfuls of corn, they are, and they know they will be, fed regularly, come what may. Every night, on coming home, no matter how cold and wet and weary he may be himself, Tam's first task is to prepare the mash and feed his dogs, and if the Queen of England were waiting for him in his cottage, Gyp would be attended to first. Auld Kenneth, on the other hand, who is of the "Cottage-dog" school, feeds his dogs when he feeds himself and shares what-ever is his supper. But since Auld Kenneth's own eating life is irregular, and since he calls at the House of Sin before going home, for "something to warm him up," he may not have a meal for the next three days, the unfortunate Tim and Meg frequently become hungry enough to steal away from snoring Kenneth's side and try to scrape a supper from the nearest garbage heap.

But back to the glen again, to ask Tam as we drive down the track about Gyp's ancestry. (As we mentioned her name, the beady eye was immedi-ately turned on us, as though to show appreciation of what we were saying, but in reality to discover if something further was required of her, or if anything had gone amiss with the struggling tup in the back of the Land-Rover beside her.)

Gyp, we were told, like practically all the good sheepdogs in the whole world, is a descendant of Old Hemp. There seemed to be a story in Old Hemp, so we listened, as Mrs. Tam took up the tale.

Old Hemp, like many founders of great dynasties, was born beyond the frontiers of the land he came to rule. To be exact, although *every* sheepdog in Scotland today is at least a remote relative of Hemp, Hemp himself was born twenty miles south of Tweed, down in England. That was in the year 1893. Again like many founders of great dynasties, he was born in very lowly estate. He was the son of an unknown rascal named Roy who was described by his owner as having "a very free eye and frank expression," and an equally unknown mother named Meg, "a shy and somewhat self-conscious bitch."

In those days the Scottish collies, to which breed Hemp rather doubtfully belonged despite his birthplace, were the best and most commonly used sheepdogs in the United Kingdom, and English and Welsh farmers and herds came north for their dogs. But Hemp came north, too, and it was quickly realized that here was something vastly superior to anything Scotland itself had yet produced. The collies were clever; but Hemp was cleverer. The collies were tough; but Hemp was tougher. The shepherds could teach the collies easily enough; but Hemp could teach the shepherds. Soon the shepherds who had always paid the collies the almost supreme Scottish compliment that they were "nae sae bad," agreed that Hemp was "bluidy marvelous."

So this scruffy little black-and-white beast strutted into Scotland rather as the little Corsican General, or Marlon Brando at least, stomped into Paris from the south. And with the same result. Arrived in the capital of sheepdogdom, Hemp met no challenger of his power and superiority. The better-bred and aristocratic natives were prepared to acknowledge and even fawn on the conquering upstart. And within a very short time he had taken to himself the sheepdog crown.

But, having achieved imperial status, Hemp behaved, not like Napoleon, but rather more like that other dynasty founder, ibn-Saud. Within a year Hemp had begotten two hundred sons, which even the Arabian Emperor would regard as "nae sae bad" a performance! And by the time Hemp was ten, no man could count his progeny.

Those that Hemp begat, and those that Hemp's sons and daughter begat, etc., etc. did not, however remain in the desert where they were begotten. Interested sheep-men began to come from all over the world, to Hemp's court, now re-established in Northumbria. They came first from all parts of the United Kingdom, and within a short space few were the working dogs in the British Isles who could not boast of a royal relative. Then they came, these farmers to buy Hemp's progeny, from New Zealand, from South Africa, and from Canada. Australia was the last British dominion to accept Hemp's suzerainty, and there they tried for some years to carry on with their peculiar locally bred dogs, but ultimately they realized the crossbred dingoes who ruled their sheep world were losing them millions in wool and mutton every year, and the House of Hemp was invited to send its scions to take over. Within ten years of his death it could truly be said that the sun never set on Hemp's offspring; and then even the republics bowed to the monarchy. Perhaps the pinnacle of Hemp's posthumous triumph was in 1940 when the North American Sheepdog Society was formed, and all Hemp's characteristics were taken as the model of the perfect sheepdog; and it was unequivocally stated that every working sheepdog in California had the blood of Old Hemp running in its veins.

Gyp, though she would recognize her California relatives by certain telltale birthmarks they have in common, can claim a rather closer relationship to the Grand Old Dog. For Gyp has a bit of paper, which Tam preserves for her more carefully than the ancient families of Scotland preserve their eleventh-century armorial writs and charters. Gyp's paper begins with the noblest of names that any dog's pedigree bears:

"Old Hemp. By Roy. Out of Meg," and proceeds in unbroken succession down to:"Gyp. By Tim. Out of Meg."

For Auld Kenneth's dogs carry the Blood Royal.

By the time we had heard this proud story, we had reached Tam's cottage and were this time horrified when Tam called to the royal personage again:"Come out o' that! Ye wee whore, you!"

But Gyp leaped obediently out of the car and went off to her lonely black box, as I think she would go to her grave, if Tam asked it of her.

And on that day which will come to her, all that will be written on her tombstone, if she gets one at all, will be:

"That'll do! Gyp!"

Nop and Hope

From *Nop's Hope*

BY DONALD McCAIG

O NLY A MAN who owns and works sheep and sheepdogs can speak about them with the authority and insight that Donald McCaig has. He says of border collies, "They are intelligent, obsessive, and physically powerful. Their handler needs both savvy and grit."

This brief excerpt is taken from McCaig's book *Nop's Hope,* which is both sentimental and true. As a border collie devotee myself, I can attest to the accuracy of what McCaig writes about them.

★　★　★　★　★

THE BANNER OVER THE TURNOFF to the Sheridan Equestrian Center said: WELCOME TO THE FIFTEENTH ANNUAL NATIONAL HANDLERS' FINALS SHEEP-DOG TRIALS. Four o'clock, Friday afternoon, a few handlers gathered in the clubhouse. Others walked the flat trial field. Dogs visited one another among the rows of motor homes. Hope came over to Nop, tail awag, and as befitted the dignity of an Older dog, Nop waited until Hope was close before offering a modest wag of his own. The Bighorn Mountains bulked up behind the field like a shy but determined wall. The lines across the face of the mountains looked like roads, but they were irrigation ditches, passing last winter's snowmelt down to the plains below.

When Hope was just six months old, Nop used to take him by the collar and roll him over in the grass while Hope growled fierce as he could. Nop had missed Hope at home, wished there was another dog to walk with and chase foolish squirrels into the air. How *does* a squirrel get from tree to tree?

"How art thou, old man," Hope bowed and yawned.

Nop inspected the course, self-importantly. "Thou hast learned nothing since last I dragged your collar," he said.

Hope grinned at him. "Tomorrow I shall work woolies. Tomorrow and the day after. Oh, I am a fine stockdog."

Nop grumbled, "There's more to life than that."

"What? What more pray? Me and my woman, we go out, we make the woolies dance. She is wise. She says good words when we talk."

"It is unwise to talk to them," the older dog grumbled. "When we talk, they learn more about us than is proper."

The Boss Dog

BY M. F. K. FISHER

MARY FRANCES KENNEDY FISHER was famous worldwide as a food writer. But she was more . . . far, far more. Her books were essays on life and loves and times past, memories of wonderful meals and how they felt, charming reminiscences, and amusing anecdotes. Yet, food was at their core—their essence.

How interesting, then, to find a book by this colossal culinary writer about . . . a dog. It is, however, also about a mother and her two daughters, as well as Provence, a friendly café, and a very special waiter. Most of all, it is about the dog who managed them all, the Boss Dog.

★　★　★　★　★

MOST PEOPLE WHO WANDER together have good things happen to them, and possibly the best thing that happened to Anne and Mary and their mother as they wandered from California to Aix-en-Provence, a serene old town near Marseille in France, was to meet the Boss Dog very soon after they arrived.

If they had not met him, and had not been selected, or so it seemed to them, to absorb some of his sinister yet beneficent spell, their lives might have been quite different.

Once, he even rescued one of them. And once he taught them about not judging too hastily as to whether a man who looks like a thug-mug-crook is that or something else again. Several times he taught them little tricks of bravery or bravado, or how to cock an ear at Fate, or how, when all is said and done, to survive, in one form or another. (In his own case, he did the last the surest way, like most of the rest of us!)

But the day the two little American girls and their mother met this gay rascal, they had no idea of what his influence would be on them. . . .

It was later in September when they first when into the Café Glacier on the big square or at least five-sided circle (a square circle or even a circle with sides is an impossibility, of course, except in Aix-en-Provence . . .), and they sat down at one of the tables just inside the windows of the restaurant.

They felt tired and a little depressed, for the town was not their own town, everybody spoke French instead of American, and an endless procession of electric- and gas-driven buses and explosive little scooters called Vespas roared around the five-sided square or square circle.

In the middle of it was the enormous and monumental and very tall fountain called *La Grande Fontaine* or *La Fontaine de la Rotonde* or simply The Big One. It was built in layers of lions-dolphins-turtles-swans-cherubs, and finally some bearded heads of men, and on top three large well-endowed women. All, except the last, spat, spurted, splashed, spluttered, and spouted in every direction.

The three small flesh-and-blood women felt confused.

Anne took off her gloves. She put them into the pocket of her coat, and then got them out again and began to bite gently at the tip of the third finger of the left one, which was of white cotton and quite dirty and her favorite, because of a lingering agreeable taste of vanilla that never seemed to wash away.

Mary put her gloves in her pocket, her elbows on the table, and her chin in her hands. She might be dozing off. . . .

The mother of the girls, one of whom was eleven and one going on nine, took off her gloves and put them in her pocket, put her chin in her hands and one finger almost in her mouth, and then said, "Anne, please take your glove out of your mouth. Mary, please take your elbows off the table. I'm tired. I'm dead. What would you like to drink?"

A waiter was, as if by magic (the kind good waiters learn early if not at birth and most people never appreciate), standing by their table. He quirked his eyes and at the same time his ears at them, the way good and even bad waiters do, and you could see his mind writing on a little piece of paper, invisible in his hand. Tired woman, it wrote. Two tired nice-looking little girls. Tourists and may be in a hurry. Probably want ice cream. . . .

"Well, what do you want, or do you?" the mother asked in a polite cranky voice.

She felt so weary and so inexplicably far away from home that what she really wanted to do was lie down in the middle of the five-sided square cir-cle, except that the Big Fountain was already there with three marble women on it, and go boohoohoo . . . more waterworks. So instead she allowed herself to snap gently at the two people she loved most in the world, which is an odd but not unusual kind of behavior.

Mary looked vaguely through the wall of the restaurant, which was of glass and therefore very easy to look through, and without seeing anything she was looking at, because she was too tired, she said, "Oh, it doesn't matter. Maybe some vodka."

Mary always said this when she was exhausted, and it was a signal to her mother that she was at the far limits of her energy, and that she was re-membering one time when she was barely old enough to walk, when she had by accident drunk a sip of vodka and gone roaring and rolling and spewing across the floor like a little wild bear.

Now the mother peered at her, and seeing that her eyes were still turned in a dreamy unfocused way on the Big Fountain, looked up once more at the waiter, standing doing what he was supposed to do, which was wait.

"Anne?" she asked somewhat more patiently, for already in this quiet glassy room she felt less tired, less alone.

Anne took the end of the vanilla-finger of the left glove out of her mouth, for suddenly it tasted really revolting. "Me? Who? Me? What?"

A few more buses gunned by. Little Vespa scooters scooted by. A man with a Siamese cat perched tiltingly on one shoulder limped by, and then a pretty lady with tiny feet in high heels and tiny twin boys in a double pram teetered by. Everybody seems to be going someplace and happy and busy ex-cept the mother and her girls, and they were really worn out and, if three people can be lonely together, they were.

The waiter was still standing there, though, and the mother looked at Anne again and said, "Well, do say what you want. *Decide.*" Then she said, "Please, darling honey-bun and sweet potato," for that was her way of admitting that she was sorry to be cross.

Anne said very nicely, "I would like some ice cream. I would like some vanilla ice cream and if there is by accident no vanilla I would like some strawberry."

The waiter, who understood a little English or at least American, glanced rather like a rabbit who can choose between a carrot and a leaf of lettuce between Anne and her mother, and then said in French, "Today there happens to be no vanilla and also by chance no strawberry because summer is almost a thing of the past, BUT today there happens to be chocolate, and it is very good but VERY good.

"I believe," he added, as firmly as if he clasped his invisible pad of paper in one hand like a little prayer book and was already writing something upon it, "that One, a Certain Young Lady, will like or even love the chocolate."

The mother savored the subtleties and the comprehension of this announcement, in a language still too subtle and all-comprehensive for her children.

Mary looked quietly around the room, empty now at a too-early "tea-time," for the traveling Englishmen who normally drank tea were at a horse-show or snoozing or sketching the countryside, and the people who lived in Aix seldom drank tea in public.

Anne, who would have liked to speak directly to the waiter and get things underway, in no matter what limping French, looked politely at her mother as she had accustomed herself to do if she wished easy sailing; her mother, who in turn would have been delighted to see somebody else take control of things but had been taught that children should let their elders talk to waiters, in no matter what language, said, "Two chocolate ice creams, please, and a small coffee. And a large brandy."

"*D'accord, Madame,*" the waiter said, which was a rather lazy slangy way of agreeing with a customer but which he did not mean at all impertinently: he felt that these three people would turn out to be his friends, and it did turn out that they would be and were. He swerved off, flushing slightly.

Whoever was in the kitchen at this odd hour of about 4:12 in the afternoon put a generous unordered dollop of whipped cream under and around the chocolate ice cream for each girl, and they licked at it as if they wished they were little kittens and not two children who had to sit up fairly straight in an empty French restaurant with people going past the windows all the time. If they had been able to grow long tails right then, they would have curled them happily around their haunches or flanks or bottoms and then later licked them in long strokes, remembering that cream.

After eating most of what the waiter had brought them, except the dishes and silverware, which in Aix is rather complicated because an ice cream is served in a stemmed metal cup on a plate and then there is a glass of cold water in which stand the spoon, cooling, to eat the ice with, with a thin brown cookie called a *gaufrette* stuck up like a signal; after attending to all this caloric panoply, Anne and Mary leaned back, feeling much better.

Their mother leaned back too; the world outside the glass wall was not as loud and dusty to her.

Anne removed a small dab of cream from one side of her mouth, which otherwise was as impeccable as that of an ivory statue.

"That is a very interesting dog who is going to come in," she said.

"What do you mean, 'That is a very interesting dog who is going to come in'?" Mary asked. "Probably what you mean is, if you really mean it, is that what you mean is, 'Look at that dog who may come in.' He may be interesting to you, but how can you state that he is also interesting to us? And how do you—?"

"What dog?" The mother asked such a question in an apologetic way that by now was quite automatic. She was always asking things like that in that way, because she was always or quite often off dreaming about this or that while the girls were talking about other thises and thats which seemed to be fairly unrelated to her own.

"Oh, for heaven's sake! Oh, murder!" they both said in a kind and patient way, for by now the cream and stuff in their stomachs was making them so, much more efficaciously than if they had drunk only the water with the spoons in it. "Look. There he is. There he goes."

They all looked toward the door onto the great square circle, where the buses went whirling by and where the fountain splashed and spat, and where there seemed to be a gentle endless tide of old and middle-aged and young women and baby carriages, all full of children either about to be born or eight months old, the latter smiling and cackling and waving.

The door closed. Some of the outside noises stopped. The waiter, who later came to be known as Léon, except on Wednesdays when Paul took over for him, opened the door and then closed it again, as if to assure himself that a human had done it and not a four-footed fellow, and Boss Dog walked slowly across the room toward Anne and Mary.

He was the doggiest dog anyone ever saw, just the way you can say that a Mexican-Yankee-Frenchman-Greek is the most Mexican-Yankee-French-Greek individual you ever saw, summing up all of himself as such, up to his cocky wonderful ears in whatever he is doing. This fellow was everything a creature could possibly be of HIM, of HE. He was Boss Dog.

Anne recognized him at once as something ultimate.

"Look at him," she said in a voice which a few years later she might well use for a person as yet unmet called a Majarajah. She spoke firmly and posedly, leaning on every syllable.

Mary was looking. Her large prune-brown eyes first grew larger and then narrowed with a kind of secondary recognition, as if she had just seen somebody like King Arthur, unexpectedly, and after a quick halt had said hurriedly, "Oh, yes! That's King Arthur!"

"Wow," she said.

The mother agreed, without a word.

The dog, who had come off the *Place de la Grande Fontaine*, took a quick sharp glance around, and then trotted toward the back of the restaurant: the dim bar, the toilets and cloakrooms, the pantries, the fine smelly kitchens. He plainly had his rounds to make, and he showed it in the stance of his black tail, which turned up arrogantly over the short white hairs of his behind.

He was a large fellow with a fat rear, mostly the kind of terrier called yippy, part Fox and part Boston and part Mystery, and rather rat-nosed, narrow-eyed, undistinguished dog esthetically, except for his unusually long plump full beautiful ear, and its peculiar mate.

The coal black one fell down soft and helpless and lovable over his left eye. The other, white and crisp as celery, stood up so proudly that it seemed to draw his right eye with it, into a merry shrewd questioning look. It was as if Boss Dog wore a hat which had been born onto him when he himself was born, pulling his face into a mask of meek velvety guile on one side and of cocky-mockery on the other.

He seemed to know it, this contradiction. As he went to the kitchens he turned fleetingly toward the table where Anne and Mary sat with their mother, and his soft black left ear had probably never looked so soft, and his stiff white ear standing out from his bold head had never looked so mocking. He new his own dramatic allure, it was clear.

He disappeared, busily.

"There's a dog for you," Anne said. " 'Wow' is right."

"He is plainly," Mary said, coming to life as if she had always been so instead of lately half-dead, "plainly and indefinitely the boss of this whole place. Indefinitely, he is KNOWN here."

"He's the kind of dog adventures would happen around," Anne said wistfully, hopefully. "Gangsters. Or witches. You can tell that he would be able to handle them."

"I think we should come back here tomorrow," Mary said as they got into gloves and so forth, and in a vague but active way the mother felt that instead of being tourists drifting about, they had suddenly got someplace, that they were indeed THERE, besides just staying in a decorous boarding-house.

Something about the way the dog had trotted efficiently in from the square circle, the way the waiter had politely opened the door and closed the door for him after he himself had done so, as if to prove that it was perfectly normal, made her feel settled and even established, and she smiled companionably at the three monumental females on top of the great busy spouting fountain.

"I think we should too," she said. "We'd better ask what the waiter's name is."

Montmorency

BY JEROME K. JEROME

J EROME K. JEROME is the author of, among many other books, *Three Men in a Boat; to Say Nothing of the Dog!*, from which this short piece is taken.

Clearly he has an inside track to the workings of his fox terrier's mind . . . and lets us into it as well.

Elsewhere he said of a dog, "You are his pal. That is enough for him, and come luck or misfortune, good repute or bad, honor or shame, he is going to stick to you, to comfort you, guard you, give his life for you, if need be—foolish, brainless, soulless dog!"

★ ★ ★ ★ ★

TO LOOK AT MONTMORENCY you would imagine that he was an angel sent upon the earth, for some reason withheld from mankind, in the shape of a small fox-terrier. There is a sort of Oh-what-a-wicked-world-this-is-and-how-I-wish-I-could-do-something-to-make-it-better-and-nobler expression about Montmorency that has been known to bring the tears into the eyes of pious old ladies and gentlemen.

When he first came to live at my expense, I never thought I should be able to get him to stop long. I used to sit down and look at him, as he sat on the rug and looked up at me, and think: "Oh, that dog will never live. He will be snatched up to the bright skies in a chariot, that is what will happen to him."

But, when I had paid for about a dozen chickens that he had killed; and had dragged him, growling and kicking, by the scruff of his neck, out of a hundred and fourteen street fights; and had had a dead cat brought round for my inspection by an irate female, who called me a murderer; and had been summoned by the man next door but one for having a ferocious dog at large, that had kept him pinned up in his own toolshed, afraid to venture his nose outside the door for over two hours on a cold night; and had learned that the gardener, unknown to myself, had won thirty shillings by backing him to kill rats against time, then I began to think that maybe they'd let him remain on earth for a bit longer, after all.

The only subject on which Montmorency and I have any serious difference of opinion is cats. I like cats; Montmorency does not.

When I meet a cat, I say, "Poor Pussy!" and stoop down and tickle the side of its head; and the cat sticks up its tail in a rigid, cast-iron manner, arches its back, and wipes its nose up against my trousers; and all is gentleness and peace. When Montmorency meets a cat, the whole street knows about it; and there is enough bad language wasted in ten seconds to last an ordinary respectable man all his life, with care.

I do not blame the dog (contenting myself, as a rule, with merely clouting his head or throwing stones at him), because I take it that it is his nature. Fox-terriers are born with about four times as much original sin as other dogs are, and it will take years and years of patient effort on the part of us Christians to bring about any appreciable reformation in the rowdiness of the fox-terrier nature.

I remember being in the lobby of the Haymarket Stores one day, and all round about me were dogs, waiting for the return of their owners, who were shopping inside. There were a mastiff, and one or two collies, and a St. Bernard, a few retrievers and Newfoundlands, a boar-hound, a French poodle, with plenty of hair round its head, but mangy about the middle; a bulldog, a few Lowther Arcade sort of animals, about the size of rats, and a couple of Yorkshire tykes.

There they sat, patient, good, and thoughtful. A solemn peacefulness seemed to reign in that lobby. An air of calmness and resignation—of gentle sadness pervaded the room.

Then a sweet young lady entered, leading a meek-looking little fox-terrier, and left him, chained up there, between the bulldog and the poodle. He sat and looked about him for a minute. Then he cast up his eyes to the ceiling, and seemed, judging from his expression, to be thinking of his mother. Then he yawned. Then he looked round at the other dogs, all silent, grave, and dignified.

He looked at the bulldog, sleeping dreamlessly on his right. He looked at the poodle, erect and haughty, on his left. Then, without a word of warning, without the shadow of a provocation, he bit that poodle's near foreleg, and a yelp of agony rang through the quiet shades of that lobby.

The result of his first experiment seemed highly satisfactory to him, and he determined to go on and make things lively all round. He sprang over the poodle and vigorously attacked a collie and the collie woke up, and immediately commenced a fierce and noisy contest with the poodle. Then Foxey came back to his own place, and caught the bulldog by the ear, and tried to throw him away; and the bulldog, a curiously impartial animal, went for everything he could reach, including the hall-porter, which gave that dear little terrier the opportunity to enjoy an uninterrupted fight of his own with an equally willing Yorkshire tyke.

Anyone who knows canine nature need hardly be told that, by this time, all the other dogs in the place were fighting as if their hearths and homes depended on the fray. The big dogs fought each other indiscriminately; and the little dogs fought among themselves, and filled up their spare time by biting the legs of the big dogs.

The whole lobby was a perfect pandemonium, and the din was terrific. A crowd assembled outside in the Haymarket, and asked if it was a vestry meeting; or, if not, who was being murdered, and why? Men came with poles and ropes, and tried to separate the dogs, and the police were sent for.

And in the midst of the riot that sweet young lady returned, and snatched up that sweet little dog of hers (he had laid the tyke up for a month, and had on the expression, now, of a new-born lamb) into her arms, and kissed him, and asked him if he was killed, and what those great nasty brutes of dogs had been doing to him; and he nestled up against her, and gazed up into her face with a look that seemed to say: "Oh, I'm so glad you've come to take me away from this disgraceful scene!"

She said that the people at the stores had no right to allow great savage things like those other dogs to be put with respectable people's dogs, and that she had a great mind to summon somebody.

Such is the nature of fox-terriers; and, therefore, I do not blame Montmorency for his tendency to row with cats, but he wished he had not given way to it that morning.

We were, as I have said, returning from a dip, and half-way up the High Street a cat darted out from one of the houses in front of us, and began to trot across the road. Montmorency gave a cry of joy—the cry of a stern warrior who sees his enemy given over to his hands—the sort of cry Cromwell might have uttered when the Scots came down the hill—and flew after his prey.

His victim was a large black tom. I never saw a larger cat, nor a more disreputable-looking cat. It had lost half its tail, one of its ears, and a fairly appreciable proportion of its nose. It was a long, sinewy-looking animal. It had a calm, contented air about it.

Montmorency went for that poor cat at the rate of twenty miles an hour; but the cat did not hurry up—did not seem to have grasped the idea that its life was in danger. It trotted quietly on until its would-be assassin was within a yard of it, and then it turned round and sat down in the middle of the road, and looked at Montmorency with a gentle, inquiring expression, that said:

"Yes? You want me?"

Montmorency does not lack pluck; but there was something about the look of that cat that might have chilled the heart of the boldest dog. He stopped abruptly, and looked back at Tom.

Neither spoke; but the conversation that one could imagine was clearly as follows:

THE CAT: Can I do anything for you?

MONTMORENCY: No—no, thanks.

THE CAT: Don't you mind speaking, if you really want anything, you know.

MONTMORENCY (backing down the High Street): Oh no—not at all-certainly—don't you trouble. I—I am afraid I've made a mistake. I thought I knew you. Sorry I disturbed you.

THE CAT: Not at all—quite a pleasure. Sure you don't want anything, now?

MONTMORENCY *(still backing)*: Not at all, thanks—not at all—very kind of you. Good morning.

THE CAT: Good morning.

Then the cat rose, and continued his trot; and Montmorency, fitting what he calls his tail carefully into its groove, came back to us, and took up an unimportant position in the rear.

To this day, if you say the word "Cats!" to Montmorency, he will visibly shrink and look up piteously at you, as if to say:

"Please don't."

Walking With a Dog

From *"Herr und Hund"*

BY THOMAS MANN

AUTHOR OF SUCH INTENSITIES as *Magic Mountain* and *Death in Venice,* Thomas Mann also had a dog. He becomes almost silly (at least as close as a heavily intellectual German writer can get) about the virtues of Bashan.

This selection, from the long story "Herr und Hund" ("A Man and His Dog"), takes us along on their morning walk. Only a very fine writer could remind us so clearly how pleasant that daily interlude is.

★　★　★　★　★

WHEN SPRING, THE FAIREST season of the year, does honor to its name, and when the trilling of the birds rouses me early because I have ended the day before at a seemly hour, I love to rise betimes and go for a half-hour's walk before breakfast. Strolling hatless in the broad avenue in front of my house, or through the parks beyond, I like to enjoy a few draughts of the young morning air and taste its blithe purity before I am claimed by the labors of the day. Standing on the front steps of my house, I give a whistle in two notes, tonic and lower fourth, like the beginning of the second phrase of Schubert's Unfinished Symphony; it might be considered the musical setting of a two-syllabled name. Next moment, and while I walk towards the garden gate, the faintest tinkle sounds from afar, at first scarcely audible, but growing rapidly louder and more distinct; such a sound as might be made by a metal license-tag clicking against the trimmings of a leather collar. I face about, to see Bashan rounding the corner of the house at top speed and charging towards me as though he meant to knock me down. In the effort he is making he has dropped his lower lip, baring two white teeth that glitter in the morning sun.

He comes straight from his kennel, which stands at the back of the house, between the props of the veranda floor. Probably, until my two-toned call set him in this violent motion, he had been lying there snatching a nap after the adventures of the night. The kennel has curtains of sacking and is lined with straw; indeed, a straw or so may be clinging to Bashan's sleep-rumpled coat or even sticking between his toes—a comic sight, which reminds me of a painstakingly imagined production of Schiller's *Die Räuber* that I once saw, in which old Count Moor came out of the Hunger Tower tricot-clad, with a straw sticking pathetically between his toes. Involuntarily I assume a defensive position to meet the charge, receiving it on my flank, for Bashan shows every sign of meaning to run between my legs and trip me up. However at the last minute, when a collision is imminent, he always puts on the brakes, executing a half-wheel which speaks for both his mental and his physical self-control. And then without a sound—for he makes sparing use of his sonorous and expressive voice—he dances wildly round me by way of greeting, with immoderate plungings and waggings which are not confined to the appendage provided by nature for the purpose but bring his whole hind quarters as far as his ribs into play. He contracts his whole body into a curve, he hurtles into the air in a flying leap, he turns round and round on his own axis—and curiously enough, whichever way I turn, he always contrives to execute these maneuvers behind my back. But the moment I stoop down and put out my hand he jumps to my side and stands like a statue, with his shoulder against my shin, in a slantwise posture, his strong paws braced against the ground, his face turned upwards so that he looks at me upside-down. And his utter immobility, as I pat his shoulder and murmur encouragement, is as concentrated and fiercely passionate as the frenzy before it had been.

Bashan is a short-haired German pointer—speaking by and large, that is, and not too literally. For he is probably not quite orthodox, as a pure matter of points. In the first place, he is a little too small. He is, I repeat, definitely undersized for a proper pointer. And then his forelegs are not absolutely straight; they have just the suggestion of an outward curve—which also detracts from his qualifications as a blood-dog. And he has a tendency to a dewlap, those folds of hanging skin under the muzzle, which in Bashan's case are admirably becoming but again would be frowned on by your fanatic for pure breeding, as I understand that a pointer should have taut skin round the neck. Bashan's coloring is very fine. His coat is a rusty brown with black stripes and a good deal of white on chest, paws, and under side. The whole of his snub nose seems to have been dipped in black paint. Over the broad top of his head and on his cool hanging ears the black and brown combine in a lovely velvety pattern. Quite the prettiest thing about him, however, is the whorl or stud or little tuft at the center of the convolution of white hairs on his chest, which stands out like the boss on an ancient breastplate. Very likely even his splendid coloration is a little too marked and would be objected to by those who put the laws of breeding above the value of personality, for it would appear that the classic pointer type should have a coat of one color or at most with spots of a different one, but never stripes. Worst of all, from the point of view of classification, is a hairy growth hanging from his muzzle and the corners of his mouth; it might with some justice be called a moustache and goatee, and when you concentrate on it, close at hand or even at a distance, you cannot help thinking of an airedale or a schnauzer.

But classifications aside, what a good and good-looking animal Bashan is, as he stands there straining against my knee, gazing up at me with all his devotion in his eyes! They are particularly fine eyes, too, both gentle and wise, if just a little too prominent and glassy. The iris is the same color as his coat, a rusty brown; it is only a narrow rim, for the pupils are dilated into pools of blackness and the outer edge merges into the white of the eye wherein it swims. His whole head is expressive of honesty and intelligence, of manly qualities corresponding to his physical structure: his arched and swelling chest where the ribs stand out under the smooth and supple skin; the narrow haunches, the veined, sinewy legs, the strong, well-shaped paws. All these bespeak virility and a stout heart; they suggest hunting blood and peasant stock—yes, certainly the hunter and game dog do after all predominate in Bashan, he is genuine pointer, no matter if does not owe his existence to a snobbish system of inbreeding. All this, probably, is what I am really telling him as I pat his shoulder-blade and address him with a few disjointed words of encouragement.

So he stands and looks and listens, gathering from what I say and the tone of it that I distinctly approve of his existence—the very thing which I am at pains to imply. And suddenly he thrusts out his head, opening and shutting his lips very fast, and makes a snap at my face as though he meant to bite off my nose. It is a gesture of response to my remarks, and it always makes me recoil with a laugh, as Bashan knows beforehand that it will. It is a kiss in the air, half caress, half teasing, a trick he has had since puppyhood, which I have never seen in any of his predecessors. And he immediately begs pardon for the liberty, crouching, wagging his tail, and behaving funnily embarrassed. So we go out through the garden gate and into the open.

We are encompassed with a roaring like that of the sea; for we live almost directly on the swift-flowing river that foams over shallow ledges at no great distance from the poplar avenue. In between lie a fenced-in grass plot planted with maples, and a raised pathway skirted with huge aspen trees, bizarre and willowlike of aspect. At the beginning of June their seedpods strew the ground far and wide with woolly snow. Upstream, in the direction of the city, construction troops are building a pontoon bridge. Shouts of command and the thump of heavy boots on the planks sound across the river; also, from the further bank, the noise of industrial activity, for there is a locomotive foundry a little way downstream. Its premises have been lately enlarged to meet increased demands, and light streams all night long from its lofty windows. Beautiful glittering new engines roll to and fro on trial runs; a steam whistle emits wailing head-tones from time to time; muffled thunderings of unspecified origin shatter the air, smoke pours out of the many chimneys to be caught up by the wind and borne away over the wooded country beyond the river, for it seldom or never blows over to our side. Thus is our half-suburban, half-rural seclusion the voice of nature mingles with that of man, and over all lies the bright-eyed freshness of the new day.

It might be about half past seven by official time when I set out; by sun-time, half past six. With my hands behind my back I stroll in the tender sunshine down the avenue, cross-hatched by the long shadows of the poplar trees. From where I am I cannot see the river, but I hear its broad and even flow. The trees whisper gently, songbirds fill the air with their penetrating chirps and warbles, twitters and trills; from the direction of the sunrise a plane is flying under the humid blue sky, a rigid, mechanical bird with a droning hum that rises and falls as it steers a free course above river and fields. And Bashan is delighting my eyes with the beautiful long leaps he is making across the low rail of the grass-plot on my left. Backwards and forwards he leaps—as a matter of fact he is doing it because he knows I like it; for I have often urged him on by shouting and striking the railing, praising him when he fell in with my whim. So now he comes up to me after nearly every jump to hear how intrepidly and elegantly he jumps. He even springs up into my face and slavers all over the arm I put out to protect it. But the jumping is also to be conceived as a sort of morning exercise, and morning toilet as well, for it smoothes his ruffled coat and rids it of old Moor's straws.

It is good to walk like this in the early morning, with senses rejuvenated and spirit cleansed by the night's long healing draught of Lethe. You look confidently forward to the day yet pleasantly hesitate to begin it, being master as you are of this little untroubled span of time between, which is your good reward for good behavior. You indulge in the illusion that your life is habitually steady, simple, concentrated, and contemplative, that you belong entirely to yourself—and this illusion makes you quite happy. For a human being tends to believe that the mood of the moment, be it troubled or blithe, peaceful or stormy, is the true, native, and permanent tenor of his existence; and in particular he likes to exalt every happy chance into an inviolable rule and to regard it as the benign order of his life—whereas the truth is that he is condemned to improvisation and morally lives from hand to mouth all the time. So now, breathing the morning air, you stoutly believe that you are virtuous and free; while you ought to know—and at bottom do know—that the world is spreading its snares round your feet, and that most likely tomorrow you will be lying in your bed until nine, because you sought it at two in the morning hot and befogged with impassioned discussion. Never mind. Today you, a sober character, and early riser, you are the right master for that stout hunter who has just cleared the railings again out of sheer joy in the fact that today you apparently belong to him alone and not to the world.

We follow the avenue for about five minutes, to the point where it ceases to be an avenue and becomes a gravelly waste along the riverbank. From this we turn away to our right and strike into another covered with finer gravel, which has been laid out like the avenue and like it provided with a cycle-path, but is not yet built up. It runs between low-lying, wooded lots of land, towards the slope which is the eastern limit of our river neighborhood and Bashan's theatre of action. On our way we cross another road, equally embryonic, running along between fields and meadows. Further up, however, where the tram stops, it is quite built up with flats. We descend by a gravel path into a well-laid-out, parklike valley, quite deserted, as indeed the whole region is at this hour. Paths are laid out in curves and rondels, there are benches to rest on, tidy playgrounds, and wide plots of lawn with fine old trees whose boughs nearly sweep the grass, covering all but a glimpse of trunk. They are elms, beeches, limes, and silvery willows, in well-disposed groups. I enjoy to the full the well-landscaped quality of the scene, where I may walk no more disturbed than if it belonged to me alone. Nothing has been forgotten—there are even cement gutters in the gravel paths that lead down the grassy slopes. And the abundant greenery discloses here and there a charming distant vista of one of the villas that bound the spot on two sides.

Here for a while I stroll along the paths, and Bashan revels in the freedom on unlimited level space, galloping across and across the lawns like mad with his body inclined in a centrifugal plane; sometimes, barking with mingled pleasure and exasperation, he pursues a bird which flutters as though spellbound, but perhaps on purpose to tease him, along the ground just in front of his nose. But if I sit down on a bench he is at my side at once and takes up a position on one of my feet. For it is a law of his being that he only runs about when I am in motion too; that when I settle down he follows suit. There seems no obvious reason for this practice; but Bashan never fails to conform to it.

I get an odd, intimate, and amusing sensation from having him sit on my foot and warm it with the blood-heat of his body. A pervasive feeling of sympathy and good cheer fills me, as almost invariably when in his company and looking at things from his angle. He has a rather rustic slouch when he sits down; his shoulder-blades stick out an his paws turn negligently in. He looks smaller and squatter than he really is, and the little white boss on his chest is advanced with comic effect. But all these faults are atoned for by the lofty and dignified carriage of the head, so full of concentration. All is quiet, and we two sit there absolutely still in our turn. The rushing of the water comes to us faint and subdued. And the senses become alert for all the tiny, mysterious little sounds that nature makes: the lizard's quick dart, the note of the bird, the burrowing of a mole in the earth. Bashan pricks up his ears—in so far as the muscles of naturally drooping ears will allow them to be pricked. He cocks his head to hear the better; and the nostrils of his moist black nose keep twitching sensitively as he sniffs.

Then he lies down, but always in contact with my foot. I see him in profile, in that age-old, conventionalized pose of the beast-god, the sphinx: head and chest held high, forelegs close to the body, paws extended in parallel lines. He has got overheated, so he opens his mouth, and at once all the intelligence of his face gives way to the merely animal, his eyes narrow and blink and his rosy tongue lolls out between his strong white pointed teeth.

Beth-Gêlert

BY WILLIAM ROBERT SPENCER

Subtitled "THE GRAVE OF THE GREYHOUND," this poem retells an ancient legend. Said to date back as early as the third century B.C., the old Aryan myth is most traditionally told about the Welsh nobleman Llewelyn the Great, who lived at the foot of Snowdon mountain. Llewelyn's father-in-law, King John, is believed to have given him the dog Gêlert in 1205.

In the eighteenth century, Spencer turned the sad story into an epic poem. But even in modern literature the essence of the old legend—the noble dog, tragically accused, innocent but banished or murdered—reappears over and over again.

★ ★ ★ ★ ★

THE SPEARMEN HEARD the bugle sound,
     And cheerily smiled the morn;
And many a brach, and many a hound
     Obeyed Llewellyn's horn.

And still he blew a louder blast,
     And gave a lustier cheer,
"Come, Gêlert, come, wert never last
     Llewellyn's horn to hear.

"O where does faithful Gêlert roam
     The flower of all his race;
So true, so brave—a lamb at home
     A lion in the chase?"

In sooth, he was a peerless hound,
     The gift of royal John;
But now no Gêlert could be found,
     And all the chase rode on.

That day Llewellyn little loved
     The chase of hart and hare;
And scant and small the booty proved,
     For Gêlert was not there.

Unpleased, Llewellyn homeward hied,
     When, near the portal seat,
His truant Gêlert he espied
     Bounding his lord to greet.

But when he gained the castle-door,
     Aghast the chieftain stood;
The hound all o'er was smeared with gore;
     His lips, his fangs, ran blood.

Llewellyn gazed with fierce surprise;
     Unused such looks to meet,
His favorite checked his joyful guise,
     And crouched, and licked his feet.

Onward, in haste, Llewellyn passed,
    And on went Gêlert too;
And still, where'er his eyes he cast,
    Fresh blood-gouts shocked his view.

O'erturned his infant's bed he found,
    With blood-stained covert rent;
And all around the walls and ground
    With recent blood besprent.

He called his child—no voice replied—
    He searched with terror wild;
Blood, blood he found on every side,
    But nowhere found his child.

"Hell-hound! my child's by thee devoured,"
    The frantic father cried;
And to the hilt his vengeful sword
    He plunged in Gêlert's side.

Aroused by Gêlert's dying yell,
    Some slumberer wakened nigh;
What words the parent's joy could tell
    To hear his infant's cry!

Concealed beneath a tumbled heap
    His hurried search had missed,
All glowing from his rosy sleep
    The cherub boy he kissed.

Nor scathe had he, nor harm, nor dread,
    But, the same couch beneath,
Lay a gaunt wolf, all torn and dead,
    Tremendous still in death.

Ah, what was then Llewellyn's pain!
    For now the truth was clear;
His gallant hound the wolf had slain
    To save Llewellyn's heir.

My Talks with Dean Spanley

BY LORD DUNSANY

E DWARD JOHN MORETON DRAX PLUNKETT, the 18th baron of
Dunsany, was an Irish dramatist and storyteller—author of short stories, plays, novels, and poems. He was known to, as the *Encyclopedia
Brittanica* says, combine "imaginative power with intellectual ingenu-
ity to create a credible world of fantasy."

I first read "My Talks with Dean Spanley", from which this excerpt is
taken, some forty years ago in a collection of dog stories given me for a birth-
day present. Too young to know what Tokay wine was, I envisioned it as rather
like honey, only intoxicating—thick, sweet, golden in color. It was very much
later that I actually tasted Tokay . . . and was mightily disappointed.

But it did the trick for Dean Spanley, whose extraordinary tale appears
here—one of the most charming and imaginative stories in all canine literature.

* * * * *

Preface

THAT THERE ARE PASSAGES in Dean Spanley's conversation that have sometimes jarred on me, the reader will readily credit. But the more that his expressions have been removed from what one might have expected of a man in his position, or indeed any member of my Club, the more they seemed to me to guarantee his sincerity. It would have been easy enough for him to have acted the part that is his duty to play; but difficult, and I think impossible, to have invented in such meticulous detail the strange story he told me. And for what reason? Upon the authenticity of Dean Spanley's experiences I stake my reputation as a scientific writer. If he has deluded me in any particular, let scientific bodies reject not only these researches, but any others that I may make hereafter. So sure am I of Dean Spanley's perfect veracity.

Should doubt be expressed of a single page of these talks, and the case against it be made with any plausibility, it is probable that I shall abandon not only this line of research, but my Investigations into the Origins of the Mentality of Certain Serious Persons, the product of years of observation, may never even be published.

1

Were I to tell you how I came to know that Dean Spanley had a secret, I should have to start this tale at a point many weeks earlier. For the knowledge came to me gradually; and it would be of little interest to my readers were I to record the hints and guesses by which it grew to a certainty. Stray conversations gradually revealed it, at first partly overheard from a little group in a corner of a room at the Olympus Club, and later addressed directly to myself. And the odd thing is that almost always it was what Dean Spanley did not say, rather than any word he uttered, a checking of speech that occurred suddenly on the top of speculations of others, that taught me he must be possessed of some such secret as nobody else, at any rate outside Asia, appears to have any inkling of. If anyone in Europe has studied the question so far, I gladly offer him the material I was able to glean from Dean Spanley, to compare and check with his own work. In the East, of course, what I have gathered will not be regarded as having originality.

I will start my story then, on the day on which I became so sure of some astonishing knowledge which Dean Spanley kept to himself, that I decided to act upon my conviction. I had of course cross-examined him before, so far as one can cross-examine an older man in brief conversation in a rather solemn club, but on this occasion I asked him to dine with me. I should perhaps at this point record the three things that I had found out about Dean

Spanley: the first two were an interest in transmigration, though only shown as a listener, greater than you might expect in a clergyman; and an interest in dogs. Both these interests were curiously stressed by his almost emphatic silences, just when it seemed his turn to speak upon either of these subjects. And the third thing I chanced to find was that the dean, though at the club a meager drinker of wine, was a connoisseur of old port. And it was this third interest of the dean's that is really the key to the strange information that I am now able to lay before the public. Well then, after many days, during which my suspicions had at first astonished me, and then excitedly ripened, I said to Dean Spanley in the reading-room of the Club, "Of course the difficulty about transmigration is that nobody ever yet remembered having lived a former life."

"H'm," said the dean.

And there and then I asked him if he would dine with me, giving as my reason what I knew to be the only one that would have any chance of bringing him, my wish to have his advice upon some vintage port that had been left me by an aunt, and which had been given to her by Count Donetschau a little before 1880. The port was as good as I had been able to buy, but I doubt he would have drunk it on that account without the name or history, any more than he would have spoken to a man who was dressed well enough, but who had not been introduced to him.

"Count Donetschau?" he said a little vaguely.

"Count Shevenitz-Donetschau," I answered.

And he accepted my invitation.

It was a failure that dinner. I discovered, what I should have known without any experience, that one cannot make a rather abstemious dean go past the point at which wit stands sentry over the tongue's utterance, merely by giving him port that he likes. He liked the port well enough, but nothing that I could say made him take a drop too much of it. Luckily I had not given myself away, had not said a word to let him see what I was after. And in a month I tried again. I said I found some port of a different vintage, hidden among the rest, and would value his opinion as to which was the better. And he accepted; and this time I had my plan.

Dinner was light, and as good as my cook could make it. Then came the vintage port, three glasses the same as last time and no more, except for half a glass of the old kind for sake of comparison, and after three and a half glasses came my plan.

"I have a bottle of Imperial Tokay in the cellar," I said.

"Imperial what!" cried the dean.

"Imperial Tokay," I said.

"Imperial Tokay," he repeated.

"Yes," I said. For I had been able to get a loan of one from a friend who in some small way had become possessed of half a dozen of this rare wine, that until a little while ago was only uncorked by command of the Emperors of Austria. When I say the loan of a bottle, I mean that I told my friend, who was totally unscientific, that there was something I wanted to draw out of this dean, and that I saw no other way of doing it than to offer him a wine, when he had come to his ordinary limit of drinking, so exciting that he would go further from that point, and that anything left in the bottle, "after you have made your dean drunk," as he put it, would be returned to him. I really think that the only reason he gave me the priceless bottle was for a certain unholy joy that his words implied. I doubt if my researches, which without that Imperial Tokay would have been impossible, will be of any interest to him.

Well the Imperial Tokay was brought in, and I poured out a glass for Dean Spanley. He drank it off at once. I don't know if a dean has a different idea of Heaven, some clearer vision of it, than the rest of us. I shall never know. I can only guess from what I saw in the eyes if Dean Spanley as that Imperial Tokay went down.

"Will you have another glass?" I asked.

"I never take more than three glasses usually," he replied.

"Oh, port doesn't count," I answered.

He had now had four and a half glasses that evening, and had just come to a point at which such remarks as my last, however silly it may seem here, appear to have wisdom. And, as I spoke, I poured into his glass that curious shining wine that has somewhat the taste of sherry strangely enchanted. It was now beside him, and we spoke of other things. But when he sipped the Tokay I said to him rather haltingly, "I want to ask you about a future life."

I said it haltingly, because, when two people are speaking, if one of them lacks confidence the other is more apt to assume it. Certainly Spanley did. He replied, "Heaven. Undoubtedly Heaven."

"Yes, ultimately of course," I said. "But if there were anything in the theories one sometimes hears, transmigration and all that, I was wondering if that might work first."

There was a certain look of caution yet on his face, and so I went rambling on, rather than leave a silence in which he would have to answer, and by the answer commit himself to concealment of all I wanted to know. "I mean," I said, "going to other lives after this one, animals and all that, and working upwards or downwards in each incarnation, according to whether or not; you know what I mean."

And then he drained the glass and I poured out another; and, sipping that almost absently, the look of caution went, and I saw instead so beautiful a contentment reigning there in its place, flickering as it seemed with the passage of old reminiscences, that I felt that my opportunity must be come, and there and then I said to him: "You see I've been rather fond of dogs; and, if one chanced to be one of them in another incarnation, I wonder if there are hints you could give me."

And I seem to have caught the right memory as it floated by on waves of that wonderful wine, for he answered at once: "Always go out of a room first: get to the door the moment it's opened. You may not get another chance for a long time."

Then he seemed rather worried or puzzled by what he had said, and cleared his throat and searched, I think, for another topic; but before he had time to find one I broke in with my thanks, speaking quickly and somewhat loudly, so as to frighten his thoughts away from any new topic, and the thoughts seemed easily guided.

"Thank you very much," I said, "very much indeed. I will say that over and over again to myself. I will get it into my very; you know, my ego. And so I shall hope to remember it. A hint like that will be invaluable. Is there anything more you could tell me, in case?"

And at the same time, while I spoke to him and held his attention, I refilled his glass with a hand that strayed outside the focus of the immediate view of either of us.

"Well," he said, "there's always fleas."

"Yes, that of course would be rather a drawback," I said.

"I wouldn't say that," he answered. "I rather like a few fleas; they indicate just where one's coat needs licking."

And a sudden look came over his face again, as though his thoughts would have strayed where I did not want them, back to strict sobriety and the duller problems of this life. To keep him to the subject that so profoundly interested me I hastily asked his advice, an act which in itself helps to hold the attention of any man.

"How can one best ingratiate oneself, and keep in with the Masters?"

"Ah, the Masters," he muttered, "the great ones. What benevolence! What wisdom! What power! And there was one incomparably greater and wiser than all of them. I remember how, when he came back, I used to mix myself a good stiff whiskey and soda and. . . ."

"But dogs," I said, "dogs don't drink whiskey."

I learned afterwards never to interrupt him, but I couldn't help it now, and I wanted to get the truth, and thought he was talking mere nonsense; and yet it wasn't quite.

"Er, er, no," said Dean Spanley, and fumbled awhile with his memories, till I was afraid I had lost touch with the mystery that I had planned so long to explore.

"I got the effect," he said, "by racing round and round on the lawn, a most stimulating effect; it seems to send the blood to the head in a very exhilarating manner. What am I saying? Dear me, what *am* I saying?"

And I pretended not to have heard him. But I got no more that night. The curtain that cuts us off from all such knowledge had fallen. Would it ever lift again?

2

A few nights later I met the dean at the Club. He was clearly vague about what we had talked of when he had dined with me, but just a little uneasy. I asked him then for his exact opinion about my port, until I had established it in his mind that that was my principal interest in the evening we spent together and he felt that nothing unusual could have occurred. Many people would have practiced that much deception merely to conceal from a friend that he had drunk a little more wine than he should have, but at any rate I felt justified in doing it now when so stupendous a piece of knowledge seemed waiting just within reach. For I had not got it yet. He had said nothing as yet that had about it those unmistakable signs of truth with which words sometimes clothe themselves. I dined at the next table to him. He offered me the wine-list after he ordered his port, but I waved it away as I thanked him, and somehow succeeded in conveying to him that I never drank ordinary wines like those. Soon after I asked him if he would care to dine again with me; and he accepted, as I felt sure, for the sake of the Tokay. And I had no Tokay. I had returned the bottle to my friend, and I could not ask him for any of that wine from him again. Now I chanced to have met a Maharajah at a party, and fixing an appointment by telephoning his secretary, I went to see him at his hotel. To put it briefly, I explained to him that the proof of the creed of the Hindus was within my grasp, and that the key to it was Imperial Tokay. If he cared to put up the money that would purchase the Imperial Tokay he would receive nothing less than the proof of an important part of his creed. He seemed not so keen as I thought he would be, though whether it was because his creed had no need of proof, or whether because he had doubts of it, I never discovered. If it were the latter, he concealed it in the end by agreeing to do what I wished; though, as for the money, he said: "But why not the Tokay?" And it turned out that he had in his cellars a little vault that was full of it. "A dozen bottles shall be there in a fortnight," he said.

A dozen bottles! I felt that with that I could unlock Dean Spanley's heart, and give to the Maharajah a strange secret that perhaps he knew already, and to much of the human race a revelation that they had only guessed.

I had not yet fixed the date of my dinner with Dean Spanley, so I rang him up and fixed it with him a fortnight later and one day to spare.

And sure enough, on the day the Maharajah had promised, there arrived at his hotel a box from India containing a dozen of that wonderful wine. He telephoned to me when it arrived, and I went at once to see him. He received me with the greatest amiability, and yet he strangely depressed me; for while to me the curtain that was lifting revealed a stupendous discovery, to him, it was only too clear, the thing was almost commonplace, and beyond it more to learn than I had any chance of discovering. I recovered my spirits somewhat when I got back to my house with that dozen of rare wine that should be sufficient for twenty-four revelations, for unlocking twenty-four times that door that stands between us and the past, and that one had supposed to be locked forever.

The day came and, at the appointed hour, Dean Spanley arrived at my house. I had champagne for him and no Tokay, and noticed a wistful expression upon his face that increased all through dinner until by the time that the sweet was served, and still there was no Tokay, his inquiring dissatisfied glances, though barely perceptible, reminded me, whenever I did perceive them, of those little whines that a dog will sometimes utter when gravely dissatisfied, perhaps because there is another dog in the room, or because for any other reason adequate notice is not being taken of himself. And yet I do not wish to convey that there was ever anything whatever about Dean Spanley that in the least suggested a dog; it was only in my own mind, preoccupied as it was with the tremendous discovery to the verge of which I had strayed, that I made the comparison. I did not offer Dean Spanley any Tokay during dinner, because I knew that it was totally impossible to break down the barrier between him and his strange memories even with Tokay, my own hope being to bring him not so far from the point by ordinary methods, I mean by port and champagne, and then to offer him the Tokay, and I naturally noted the precise amount required with the exactitude of a scientist; my whole investigations depended on that. And then the moment came when I could no longer persuade the dean to take another drop of wine; of ordinary wine, I mean; and I put the Tokay before him. A look of surprise came into face, surprise that a man in possession of Tokay would let so much of the evening waste away before bringing it out. "Really," he said, "I hardly want any more wine, but . . ."

"It's a better vintage than the other one," I said, making a guess that turned out to be right.

And it certainly was a glorious wine. I took some myself, because with that great bundle of keys to the mysterious past that the Maharajah's dozen bottles had given me I felt could afford this indulgence. A reminiscent look came over Dean Spanley's face, and deepened, until it seemed to be peering over the boundaries that shut in this life. I waited a while and then I said: "I was wondering about rabbits."

"Among the worst of Man's enemies," said the dean. And I knew at once from his vehemence that his memory was back again on the other side of the veil that shuts off so much from the rest of us. "They lurk in the woods and plot, and give Man no proper allegiance. They should be hunted whenever met."

He said it with such intensity that I felt sure the rabbits had often eluded him in that other life; and I saw that to take his side against them as much as possible would be the best way to keep his memory where it was, on the other side of the veil; so I abused rabbits. With evident agreement the dean listened, until, to round off my attack of them, I added: "And over-rated animals even to eat. There's no taste in them."

"Oh, I wouldn't say that," said the dean. "A good hot rabbit that has been run across a big field has certainly an, an element of . . ." And he did not complete his sentence; but there was a greedy look in his eyes.

I was very careful about refilling the dean's glass; I gave him no more for some while. It seemed to me that the spiritual level from which he had this amazing view, back over the ages, was a very narrow one; like a ridge at the top of a steep, which gives barely a resting place to the mountaineer. Too little Tokay and he would lapse back into orthodoxy; too much, and I feared he would roll just as swiftly down to the present day. It was the ridge from which I feared I had pushed him last time. This time I must watch the mood that Tokay had brought, and neither intensify it nor let it fade, for as long as I could hold it with exactly the right hospitality. He looked wistfully at the Tokay, but I gave him no more yet.

"Rabbits," I said to remind him.

"Yes, their guts are very good," he said. "And their fur is good for one. As for their bones, if they cause one any irritation, once can always bring them up. In fact, when in doubt, always bring anything up: it's easily done.

"But there is a bit of advice I would give to you. Out-of-doors. It's always best out-of-doors. There are what it is not for us to call prejudices: let us rather say preferences. But while these preferences exist amongst those who hold them, it is much best out-of-doors. You will remember that?"

"Certainly," I said. "Certainly."

And as I spoke I carefully watched his eyes, to see if he was still on that narrow ledge that I spoke of, that spiritual plane from which a man could gaze out on the past ages. And he was. A hand strayed tentatively toward the Tokay, but I moved it out of his reach.

"Rats!" I said. And he stirred slightly, but did not seem greatly interested.

And then, without any further suggestion from me, he began to talk of the home life of a dog, somewhere in England in the days long before motors.

"I used to see off all the carts that drove up to the back-door every day. Whenever I heard them coming I ran round; I was always there in time; and then I used to see them off. I saw them off as far as a tree that there was a little way down the drive. Always about a hundred barks, and then I used to stop. Some were friends of mine, but I used to see them off the same as the rest. It showed them the house was well guarded. People that didn't know me used to hit at me with the whip, until they found out that they were too slow to catch me. If one of them ever had hit me I should have seen him off the whole way down the drive. It was always pleasant to trot back to the house from one of these little trips. I have had criticism for this; angry words, that is to say; but I knew from the tone of the voices that they were proud of me. I think it best to see them off like that, because, because . . ."

I hastily added: "Because otherwise they might think that the house wasn't properly guarded."

And the answer satisfied him. But I filled the dean's glass with Tokay as fast as I could. He drank it and remained at that strange altitude from which he could see the past.

"Then sooner or later," he continued, "the moon comes over the hill. Of course you can take your own line about that. Personally, I never trusted it. It's the look of it I didn't like, and the sly way it moves. If anything comes by at night I like it to come on footsteps, and I like it to have a smell. The you know where you are."

"I quite agree," I said, for the dean had paused.

"You can hear footsteps," he went on, "and you can follow a smell, and you can tell the sort of person you have to deal with, by the kind of smell he has. But folk without any smell have no right to be going about among those that have. That's what I didn't like about the moon. And I didn't like the way he stared one in the face. And there was a look in his stare as though everything was odd and the house was not properly guarded. The house was perfectly well guarded, and so I said at the time.

"But he wouldn't stop that queer look. Many's the time I've told him to go away and not to look at me in that odd manner; and he pretended not to hear me. But he knew all right, he knew he was odd and strange and in league with magic, and he knew what honest folks thought of him: I've told him many a time."

"I should stand no nonsense from him," I said.

"Entirely my view," said the dean.

There was silence then such as you sometimes see among well satisfied diners.

"I expect he was afraid of you," I said; and only just in time, for the dean came back as it were with a jerk to the subject.

"Ah, the moon," he said. "Yes, he never came any nearer. But there's no saying what he'd have done if I hadn't been there. There was a lot of strangeness about him, and if he'd come any nearer everything might have been stranger. They only had me to look after them.

"Only me to look after them," he added reflectively. "You know, I've known them to talk to a man that ought at least to be growled at, stand at the front door and talk to him. And for what was strange or magical they never had any sense; no foreboding I mean. Why, there were sounds and smells that would make my hair rise on my shoulders before I had thought of the matter, while they would not even stir. That was why they so much needed guarding. That of course was our *raison d'être,* if I may put it in that way. The French often have a way of turning a phrase, that seems somehow more deft than anything that we islanders do. Not that our literature cannot hold its own."

"Quite so," I said to check this line of thought, for he was wandering far away from where I wanted him. "Our literature is very vivid. You have probably many vivid experiences in your own memory, if you cast your mind back. If you cast your mind back you would probably find material worthy of the best of our literature."

And he did. He cast his mind back as I told him. "My vividest memory," he said, "is a memory of the most dreadful words that the ear can hear, 'Dirty dog.' Those unforgettable words; how clear they ring in my memory. The dreadful anger with which they were always uttered, the emphasis, the miraculous meaning! They are certainly the most, the most prominent words of all I have ever heard. They stand by themselves. Do you not agree?"

"Undoubtedly," I said. And I made a very careful mental note that, whenever he wandered away from the subject that so much enthralled me, those might be the very words that would call him back.

"Yes, dirty dog," he went on. "Those words are never uttered lightly."

"What used to provoke them?" I asked. For the dean had paused, and I feared lest at any moment he should find a new subject.

"Nothing," he said. "They came as though inspired, but from no cause. I remember once coming into the drawing-room on a lovely bright morning, from a very pleasant heap that there was behind the stable yard, where I sometimes used to make my toilet; it gave a very nice tang to my skin, that lasted some days; a mere roll was sufficient, if done in the right place; I came in very carefully smoothed and scented and was about to lie down in a lovely patch of sunlight, when these dreadful words broke out. They used to come like lightning, like thunder and lightning together. There was no cause for them; they were just inspired."

He was silent, reflecting sadly. "There was nothing else to do. I slunk out and rolled in ordinary grass and humbled myself and came back later with my fur all rough and untidy and that lovely aroma gone, just a common dog. I came back and knocked at the door and put my head in, when the door was opened at last, and kept it very low, and my tail low too, and I came in very slowly, and they looked at me holding their anger back by the collar, and I went slower still, and they stood over me and stooped, and then in the end they did not let their anger loose, and I hid in a corner I knew of. Dirty dog. Yes, yes. There are few words more terrible."

The dean fell then into a reverie, till presently there came the same look of confusion, and even alarm, on his face that I had noticed before when he suddenly cried out, "What am I taking about?" And to forestall any such uncomfortable perplexity I began to talk of myself. "The lightning, the upkeep and the culinary problems," I said, "are on the one hand. On the other, the Committee should so manage the Club that its amenities are available to all, or even more so. You, no doubt, agree there."

"Eh?" he said. "Oh yes, yes."

I tried no more that night, and the rest of our conversation was of this world, and of this immediate sojourn.

3

"I was the hell of a dog," said the dean, when next I was able to tempt him with the Tokay to that eminence of the mind from which he had this remarkable view down the ages, but it was not easily done; in fact it took me several weeks. "A hell of a dog. I had often to growl so as to warn people. I used to wag my tail at the same time, so as to let them know that I was only meaning to warn them, and they should not think I was angry.

"Sometimes I used to scratch up the earth, merely to feel my strength and to know that I was stronger than the earth, but I never went on long enough to harm it. Other dogs never dared do more than threaten me; I never had to bite them, my growl was enough, and a certain look that I had on my face and teeth, and my magnificent size, which increased when I was angry, so that they could see how large I really was.

"They were lucky to have me guard them. It was an inestimable privilege to serve them; they had unearthly wisdom; but ..."

"But they needed guarding," I said. For I remembered this mood of his. And my words kept him to it.

"They needed it," he said. "One night I remember a fox came quite near the house and barked at them. Came out of the woods and on to our lawn and barked. You can't have that sort of thing. There's no greater enemy of man than the fox. They didn't know that. They hunted him now and then for sport; but they never knew what an enemy he was. I knew. They never knew that he has no reverence for man, and no respect for his chickens. I knew. They never knew of his plots. And here he was on the lawn barking at men. I was unfortunately in the drawing-room, and the doors were shut, or my vengeance would have been frightful. I should have gone out and leapt on him, probably in one single bound from the hall door, and I should have torn him up into four or five pieces and eaten every one of them. And that is what I told him, holding back nothing. And then I told him all over again. Somebody had to tell him.

"Then one of the wise ones came and told me not to make so much noise; and out of respect to him I stopped. But when he went away the fox was still within hearing, so I told him about it again. It was better to tell him again, so as to make quite sure. And so I guarded the house against all manner of dangers and insults, of which their miraculous wisdom had never taken account."

"What other dangers?" I asked. For the dean was looking rather observantly at objects on the table, peering at them from under his thick eyebrows, so that in a few moments his consciousness would have been definitely in the world of the outer eye, and far away from the age that has gone from us.

"Dangers?" he said.

"Yes," I replied.

"The dark of the woods," he answered, "and the mystery of night. There lurked things there of which man himself knew nothing, and even I could only guess."

"How did you guess?" I asked him.

"By smells and little sounds," said the dean.

It was this remark about the woods and the night, and the eager way in which he spoke of the smells and the sounds, that first made me sure that the dean was speaking from knowledge, and that he really had known another life in a strangely different body. Why these words made me sure I cannot say; I can only say that it is oddly often the case that some quite trivial remark in a man's conversation will suddenly make you sure that he knows what he is talking about. A man will be talking perhaps about pictures, and all at once he will make you feel that Raphael, for instance, is real to him, and that he is not merely making conversation. In the same way I felt, I can hardly say why, that the woods were real to the dean, and the work of a dog no less to him than an avocation. I do not think I have explained how I came to be sure of this, but from that moment any scientific interest in what my Tokay was revealing was surpassed by a private anxiety to gather what hints I could for my own ends. I did not like to be adrift as I was in a world in which transmigration must be recognized as a fact, without the faintest idea of the kind of problems with which one would have to deal, if one should suddenly find oneself a dog in what was very likely an English rectory. That possibility came on me with more suddenness than it probably does to my reader, to whom I am breaking it perhaps more gently. From now on I was no longer probing a man's eccentric experience, so much as looking to him for advice. Whether it is possible to carry any such advice forward to the time one might need it is doubtful, but I mean to try my best by committing it carefully to memory, and all that I gleaned from the dean is of course at my reader's disposal. I asked him first about the simple things: food, water and sleep. I remember particularly his advice about sleep, probably because it confused me and so made me think; but, whatever the cause, it is particularly clear in my memory. "You should always pull up your blanket over your lips," he said. "It insures warm air when you sleep, and is very important."

It was some time since he had had a glass of Tokay, and to have questioned him as to his meaning would have induced in him a logical, or reasonable, frame of mind. We boast so much of our reason, but what can it see compared to that view down the ages that was now being laid before me? It is blind, compared to the dean.

Luckily I did not have to question him, for by a little flash of memory I recalled a dog sleeping, a certain spaniel I knew; and I remembered how he always tucked the feathery end of his tail over his nostrils in preparation for going to sleep: he belonged to an ignorant man who had neglected to have his tail cut off as a puppy. It was a tail that the dean meant, not a blanket.

Clear though the meaning was to me at the moment I thought of the spaniel, I saw that the confusion of the dean's remark could only mean that the mist was beginning to gather over his view of time, and I hastily filled his glass. I watched anxiously till he drank it; it must have been his third or fourth; and soon I saw from the clearness of his phrases, and a greater strength in all his utterances, that he was safely back again looking out over clear years.

"The wise ones, the great ones," he went on meditatively, "they give you the straw. But they do not, of course, make your bed for you. I trust one can do that. One does it, you know, by walking round several times, the oftener the better. The more you walk around, the better your bed fits you."

I could see from the way he spoke that the dean was speaking the truth. After all, I had made no new discovery. *In vino veritas*; that was all. Though the boundaries of this adage had been extended by my talks with Dean Spanley, beyond, I suppose, any limits previously known to man; at any rate this side of Asia.

"Clean straw is bad," continued the dean, "because there is no flavor to it at all. No."

He was meditating again, and I let him meditate, leaving him to bring up out of that strange past whatever he would for me.

"If you find anything good, hide it," he continued. "The world is full of others; and they all seem to get to know if you have found anything good. It is best therefore to bury it. And to bury it when no one is looking on. And to smooth everything over it. Anything good always improves with keeping a few days. And you know it's always there when you want it. I have sometimes smoothed things over it so carefully that I have been unable to find it when requiring it, but the feeling that it's there always remains. It is a very pleasant feeling, hard to describe. Those buryings represent wealth, which of course is a feeling denied to those greedy fellows who eat every bone they find, the moment they find it. I have even buried a bone when I've been hungry, for the pleasure of knowing that it was there. What am I saying! Oh Heavens, what am I saying!"

So sudden, so unexpected was this rush back down the ages, and just when I thought that he had had ample Tokay, that I scarcely knew what to do.

But, whatever I did, it had to be done instantly; and at all costs I had to preserve from the dean the secret that through his babblings I was tapping a
source of knowledge that was new to this side of the world, for I knew instinctively that he would have put a stop to it. He had uttered once before in my
hearing a similar exclamation, but not with anything like the shocked intensity
with which he was now vibrating, and his agitation seemed even about to in-
crease. I had, as I say, to act instantly. What I did made a certain coolness between me and the dean, that lasted unfortunately for several weeks, but at least
I preserved the secret. I fell forward over the table and lay unconscious, as
though overcome by Tokay.

4

There was one advantage in the awkwardness that I felt when I next saw the
dean at the Club, and that was that my obvious embarrassment attracted his attention away from the direction in which a single wandering thought might
have ruined everything. It was of vital importance to my researches that any
question about over-indulgence in a rare wine should be directed solely at me.
My embarrassment was not feigned, but there was no need to conceal it. I
passed him by one day rather sheepishly, as I crossed the main hall of the Club
and saw him standing there looking rather large. I knew he would not give me
away to the other members, nor quite condone my lapse. And then one day I
very humbly apologized to him in the reading-room.

"That Tokay," I said. "I am afraid it may have been a little bit stronger
than I thought."

"Not at all," said the dean.

And I think we both felt better after that; I for having made my apol-
ogy, he for the generosity with which his few kind words had bestowed for-
giveness. But it was some while before I felt that I could quite ask him to dine
with me. Much roundabout talk about the different dates and vintages of
Imperial Tokay took place before I could bring myself to do that; but in the
end I did, and so Dean Spanley and I sat down to dinner again.

Now I don't want to take credit for things that I have not done, and I
will not claim that I maneuvered my guest to take up a certain attitude; I think
it was merely due to a mood of the dean. But certainly what happened was
that the dean took up a broad and tolerant line and drank his Tokay like a man,
with the implication made clear, in spite of his silence, that there was no harm
in Tokay, but only in not knowing when to stop. The result was that the dean
arrived without any difficult, and far more quickly than I had hoped, at that

point at which the truth that there is in wine unlocked his tongue to speak of that clear vision that the Tokay gave him once more. No chemist conducting experiments in his laboratory is likely to have mixed his ingredients with more care than I poured out the Tokay from now on. I mean, of course, for the dean. I knew bow how very narrow was the ridge on which his intellect perched to peer into the past; and I tended his glass with Tokay with the utmost care.

"We were talking, last time, about bones," I said. And if it had turned out to be the wrong thing to say I should have turned the discussion aside onto grilled bones. But no, there was nothing wrong with it. I had got him back to just the very point at which we left off last time.

"Ah, bones," said the dean. "One should always bury them. Then they are there when you want them. It is something to know that, behind all the noise and panting that you may make, there is a good solid store of bones, perhaps with a bit of meat on them, put away where others can't find it. That is always a satisfaction. And then, however hungry one may feel, one knows that the meat is improving all the time. Meat has no taste until it has been hidden awhile. It is always best to bury it. Very often, when I had nothing special to do, I would tear up a hole in the ground. I will tell you why I did that: it attracted attention. Then, if eavesdropping suspicious busybodies wanted to get your bone, they probably looked in the wrong place. It is all part of the scheme of a well-planned life: those that do not take these little precautions seldom get bones. Perhaps they may pick up a dry one now and again, but that is about all. Yes, always bury your bones."

I noticed the dawn of what seemed a faint surprise in his face, as though something in his words had struck him as strange, and I hastily filled his glass and placed it near his hand, which throughout the talks that I had with him had a certain wandering tendency reminiscent to me of a butterfly in my garden; it hovered now over that golden wine, then lifted the glass, and at once he was back where his own words seemed perfectly natural to him; as indeed they did to me, for I knew that he drew them straight from the well of Truth, that well whose buckets are so often delicate glasses such as I had on my table, and which were bringing up to me now these astonishing secrets. So often I find myself referring to this Tokay, that, borrowed though it was, it may be thought I am overproud of my cellar; but I cannot sufficiently emphasize that the whole scientific basis of my researches was the one maxim, *in vino veritas;* without that the dean might have exaggerated or misinterpreted, or even have invented the whole of his story. What the law of gravity is to astronomical study, so is this Latin maxim to those investigations that I offer now to the public.

"Yes, bury your bone," said the dean. "The earth is often flavorless; yet, if you choose with discrimination, in farms, beside roads, or in gardens, you hit on a delightful variety of flavors that greatly add to your bone. I remember a favorite place of mine, just at the edge of a pig-sty, which well bore out my contention that, by a careful choice of earth, there is hardly any limit to the flavoring that may improve a buried bone or a bit of meat. For pigs themselves I have nothing at all but contempt. Their claim to be one of us is grossly exaggerated. Always chase them. Chase cows too; not that I have anything particular against them: my only reason for giving you this advice is that by this means you have their horns pointing the right way. Horns are dangerous things and, unless you chase them, they are always pointing the wrong way, which, as I need hardly say, is towards you. There is very likely some scientific reason for it, but whenever you see cows they are always coming toward you; that is to say, until you chase them. Whatever the reason is, I do not think I have ever known an exception to this natural law. Horses one should chase too: I do not exactly know why, but that is the way I feel about it. I leave them alone on a road, but if I find them in a field or on paths I always chase them. It always makes a bit of a stir when horses come by; and if you don't chase them, the idea gets about that it is they that are making the stir and not you. That leads to conceit among horses, and all kinds of undesirable things. That's the way I feel about it. There's just one thing to remember and that is that, unlike cows, their dangerous end is towards you when you chase them; but no one that has ever heard the jolly sound of their hooves while being really well chased will ever think twice about that. While standing still they can kick with considerable precision, but one is not there on those occasions. While galloping their kicking is often merely silly; and, besides that, one is moving so fast oneself that one can dodge them with the utmost facility. Nothing is more exhilarating than chasing a horse. Chasing anything is good as a general rule; it keeps them moving, and you don't want things hanging around, if you will excuse the modern expression."

The phrase made me a little uneasy, but I needn't have been, for he went straight on. "And that brings us," said the dean, "to the subject of cats. They are sometimes amusing to chase, but on the whole they are so unreliable that chasing cats can hardly be called a sport, and must be regarded merely as a duty. Their habit of going up trees is entirely contemptible. I never object to a bird going into a tree, if I happen to have chased it off the lawn, so as to keep the lawn tidy. A tree is the natural refuge of a bird. And, besides, one can always get it out of the tree by barking. But to see a four-footed animal in a tree is a sight so revolting and disgusting that I have no words in which to describe it.

Many a time I have said what I thought about that, clearly and unmistakably, and yet I have never felt that I have finally dealt with the subject. One of these days perhaps my words will be attended to, and cats may leave trees for good. Till then, till then...."

And I took the opportunity of his hesitation to attempt to turn the talk in a direction that might be more useful to me, if ever the time should come when this, that I call I, should be what Dean Spanley had evidently been once.

5

There was a matter that seemed to me of vital importance if one could only get it fixed so firm in the core of one's memory that it would have a chance of survival, of surviving in fact the memory itself. This was the matter of wholesome food and water. How could one be sure of obtaining it? Sitting over a tidy table, with a clean tablecloth on it, and clean knives and forks, one may have exaggerated the importance of cleanliness; though I still feel that in the case of water such exaggeration is hardly possible. And then again I exaggerated the probability of finding oneself one day in the position I contemplated. But the vividness and sheer assurance of the dean's memories were most conducive to this. Add to that vividness and assurance a glass or two of Tokay, and I hardly know who would have held out against the belief that such a change was quite likely. And so I said to him, "I should object, as much as anything, to drinking bad water."

And the dean said: "There is no such thing as bad water. There is water with different flavors, and giving off different smells. There is interesting water and uninteresting water. But you cannot say there is bad water."

"But if there are really great impurities in it," I said.

"It makes it all the more interesting," said the dean. "If the impurities are so thick that it is solid, then it ceases to be water. But while it is water it is always good."

I may have looked a trifle sick; for the dean looked up and said to me reassuringly, "No, no, never trouble yourself about that."

I said no more for a while: it seemed hardly worth the trouble to drive and drive into one's memory, till they became almost part of one's character, little pieces of information that might perhaps survive the great change, if the information was no better than this. Of food I had heard his views already; the whole thing seemed disgusting; but I decided that in the interests of science it was my duty to get all the facts I could from the dean. So I threw in a word to keep him to the subject, and sat back and listened.

"It is the same with meat," he went on. "When meat can no longer be eaten, it is no longer there. It disappears. Bones remain always, but meat disappears. It has a lovely smell before it goes; and then fades away like a dream."

"I am not hungry," I said. And indeed truer word was never spoken, for my appetite was entirely lost. "Shall we talk of something else for a bit? If you don't mind. What about sport? Rats for instance."

"Our wainscot was not well stocked with game," said the dean, "either rats or mice. I have hunted rats, but not often. There is only one thing to remember at this sport: shake the rat. To shake the rat is essential.

"I need hardly tell you how to do that, because I think everybody is born to it. It is not merely a method of killing the rat, but it prevents him from biting you. He must be shaken until he is dead. Mice of course are small game."

"What is the largest game you have ever hunted?" I asked. For he had stopped talking, and it was essential to the interests of these researches that he should be kept to the same mood.

"A traction-engine," replied the dean.

That dated him within fifty years or so; and I decided that that incarnation of his was probably some time during the reign of Queen Victoria.

"The thing came snorting along our road, and I saw at once that it had to be chased. I couldn't allow a thing of that sort on our flower-beds, and very likely coming into the house. A thing like that might have done anything, if not properly chased at once. So I ran around and chased it. It shouted and threw black stones at me. But I chased it until it was well past our gate. It was very hard to the teeth, very big, very noisy and slow. They can't turn round on you like rats. They are made for defense rather than for attack. Much smaller game is often more dangerous than traction-engines."

So clearly did I picture the traction-engine on that Victorian road, with a dog yapping at the back wheels, that I wondered more and more what kind of dog, in order to complete the mental picture. And that was the question I began to ask the dean. "What kind of a dog . . .?" I began. But the question was much harder to ask than it may appear. My guest looked somehow so diaconal that the words froze on my lips; and, try as I would, I could not frame the sentence: what kind of a dog were you?

It seems silly, I know, to say that it was impossible merely to say seven words; and yet I found it so. I cannot explain it. I can only suggest to any that cannot credit this incapacity, that they should address those words themselves to any senior dignitary of the church, and see whether they do not themselves feel any slight hesitancy. I turned my question aside, and only lamely asked, "What kind of a dog used they to keep?"

He asked me who I meant. And I answered: "The people that you were talking about."

Thus sometimes conversations dwindle to trivial ends.

Many minutes passed before I gathered again the lost threads of that conversation. For nearly ten minutes I dared hardly speak, so near he seemed to the light of today, so ready to turn away from the shadows he saw so clearly moving in past years. I poured out for him more Tokay, and he absently drank it, and only gradually returned to that reminiscent mood that had been so gravely disturbed by the clumsiness of my question. Had I asked the dean straight out, "What kind of dog were you?" I believe he would have answered satisfactorily. But the very hesitancy of my question had awaked suspicion at once, as though the question had been a guilty thing. I was not sure that he was safely back in the past again until he made a petulant remark about another engine, a remark so obviously untrue that it may not seem worth recording; I repeat it here as it showed that the dean had returned to his outlook over the reaches of time and that he seems to have been contemporary with the threshing machine. "Traction-engines!" he said with evident loathing. "I saw one scratching itself at the back of a haystack. I thoroughly barked at it."

"They should be barked at," I said, as politely as I could.

"Most certainly," said the dean. "If things like that got to think they could go where they liked without any kind of a protest, we should very soon have them everywhere."

And there was so much truth in that that I was able to agree with the dean in all sincerity.

"And then where should we all be?" the dean asked.

And that is a question unfortunately so vital to all of us that I think it is sufficient to show by itself that the dean was not merely wandering. It seemed to me that the bright mind of a dog had seen, perhaps in the seventies of the last century, a menace to which the bulk of men must have been blind; or we should never be over-run by machines as we are, in every sense of the word. He was talking sense here. Was it not therefore fair to suppose he was speaking the truth, even where his words were surprising? If I had faintly felt that I was doing something a little undignified in lowering myself to the level of what, for the greater part of these conversations, was practically the mind of a dog, I no longer had that feeling after this observation the dean had uttered about machinery. Henceforth I felt that he was at least my equal; even when turning, as he soon did, from philosophical speculation, he returned to talk of the chase.

"To chase anything low," he said, "is always wearisome. You are continually bumping into what you are chasing. There is nothing so good as a ball. A ball goes so fast that it draws out your utmost speed, in a very exhilarating manner, and it can jump about as far as one can oneself, and before one can begin to be tired it always slows down. And then it takes a long time to eat; so that, one way and another, there is more entertainment in a ball than perhaps anything else one can chase. If one could throw it oneself, like the masters, I cannot imagine any completer life than throwing a ball and chasing it all day long."

My aim was purely scientific; I desired to reveal to Europeans a lore taught throughout Asia, but neglected, so far as I knew, by all our investigators; I desired to serve science only. Had it been otherwise, the momentary temptation that came to me as the dean spoke now might possibly have prevailed; I might possibly have hurried on some slight excuse from the room and come back with an old tennis ball, and perhaps have suddenly throw it, and so have gratified that sense of the ridiculous that is unfortunately in all of us, at the expense of more solid study.

6

The temptation to which I referred in the last chapter was far too trivial a thing to have its place in this record, or indeed in any summary of investigations that may claim to be of value to science. It should certainly have never arisen. And yet, having arisen, it enforces its place amongst my notes; for, my researches being of necessity conversational, whatever turned the current of the conversation between the dean and myself becomes of scientific importance. And that this unfortunately frivolous fancy, that came so inopportunely, did actually affect the current of our conversation is regrettably only too true. For about five minutes I was unable to shake it off, and during all that time, knowing well how inexcusable such action would be, I dared scarcely move or speak. Dean Spanley therefore continued his reminiscences unguided by me, and sometimes wandered quite away from the subject. I might indeed have lost him altogether; I mean to say, as a scientific collaborator; for during that five minutes I never even filled his glass. Luckily I pulled myself together in time, banished from my mind entirely that foolish and trivial fancy, and resumed the serious thread of my researches by saying to the dean: "What about ticks?"

"It is not for us to deal with them," said the dean. "The wise ones, the masters, can get them out. Nobody else can. It is of no use therefore to scratch. One's best policy towards a tick is summed up in the words, 'Live and let live.'

That is to say, when the tick has once taken up his abode. When the tick is still wild it is a good thing to avoid him, by keeping away from the grasses in which they live, mostly in marshy places, unless led there by anything exciting, in which case it is of course impossible to think of ticks."

This fatalistic attitude to a tick, when once it has burrowed in, so strangely different from the view that we take ourselves, did as much as anything else in these strange experiences to decide me that the dean was actually remembering clearly where the rest of us forget almost totally; standing, as it were, a solitary traveler near one bank of the river of Lethe, and hearing his memories calling shrill through the mist that conceals the opposite shore. From now on I must say that I considered the whole thing proved, and only concerned myself to gather as many facts as possible for the benefit of science, a benefit that I considered it only fair that I should share myself, to the extent of obtaining any useful hints that I could for use in any other sojourn, in the event of my ever meeting with an experience similar to Dean Spanley's and being able to preserve the memory of what I had learned from him. Now that I considered his former sojourn proved (though of course I do not claim to be the sole judge of that) I questioned Dean Spanley about what seems to many of us one of the most mysterious things in the animal world, the matter of scent. To the dean there seemed nothing odd in it, and I suppose the mystery lies largely in the comparative weakness of that sense among us.

"How long would you be able to follow a man," I said, "after he had gone by?"

"That depends on the weather," said the dean. "Scent is never the same two days running. One might be able to follow after he had gone half an hour. But there is one thing that one should bear in mind, and that is that, if any of the masters in their superb generosity should chance to give one cheese, one cannot, for some while after that, follow with any certainty. The question of scent is of course a very subtle one, and cannot be settled lightly. The view that the archbishop takes, er, er, is . . ."

The moment had come for which I had been watching all the evening, the moment when the dean was waking up from the dream, or falling asleep from the reality, whichever way one should put it, the moment at which any words of his own describing his other sojourn would upon penetrating those diaconal ears, cause the most painful surprise. Twice before it had happened; and I felt that if it happened again I might no more be able to get the dean to dine with me. Science might go no further in this direction, in Europe. So I said, "Excuse me a moment. The telephone, I think." And I rushed out of the room.

When I came back our conversation was not, I trust, without interest; but as it was solely concerned with the new lift that it is proposed to install in the club to which Dean Spanley and I belong, not many of my readers would easily follow the plans, were I to describe them here, or understand the importance of the new lift.

I pass over the next few weeks. The dean dined with me once more, but I was not able to persuade him to take sufficient Tokay to enable him to have that wonderful view of his that looked back down the ages, or indeed to see anything of interest at all. He talked to me, but told me nothing that any reasonably well-educated reader could not find out for himself in almost any library. He was far far short of the point to which I hoped my Tokay would bring him. I felt a renegade to science. There are those who will understand my difficulties; he was naturally an abstemious man; he was a dean; and he was now entirely familiar with the exact strength of Tokay; it was not so easy to persuade him by any means whatever to go so far with that wine as he had gone three times already, three lapses that he must have suspected, if he did not even know exactly all about them. There are those who will understand all this. But there are others who in view of what was at stake will be absolutely ruthless; scientists who, in the study of some new or rare disease, would not hesitate to inoculate themselves with it, were it necessary to study it so, men who would never spare themselves while working for Science, and who will not withhold criticism from me. What prevented me, they will ask, from forcing upon Dean Spanley, by any means whatever, sufficient alcohol for these important researches? For such a revelation as was awaiting a few more glasses of wine, any means would have been justified. It is easy to argue thus. But a broader mind will appreciate that you cannot ask a man to dine with you, let alone a dean, and then by trickery or violence, or whatever it is that some may lightly recommend, reduce him to a state that is far beyond any he would willingly cultivate. All the permissible arts of a host I had already exercised. Beyond that I would not go. Meanwhile what was I to do? I felt like Keats' watcher of the skies when some new planet swims into his ken, and when almost immediately afterwards some trivial obstacle intervenes; a blind is drawn down, a fog comes up, or perhaps a small cloud; and the wonder one knows to be there is invisible. Much I had learned already, and I trust that what I have written has scientific value, but I wanted the whole story. I was no more content than a man would be who had obtained twenty or thirty pages of an ancient codex, if he knew there were hundreds of pages of it. And what I sought seemed so near, and yet out of my grasp, removed from by perhaps two small glasses. I never lost my temper with the dean, and when I found I could no more question him stimulated, I questioned him sober. This was perhaps the most enraging experience of all; for not only was Dean Spanley extremely reticent, but he did really know anything. An intense understanding of dogs, a sympathy for their more reputable emotions, and a guess that a strange truth revealed to the Hindus, was about all he had to tell. I have said already that I knew he had a secret; and this knowledge was what started my on my researches; but this secret of his amounted to no more knowledge, as a scientist uses the word, than a few exotic shells bought in some old shop on a trip to the seaside can supply knowledge of seafaring. Between the dean sober at the Olympus Club, and the same dean after his fourth glass of Tokay, was all the difference between some tripper as I have indicated and a wanderer familiar with the surf of the boundaries of the very furthest seas. It was annoying, but it was so. And then it seemed to me that perhaps where I had just failed alone I might be able to succeed with the help of example, if I asked one or two others to meet the dean. I was thinking in the form of a metaphor particularly unsuited to Tokay, "You may lead the horse to water, but you cannot make him drink." And from thinking of horses I got the idea of a lead out hunting, and so the idea of a little company at dinner easily came to me, one or two of the right kind who could be trusted to give a lead.

And I found the very man, and the moment I found him I decided that no more was necessary; just he and I and the dean would make a perfect dinner-party, from which I hoped that so much would be revealed. I found him sitting next to me at a public dinner, a man of the most charming address, and with an appreciation of good wine that was evidently the foremost of his accomplishments. He was so much in contrast to the man on the other side of me that I turned to Wrather (that was his name) quite early in the dinner and talked to him for the rest of the evening. The man on the other side of me was a teetotaler, which anybody may be, but one that wanted to convert his neighbors, and he started on me as soon as the sherry came round; so that it was a pleasure to hear from Wrather what was almost his first remark to me: "Never trust a teetotaller, or a man that wears elastic-sided boots." The idea struck me at once that he might be the man I wanted; and when I saw how well he was guided by the spirit of that saying, both in dress and in habits, I decided that he actually was. Later in that evening he put an arm round my shoulders and said: "You're younger than me; not with your whole life before you, but some of it; and this advice may be useful to you: Never trust a teetotaller or a man that wears elastic-sided boots."

One doesn't see elastic-sided boots as much now as one used to, and I fancied that he had evolved his saying early in life, or perhaps it was handed down to him.

We made great friends, and as we went out from the dinner together I tried to help him into his coat. He could not find the armhole, and said, "Never mind. I shall never find it. Throw the damned thing over my shoulders."

Which I did. And he added, "But for all that, never trust a teetotaller, or a man that wears elastic-sided boots."

We shared a taxi and, in the darkness of it, he talked as delightfully as he had in the bright hall where we had dined; until, suddenly seeing a policeman, he stopped the cab and leaned out and shouted, "Bobby! There's something I want to tell you; and it's worth all you've ever learned at Scotland Yard."

The constable came up slowly.

"Look here," said Wrather. "It's this. Never trust a teetotaller, or a man that wears elastic-sided boots.

"We've been dining at the Woolgatherers," I said through a chink beside Wrather.

And the constable nodded his head and walked slowly away.

"Sort of thing that will set him up," said Wrather, "if only he can remember it."

7

I called on Wrather the very next day and told him about the dinner with the dean. I did not talk science or philosophy with Wrather, because he was not interested in science, and I far as I could gather from the talk of a single evening the tenets of transmigration did not appeal to him. But I told him that the dean kept a dog, and knew a great deal about dogs, and that when he had a few glasses he thought he *was* a dog, and told dog-stories that were amusing and instructive. I told Wrather straight out that the dean went very slow with wine, and that to get any amusement out of him he must be encouraged to take his whack like a reasonable sportsman. Wrather said very little, but there was a twinkle in his eyes that showed me I could rely on him whenever I should be able to get the dean. And I think that there may have been also in Wrather's mind, like a dim memory, the idea that I had helped him with the policeman, and he felt grateful. I watched next for the dean at the Club, and soon found him, and said that I hoped he would dine with me one day again, as I particularly want to ask him about the Greek strategy at Troy, a subject that I had found out he was keen on. He may have been a little afraid of the Tokay; on the other hand it attracted him. A man of the dean's degree of refinement could hardly fail to have been attracted to the Tokay, if he knew anything about wine at all; and Dean Spanley certainly did. He was not unpleased to be consulted by me about the Greek strategy, no man is entirely unmoved by being asked for information upon his particular subject; and he was very anxious to tell me about it. The final touch that may have decided him to accept my invitation was that he had beaten the Tokay last time, and so may well have thought that his fear of it was ungrounded. But an estimate of the dean's motives in accepting my invitation may not be without an element of speculation; the bare fact remains that he did accept it. It was to be for the Wednesday of the following week, and I hurried round to Wrather again and got him to promise to come on that day. I told him now still more about the dean: I said that I was a writer, and wanted to get some of the dean's stories; but there are many different kinds of writers, and I was far from telling Wrather what kind I was, for I knew that, had I told him I was a scientist, I should merely have bored him; I let him therefore suppose that I wanted the dean's dog-stories only for what might be humorous in them, and he never at any time had an inkling of the value of what I sought, the Golconda of knowledge that was lying so close to me. I told him that the Tokay was the key to what I was after, and the dean was rather difficult. "Did I ever tell you," asked Wrather, "a maxim that my father taught me? Never trust a teetotaller, or a man who wears elastic-sided boots."

"Yes, I think you did," I answered. "But Dean Spanley is not a teetotaller. Only goes a bit slow, you know."

"We'll shove him along," said Wrather.

And I saw from the look in his eyes that Wrather would do his best.

And certainly Wrather did do his best when the night came. To begin with he appreciated the Tokay for its own sake. But there was a certain whimsical charm about him that almost compelled you to take a glass with him when he urged you to do so in the way that he had. I know that what I am telling you is very silly. Why should a man take a glass of wine for himself because another man is taking one for *himself*? And yet it is one of the ways of the world that I have not been able to check. Some abler man than I may one day alter it. We did not come to the Tokay at once; we began on champagne. And certainly Dean Spanley went very slow with it, as I saw from a certain humorous and mournful look on the face of Wrather, as much as I did by watching the glass of the dean. And in the end we came to the Tokay; and Wrather goaded the dean to it.

"I don't suppose that a dean drinks Tokay," said Wrather, gazing thoughtfully at his own glass.

"And why not?" asked the dean.

"They are so sure of Heaven hereafter," said Wrather, "that they don't have to grab a little of it wherever they can, like us poor devils."

"Ahem," said the dean, and looked at the glass that I had poured out for him, the merits of which he knew just as well as Wrather.

"And then they're probably afraid of doing anything that people like me do, thinking we're all bound for Hell, and that their names might get mixed up by mistake with ours on the Day of Judgment, if they kept company with us too much."

"Oh, I wouldn't say that," said the dean.

I tried to stop Wrather after a while, thinking he went too far; but he wouldn't leave Dean Spanley alone; I had set Wrather onto him, and now I found I could not call him off. At any rate the dean drank his Tokay. "Well, what more do you want?" Wrather seemed to say to me with a single glance of his expressive eyes, knowing perfectly well that I was trying to stop him. It was then that I asked the dean about the Greek strategy at Troy. Dean Spanley put down his third glass of Tokay and began to tell me about it, and a look came over Wrather's face that was altogether pro-Trojan, or at any rate against everything to do with Greeks. As the dean talked on I poured out another glass of Tokay for him and watched him, and Wrather watched too. He was getting near to that point at which the curious change took place: I knew that by little signs that I had noted before. Wrather sat now quite silent, seeming to know as much as I did of the effect of the Tokay on the dean, though he had not seen him drink it before. But he was not there yet. I need not say what a thousand writers had said, that alcohol dulls the memory; I need not say what has been said for three thousand years, that wine sharpens the wit; both of these things are true; and both were to be observed in the same dean. Some minds are more easily affected than others; when forgetfulness came to the dean it came suddenly and very completely; had it not done so he would never have spoken out as he did. And right on top of the forgetfulness came this other phenomenon, the intense brightening of another part of the mind, a part of the mind that others of us may not possess, but far more likely, I think, a part that in most of us has never happened to be illuminated. It was, as I have said before, on only a narrow ridge that this occurred even with the dean, only for a short while, only after that precise glass, that exact number of drops of Tokay, that makes the rest of us think, upon careful reflection long after, that we may have perhaps taken a drop more that was strictly advisable. This ridge, this moment, this drop, was now approaching the dean, and Wrather and I sat watching.

"If we compare the siege of Troy with more modern sieges," said the dean, "or the siege of Ilion, as I prefer to call it, one finds among obvious differences a similarity of general principle."

Only he did not say the word principle; his tongue bungled it, went back and tried it again, tripped over it and fell downstairs. An effort that he made to retrieve the situation showed me the moment had come.

"Good dog," I said.

A momentary surprise flickered on Wrather's face, but with the dean bright memory shone on the heels of forgetfulness.

"Eh?" he said. "Wag was my name. Though not my only one. On rare occasions, very precious to me, I have been called 'Little Devil.' "

The surprise cleared from Wrather's face, and a look of mild interest succeeded it, as when a connoisseur notes a new manifestation.

Any difficulty the dean had had with his tongue had entirely disappeared.

"Ah, those days," he said. "I used to spend a whole morning at it."

"At what?" I asked.

"At hunting," said the dean, as though that should have been understood. "Ah, I can taste to this day, all the various tastes of digging out a rabbit. How fresh they were."

"What tastes?" I asked. For however tedious exactitude may be to some, it is bread and jam to a scientist.

"The brown earth," he said. "And sometimes chalk when one got down deeper, a totally different taste, not so pleasant, not quite so meaty. And then the sharp taste of the juicy roots of trees that almost always have to be bitten in two while digging out a rabbit. And little unexpected tastes, dead leaves, and even a slug. They are innumerable, and all delightful. And all the while, you know, there is that full ample scent of the rabbit, growing deeper and deeper as you get further in, till it is almost food to breathe it. The scent grows deeper, the air grows warmer, the home of the rabbit grows darker, and his feet when he moves sound like thunder; and all the while one's own magnificent scratchings sweep towards him. Winds blowing in past one's shoulders with scents from outside are forgotten. And at the end of it all is one's rabbit. That is indeed a moment."

"Some dean," muttered Wrather. An interruption such as no student of science would welcome at such a time. But I forgave him, for he had served science already far better than he could know, and I hushed him with a look, and the dean went on.

"It may be," said the dean, "though I cannot analyze it, but it may be that the actual eating of one's rabbit is no more thrilling that that gradual approach as one gnaws one's way through the earth. What would you say?"

"I should say it was equal," I answered.

"And you, Mr. Wrather?" said the dean.

"Not very good at definitions, you know," said Wrather. "But I will say one thing: one should never trust a teetotaller, or a man that wears elastic-sided boots."

And I could see that he was warming towards the dean; so that, trivial though such a thought is for a scientist to entertain in the middle of such researches, I saw that my little dinner-party would at any rate go well, as the saying is.

"There is one thing to bear in mind on those occasions," said the dean, fingering his collar with a touch of uneasiness, "and that is getting back again. When one's dinner is over one wants to get back. And if the root of a tree, that one has perhaps bitten through, or a thin flint pointing the wrong way, should get under one's collar, it may produce a very difficult situation."

His face reddened a little over his wide white collar even at the thought. And it is not a situation to laugh at.

"Where your head and shoulders have gone they can get back again," the dean continued, "were it not for the collar. That is the danger. One does not think of that while eating one's rabbit, but it is always a risk, especially where there are roots of trees. There have been cases in which that very thing has happened; caught by the collar. I knew of a case myself. Someone was lost, and men were looking for him in our woods. Of course they could not smell. But I happened to be out for a walk, and I noticed a trail leading straight to a rabbit-hole, a very old trail indeed, but when one puts one's nose to the hole the dog was undoubtedly down there and had been there a long time. He must have been caught. I expect by the collar."

"And what did you do for him?" I couldn't help blurting out.

"He was nobody I knew," said the dean.

8

Wrather turned his face slowly round and looked at me; and I could see that the feeling of friendship that he had had for the dean when he found he was not a teetotaller had suddenly all veered away. For myself I cared nothing for the dean, one way or the other, except as the only link that Europe is known to have between the twentieth century and lives that roamed other ages. As such he was of inestimable value, so that the callousness that was so repulsive to Wrather had no more effect upon me than a distorted bone has on a surgeon; it was just one manifestation of a strange case.

"Are you sure he hasn't elastic-sided boots?" murmured Wrather to me. An absurd question about any member of the Olympus Club. And I treated it with silence accordingly. And out of that silence arose Dean Spanley's voice, with a touch of the monotony that is sometimes heard in the voice of a man who is deep in reminiscences, far away from those he addresses.

"It's a grand life, a dog's life," he said.

"If one thinks one's a dog," muttered Wrather to me, "one should think one is a decent kind of a dog."

Dean Spanley never heard him, and rambled on: "It is undoubtedly the most perfect form of enjoyment that can be known. Where else shall we find those hourly opportunities for sport, romance and adventure combined with a place on the rugs of the wisest and greatest? And then the boundless facilities for an ample social life. One has only to sniff at the wheel of a cart to have news of what is going on, sometimes as much as five miles away. I remember once sniffing at a wheel myself and I found that there was a fellow who had been doing the same at a distance of nearly ten miles. And in the end I got to know him. He came one day with the cart, and I recognized him at once. We had a bit of a fight at first; on my part because I had to show him that the house was properly guarded and that it could not allow strangers, and he in order to show that that wheel was his. We fought on a patch of grass that there was near the back door. There was a grip that I used to be fond of; the ear. The throat-grip is of course final, but as nobody ever lets you in at it, or hardly ever, I used to think that it was waste of time to try for it, and I concentrated upon an ear. The ear was my specialty. Well, I got him by one of the ears and he shouted : I am a poor dog! I am being most dreadfully maltreated! I am far away from home and I am being killed in a cruel country! I am the favorite dog of very great and magnificent people! They would weep to see me killed like this. They brought me up very nicely! I am a poor dog! Oh! Oh! Oh! All is over with me now! It is the end! I was a poor good dog. But now I am quite dead.' I remember his words to this day. And then a lady came out from the kitchen with a bucket; and she had always a very high opinion of me, a very high opinion indeed, and treated me with the utmost consideration; but today she must have had some disappointment, for she acted with the bucket in a way quite unlike herself. Indeed I will not even say what she did with the bucket. It was a hasty act, and quite spoiled the fight. She did it without reflection. The other fellow licked the side of his paw and smoothed down his ear with it. 'Very powerful and angry people you have here,' he said.

" 'Not at all,' I said. 'She's never like that as a rule. She must have had some disappointment.'

" 'Never mind,' he said, 'it was a good fight as far as it went.'

" 'But I can't understand her spoiling it,' I said. 'I don't know what disappointed her.'

" 'Oh, they're the same everywhere,' he said. 'I have seen people act just as hastily with a broom.'

"We sat and talked like that: how clearly it all comes back to me. And from that we came to talking about sport. And I said that our woods held a lot of very big game. And we arranged a little party of him and me, and set out to hunt the woods there and then. And the very first thing we came to was a great big smell of an enormous animal, and a great enemy of man, and much too near the house, a fox. And we sat down and said should we hunt him? He was somewhere quite close, the smell was lying on the ground in great heaps and stretched as high up as you could jump. And we sat and thought for a while as to whether we ought to hunt him. And in the end the other fellow decided. I remember his words to this day. 'Perhaps not,' he said. So we went on then after rabbits. The woods were on a slope, and near the top there were brambles. I put him into the brambles and ran along the outside a little ahead of him at the edge of the trees. There were rabbits in those brambles that didn't properly belong to our wood at all: they came in there from the open land, to keep warm. So when my friend put one out, he ran to the open country that he had come from, over the top of the hill; and I gave a shout or two and we both went after him, and it was just the country for a hunt, no bushes or brambles where the rabbit could play tricks, good short grass very nice for the feet, and fine air for shouting in.

"The rabbit, as you know, has been given a white tail to guide us, so that we did not need to take any trouble to keep him in sight. He went over the top of the hill, smooth grass all the way, with nothing else but a few antheaps, and down the side of a valley: his home was a long way off, and it would have been a lovely hunt had he not resorted to trickery. We came to a thick hedge, full of trees, and he went in and hopped about the thorns and round the trunks of the trees in a silly sort of way, and in and out among brambles; in fact the whole thing got so stupid that after a while we decided to have no more to do with the silly thing. I said, 'Let's hunt something more sensible.'

"And he said, 'Let's.'

"I don't waste my time on folk that fool about among brambles. Well, we got back to the wood, and we went along taking observations in the air. Winds, you know, blew down paths and between trees, and we noted what was at the other end of the wind. And we hadn't gone far when there was a very strange scent indeed, quite close and there was a big hole in the chalk and the scent coming pouring out of it. 'You have big game in your woods,' said my friend.

" 'Very big game indeed,' I said.

"And we went up to the hole. There was a badger at home down there and he seemed to be asleep. So we decided to wake him up. We just put our mouths right into the hole and barked at him. He was a long way down, but he must have heard us. We barked at him for ten minutes. It was the greatest fun. Then we went out on through the wood and presently what should we see but a very showy young rabbit who was out on a long walk, no doubt for social reasons. So we chased the young fellow all through the wood and back to his own house. It was a very populous neighborhood, and we didn't stop and dig: too many passages, you know, running in all directions. So I said: 'Let's come and hunt a large bad animal.'

"It was a pig that I meant, but that's how one puts it. You know the sniff beside the other fellow's face, and the beckoning of the head, that means that?"

I merely nodded: I was not going to interrupt the dean just now with a request for explanations. And I looked at Wrather, in case he was going to do so; but Wrather sat silent and interested.

"He said, 'Let's.' And I said, 'I know where there is one.' And I ran on in front.

"So we came to the pig's house and looked in through his door at him and shouted 'Pig.' He didn't like that. He looked just like a pig; he was a pig; and he knew it. He came towards his door saying silly surly things in a deep voice. You know the kind of talk. And we just shouted, 'Pig. Pig. Pig.' Both of us, for nearly half an hour. It was perfectly splendid and we enjoyed it immensely."

"What did he say?" asked Wrather.

"What could he say?" said the dean. "He knew he was a pig. But he didn't like being told about it. I've seldom enjoyed myself more. It made up for that fool of a rabbit that was so silly in the hedge on the hill.

"Then we went to the back of the stables and rolled in something nice, till our coats were smooth and we both had a beautiful scent. Then we killed a hen for the fun of it. It was a lovely evening.

"It was getting all dark and late now. In fact, if I stayed any longer, there would be terrible beatings. So I said: 'What about your cart?'

"And he said: 'It's a long way to go. I can catch that up when I like. We live three overs away.' "

"Overs?" I said.

"Dips over the hills," said the dean.

And I did not like to question him further for fear that it would bring him back to our day. But what I think he meant was a distance of three horizons.

"I said, 'Very well, old fellow, then we'll have a bit more sport.'

"'What shall it be?' he said.

"And even as he spoke a thing I had been suspecting happened on top of the hill. There'd been a suspicious light there for some time; not the right kind of light; a touch too much of magic in it to my liking; a thing to be watched. And sure enough the moon rose. It was of course my job to guard the house when the moon came large and sudden over that hill, as I have known it to do before, but now that I had my friend with me I said, 'Shall we hunt it?' And he said, 'Oh, let's.' And we went up that hill quicker than we went after the rabbit; and when we got to the top we barked at the moon. And lucky for the moon he didn't stay where he was. And the longer we stayed the stranger the shadows got. Soon it was magic all round us, and more than one dog could bark at. Very magic indeed. When we had hunted the moon enough we came back through the wood; and we both of us growled as we came to the trees so as to warn whatever there was in the darkness, in case it should try to threaten us. There were lots of things in the wood that were hand-in-glove with the moon, queer things that did not bark or move or smell, and one could not see them, but one knew they were there. We came back down the hill with our mouths wide open, so as to breathe in all the pleasantness of that day: we had hunted a badger, two rabbits, a hen, a pig and the moon, and very nearly a fox; and I had a feeling I have not often had, that it was almost enough. And my friend said, 'I must go after my cart now, or the man will be thinking he's lost.' And I said, 'Let me know how you are, next time your cart is coming this way.' And he promised he would. And I promised to let him know how I was, whenever the cart came."

"He thinks he is one, all right," said Wrather to me.

"I beg your pardon?" said the dean.

"Nothing," said Wrather. "Something we were talking about the other day. I've let the Tokay stop in front of me. I *beg* your pardon." And he passed it on to the dean. We watched Dean Spanley, thus encouraged, pour out another glass. He drank a little, and Wrather continued, "But you were telling me about a very interesting evening."

"Yes, it was interesting," said the dean. "I remember coming back to the house and it was late and the door was unfortunately shut. And I knocked, but nobody came to it. And I had to shout, 'I am out in the cold.' 'I am out in the cold,' I shouted, 'and the moon is after me. It is a terrible terrible night and

I shall die in the cold, and my ghost will haunt this house. My ghost will wail in the house when the cold and the moon have killed me. I am a poor dog out in the dark.'

"I went into the kitchen then and said to them there: 'I have had a splendid beating, and I am not at all the dog that I was before, but am utterly purged of sin, and I am wise now and good and never shall sin again, but I am very hungry.' I am telling you the exact words that I used, because they happen to be very clear in my memory. I don't know if my reminiscences interest you."

"Profoundly," said Wrather. "But I hope you aren't expecting me to drink all the Tokay by myself, and then perhaps going to laugh at me afterwards."

"Not at all," said the dean.

And he took a little more, though not much, and went on with his reminiscences, while I applauded Wrather as far as one can by a look. "They gave me a very beautiful dinner. They were good women of great wisdom. And when I had finished what they had given me, and I had cleaned the plate as one should, I was fortunate enough to find a good deal of bacon-rind, which was kept in a treasury that I knew of, and which by a great piece of luck was well mixed with some jam and some pieces of cheese, and a good deal of broom-sweepings with several different flavors, and one sausage, which happened to be old enough to give a distinct taste to the whole dish. It was a lovely dinner; and I knew that the moon would not dare to come back again after all I and the other fellow had said to him, so there was really no more to be done when they took me to bed. And I walked round eight or nine times on the straw, till my bed was just right, and I lay down and the night went away, and all the world was awake again."

9

"When all the world woke up," the dean went rambling on, "there were the voices of a great many things that had come too close, impudent folk like birds, that had to be chased. So I shouted, asking to be let out at once. For a long while no one came, and then I heard a voice saying something about all this noise, which was just what I had been calling his attention to; and he let me out, but I think he had been worried overnight by the moon or one of those prowling things, for he did not look glad. And I ran out and chased everything that needed chasing. And so another day started."

"You must have been the hell of a dog," said Wrather suddenly.

That spoiled everything. To begin with, talk of any sort was rather liable to bring him back to the present day; and, besides that, it was not the way to address a dean. That he had once used similar words himself did not excuse Wrather.

In any case Dean Spanley, so far as I had observed him, never stayed for very long with his mind's eye open upon that strange past and shut to this age of ours. He started slightly now, and I indicated the bottle of Tokay, nearly empty, and then glanced towards Wrather, to account for, if not to excuse, the unfortunate words.

"When I was up at Oxford," said the dean, "I was certainly a young man of some, shall I say, considerable activity. But a dog in any sense of the word, let alone one qualified by the word you used, would be a much exaggerated way of describing me."

"Certainly. Quite so," I said.

And the incident passed off, while we both turned somewhat pitying eyes upon Wrather.

"You know, you're a bit overcome," I said to Wrather.

And Wrather understood me.

"I expect that's it," he said. And he took the line that I indicated.

It is curious that, of all the amazing things said in that room, the words that made far the most stir were the almost innocent remark of Wrather. And I am sure that Dean Spanley believed that this remark was the strangest that had been made there that evening. This was as it should be; but, while it left the way open for another dinner, it certainly made it difficult to get the dean to meet Wrather.

Our little dinner-party soon broke up; the dean was a trifle shocked at Wrather's lapse with the Tokay; Wrather was a bit ashamed of himself for having spoiled the sport, as he put it afterwards; and I had no longer any scientific interest in the dinner, as I realized that the dean would not go back through the years any more that night. I merely remained an ordinary host. I do not think it was any hardship on Wrather to have been suspected of drunkenness, for he had brought it all on himself; incidentally he had had an enormous amount of Tokay, but only incidentally, for it had no real effect on Wrather. We all went downstairs, and I called a taxi, into which I put the dean. Then Wrather came back into the house with me. Going upstairs he apologized for having "undogged the dean," and then we came to a room in which I sit and smoke a good deal, and we sat in front of the fire in armchairs and talked of Dean Spanley. And Wrather, with the air of a man who has been slightly cheated, said: "Have you noticed that he told us nothing of any love-affair?"

"No," I said. "He didn't. I wonder why."

"Too much dean still left in him," said Wrather. "You must get him deeper."

"Deeper?" I said.

"More Tokay," said Wrather.

It was all very well for Wrather to say that, but it couldn't be done. Besides which, I was by no means certain how wide that ridge was from which the dean saw the past: at a certain number of glasses he arrived there; might not two extra glasses topple him down beyond it, and, if so, where? Then Wrather, though he had no idea how much was at stake scientifically, was distinctly helpful. "I think he is there all the time; in his dog-kennel, you know," he said. "Only, in the glare of today, he can't see it. That Tokay of yours is just like pulling down a blind on the glare, and then the old dog can see. Keep him full of it and you should have some sport with him."

The flippancy of these remarks is obvious. But I give them to my reader for the element of truth that I think they contained, for flashes of truth may often appear to an insight even as unscientific as Wrather's. Moreover, Wrather's view bore out the idea that I had long ago formed, that Dean Spanley in broad daylight at his club knew something veiled from the rest of us, though too little to be of any real value, until he was entirely removed from unfavorable conditions. And this removal my Tokay seemed to accomplish.

"It's all very well," I said rather crossly, "for you to say keep him full of Tokay. But he won't drink it for me, not to any extent. He would for you somehow; but you've spoiled it all by calling him a dog, which is a thing no dean would stand."

"I'm sorry," said Wrather. "Let's think what we can do. You know I'm as keen as you are to hear the old dog talk."

That this was not the way to speak of Dean Spanley will be clear to my readers, but I said nothing of that then, and instead of touching on any such delicate matter we hatched a somewhat childish plot between us.

The plot went like this, and it was mainly Wrather's idea: the dean would not want to meet a drunken fellow like Wrather again; no dignitary of the church, no member of an important club, would. But represent Wrather as a man needing guidance, represent him as something much worse than what he had appeared to Dean Spanley, or anything he had ever been, a man about to be wrecked on the rocks of Tokay (if a liquid may be compared to a rock), and Wrather argued and I came to agree, and we hatched the thing out together, the dean would come to save an almost hopeless case; and, if he got a few glasses of the finest Tokay while he was doing it, who would deserve them more?

"Tell him it's no case for the pledge," said Wrather. "Tell him I'm past all that. And there's a certain amount of truth in that too. Say that I didn't drink fair. *He* didn't as a matter of fact: he wouldn't keep up. But say it was me. And say that I must be watched, and taught to drink at the same pace as other men, reasonable men like the dean, I mean; or otherwise the black fellow will get me. And I shouldn't be surprised if he did in any case, but that's neither here nor there. You get him drinking level with me, and we'll soon bring out the dog in him, and we'll have a whale of an evening."

It wasn't quite the way to talk, but I agreed. And I would have agreed to odder arrangements than that in the interests of science.

A few days later I had a talk with the dean in the Club, on the lines that Wrather and I had arranged.

"I am a good deal worried about that man Wrather," I said.

"He is a bit crude, somewhat uncouth, somewhat perhaps. . . ." said Dean Spanley.

And while he pondered some exacter word, I broke in with, "It's worse than that. The man of course will never be a teetotaller, but he does not notice what other men drink, reasonable men, I mean. His only chance would be to learn how much wine can be taken in safety."

"That's not always so easy to teach, in a case like that," said the dean.

"No," I said, "and I have come to you for advice about it, for I shouldn't like to see Wrather, or any man, utterly ruined, as he soon must be if he goes on like that. What I thought was that if he could be guided by some sensible man, he might learn what was good for him and limit himself to that."

"How do you mean?" said the dean.

"Well, drinking glass for glass," I said. "I would see that the wine was passed round continually, and that each man had only his share."

"H'm," said the dean.

"It's a rare wine, you see, and he's unfamiliar with it, and he'd learn, that way, how much he could take in safety. It might save him altogether."

But still the dean seemed suspicious, or at any rate not quite satisfied. "I take it you can do that yourself," he said.

It was then that I played, if I may say so, my master-stroke.

"I'm afraid not," I said.

"Eh?" said the dean.

"I am afraid," I said, "where so much is at stake for Wrather, I could not select myself as the perfect mentor."

"I see," said the dean.

He remembered the occasion when I had given way to Tokay, a surrender by no means enforced on me, but still a surrender.

"Of course if you think he can be checked and brought round in that way," said the dean, "and I dare say it may not be impossible—then of course you should be very careful how it is done."

"That is why I have come to you," I said.

"To me, eh?"

"Yes."

Things hung in the balance then, while the dean pondered.

"I don't see how giving him more wine can teach him to take less," he said, but there was doubt in his voice.

"If one tried to stop a case like that from taking any wine at all, one would lose the last vestige of influence over him, and he would be utterly lost. It's worth trying."

"Oh, I suppose so," said the dean, and without enthusiasm, for Wrather had been distinctly rude to him.

And then I flashed out on him the ace of trumps. "You suppose so! Can you doubt, Mr. Dean, that any soul is worth saving?"

The ace of trumps at his own game, and it had to take the trick.

"I will certainly be glad to try," he said.

So I arranged what at one time I had thought to have been impossible, another dinner at my house, at which Dean Spanley was to meet Wrather.

Then I went off to tell Wrather what I had done, and to book him for the date. And at the same time I tried, as tactfully as I could, to check in advance any levity in remarks he might make to the dean.

"You've got to damned well save my soul," said Wrather. "Never you mind about anything else."

"You'll bring him right back with a jerk," I said, "if you talk like that when he's there. The split infinitive alone would be almost enough to do it."

But all Wrather said was: "We'll have him so far under, that nothing will bring him back."

It is almost inconceivable to me, looking back on it, that such talk should have been the preliminary of a research of the first importance.

10

It was exactly as Wrather had said, when the dinner came off; he did lead the dean to the point which we both of us, for very different reasons, desired: and today with all its trappings—sights, noises and points of view—fell away from him with the sudden completeness of snow on a southern slope, when the spring sun charms it thence and the sleeping grass is laid bare. At a certain stage of our dinner, and evidently just the right one, I had referred to his reminiscences. And at that moment I had addressed him not as Mr. Dean but by his earlier name of Wag. Just plain Wag.

"As soon as they brought me round from my own house," said the dean, "I used to have breakfast. And after that I used to run round to look for some food, in various places I knew of. There was the pigsty for one. A very greedy devil, the pig, and a lot of good stuff was brought to him; and, if one knew just where to look, there was always a lot of it to be found that had slopped over into the mud; and even when one found nothing to get one's teeth into, there was always a very meaty taste in the water of all the puddles around there. And then there was a heap near the stables where a lot of good things were put. Various places, you know. On a lucky day I would sometimes eat till dinner-time, then have dinner, and go out to look for a bit more. That is one way of eating, and a very satisfying way. Another way is to hunt your own game and eat it nice and hot. They say it gives one an appetite, which of course it does; but there is no need for that; one always has an appetite. Still, life would not be complete without hunting. Hunting and dog-fighting should be one's main pursuits, as guarding is a duty, and eating a pastime.

"I shouldn't like you to go away with the idea, by the way, that I would eat anything. That was not so. One has a certain position to keep up, and a certain (shall I say?) dignity to preserve; and to preserve it I made a point of never eating bread. There were those that offered it to me, until they got to know me, but I always had to leave it on the carpet. There is no harm in bread, yet it has not only no flavor, but is one of those things that do not develop a flavor even when buried for a long time, so that it can never become interesting.

"To be a bread-eater is to my mind to be lacking in refinement or self-respect. I do not of course refer to soft toast, on which perhaps a snipe has been lying, all saturated with gravy: such things may be very precious.

"And cake of course is never to be confused with bread; it has a similar taste and the same disabilities, but is a far more important food, so that there can never be any loss of dignity in eating a piece of cake. The wise ones eat cake by itself, but to bread they always add something before eating it, which shows the unimportance of bread. And from this I come to table manners. One should catch one's food as neatly as possible. By fixing one's eyes on the wise ones before they throw it is almost impossible to miss."

Wrather moved slowly nearer to me, sideways.

I knew what he was going to say.

"Do you think," he whispered, "that the old dog would catch anything now?"

I could not explain to Wrather at this time what in any case I had led him to believe was not the case, that this was research work on my part, not mere amusement. So all I said to him was, "Don't whisper," a rudeness that he forgave me at once with a twinkling eye.

"Eh? What?" said the dean. "I was saying that one should fix one's eyes on the wise ones. There are those that do not appreciate intense devotion at meal-times. But it is not for us to withhold our devotion on that account. It is born in all of us, and increased by beatings. A few sharp words should not diminish it. And sometimes it brings us abundant bones."

"I say," said Wrather, "the old dog wants bucking up a bit."

"Don't!" I said in an undertone. "You'll bring him round."

"No, I shan't," said Wrather. And to the dean he said, "Did you never have any more exciting experiences?"

"Exciting?" replied the dean. "Life is full of excitement, except while one is sleeping."

"Anything specially thrilling, I mean," said Wrather.

I couldn't stop him. But Dean Spanley, far from being brought back by him to our own time, leaned forward and looked at Wrather, and said: "I was out once for a walk by myself, and I saw a nursery-maid and two children and a dog coming my way, and a strange new smell ran past me, and I glanced up and saw the look in the eyes of the dog. And I ran. I started just in time and he never came after me. It was rabies. And the nursery-maid and the children came quietly on, walking as they do on a Sunday."

"Rabies!" said Wrather, all hushed. "How did you know?"

"How did I know?" said the dean. "I saw his eyes, and the look was there."

"And you couldn't have been mistaken?" I asked.

"It was glaring," replied the dean.

And that was one thing I learned from him.

Wrather drank off a whole glass of Tokay and said: "Tell us something more cheerful."

I was afraid every moment that Wrather would bring him back.

"Down," I said to Wrather, who understood what I meant, and the sharp command helped, I think, to keep the dean where he was among his old memories. Nevertheless, he answered Wrather, and seemed to do what he asked.

"I remembered the hounds coming once to our house; professional hunters, you know. I should have liked to have asked them whether they had been permitted to come there by the wise master, and whether their intentions were entirely correct, and indeed a great many other things; and, if their answers had been satisfactory, I should have liked to have told them all about our woods and all about who lived in them. I could have helped them in hundreds of ways. But unfortunately I was shut up. I shouted a good deal to them from my house; but I should have liked to have gone with them and showed them the way; I should have liked to have gone round and seen that they were all quite well. And I should have liked to have chased the horses so that they should not think, on account of their size, that they were more important than me. But there it was, I was shut up.

"I had an enormous amount to do when they left. I had to go and find out who they all were, and where they had come from and if they were all quite well. Every tuft of grass had news of them. There were the scents of the hounds themselves, and scents from the roads they had come by, and tracks and scents of the horses: the field in front of our house was nothing less than a history; and it took me a long time to go through it. I was a bit behindhand owing to having been shut up, but scents that had gone from lawns and paths still hung in the taller grasses, and I was able to gather all the information that I required."

"What for?" blurted out Wrather, before I could stop him.

"To guard the house," said the dean. "It was my duty to guard it and I had to know who had come near it, and what their business was. Our house was sacred, and we couldn't have people coming near it unless we knew what they had come for: there might have been an enemy among them. You will not suggest, I trust, that anybody and everybody should be allowed without enquiry, and without the most careful enquiry, near a sacred house."

"Not at all," said Wrather.

And I felt it necessary to add: "Of course not."

"Ours was a particularly sacred house," said the dean, still somewhat nettled. "Even the butcher's cart had to be barked at, though at many houses such a cart as that would be allowed to drive up without question. I certainly could not have all those people coming without enquiring into their motives and, as a matter of general interest, their state of heath. So I naturally had a very busy morning. They went visiting in our wood while I was still shut up, and I heard them leave the wood hunting. They all shouted out that they were after a fox, and quite right too, but I could not allow them merely on that account to come near a house such as ours without proper investigations.

"And there were two or three light carriages that had come to our stables and that were fortunately still there when I was let out. So I sniffed at the wheels to get news of what was going on in the world, and I left a message with all of them to say that I was quite well."

11

One more story we got from the dean that night; he had met his friend again, the one that lived three overs away; he had come to the house we had heard of, running behind his cart. The dean had gone up to him at once, or Wag, I should say, no doubt putting his nose right up to the other dog's, and flicking it away and trotting off, and the other dog had followed.

"I invited him to come hunting," said the dean, "and he said he would like to, and we went off at once."

"What was your friend's name?" put in Wrather.

"Lion-hunter," replied the dean.

"Did he hunt lions?" asked Wrather.

"No," said the dean, "but he was always ready to; he was always expecting a lion in his garden, and he thought of himself as Lion-hunter, therefore it was his name."

"Did you think of yourself as Wag?" asked Wrather, not in any way critically, but only, I think, to get the details right.

"No," said the dean, "I answered to it. I came to them when the great ones called that name. I thought of myself as Moon-chaser. I had often hunted the moon."

"I see," said Wrather.

And he had spoken so suavely that he never brought the dean around, as I feared a jarring note might have done.

"When we came to the wood," continued the dean, "we examined several rabbit-holes; and when we came to a suitable one, a house with only two doors to it, and the rabbit at home, I set Lion-hunter to dig, and stood myself at the back-door. He did all the barking, while I waited for the rabbit to come out. Had the rabbit come out I should have leaped on him and torn him to pieces, and eaten up every bit, not allowing Lion-hunter or anyone in the world to have a taste of it. When my blood is up no one can take anything from me, or even touch it. I should have caught it with one leap, and killed it with one bite, and eaten even the fur. Unfortunately the rabbit lived deeper down than we thought.

"But it was not long before a very strange and beautiful scent blew through the wood, on a wind that happened to come that way from the downs outside. We both lifted our noses, and sure enough it was a hare. We ran out of the wood, and we very soon saw him; he was running over the downs on three legs, in that indolent affected manner that hares have. He stopped and sat up and looked at us, as though he hadn't expected to meet two great hunters. Then he went on again. We raced to a point ahead of him, so as to meet him when he got there, and we soon made him put down that other hind leg. Unfortunately before he got to the point that we aimed at, he turned. This happened to leave us straight behind him. We shouted out that we were hunting him, and that we were great hunters, Lion-hunter and I, and that nothing ever escaped from us, and that nothing ever would. This so alarmed him that he went further. When he came to a ridge of the downs he slanted to his left, and we slanted more, so as to cut him off, but when we got over the ridge he had turned again. We shouted to him to stop, as it was useless to try to escape from us, but the tiresome animal was by now some way ahead. He had of course the white tail that is meant to guide us, the same as the rabbit has; and we kept him in sight for a long while. When he was no longer in sight we followed the scent, which Lion-hunter could do very well, though he was not as fast as I; and it led us to places to which I had never been before, over a great many valleys. We puzzled out the scent and followed on and on, and we did not give up the hunt until all the scent had gone, and nothing remained except the smell of grass, and the air that blew from the sheep. Night came on rather sooner than usual, and we did not know where we were, so we turned for home."

"How did you do that," asked Wrather, "if you did not know where you were?"

"By turning towards it," replied the dean. "I turned first, and then Lion-hunter turned the same way."

"But how did you know which way to turn?" persisted Wrather.

"I turned towards home," said the dean.

There was something here that neither Wrather nor I ever quite understood, though we talked it over afterwards, and I was never able to get it from the dean. My own impression is that there was something concerned which we should not have understood in any case, however it had been explained. My only contribution to any investigation that there may be on these lines is merely that the queer thing is there: what it is I have failed to elucidate.

"We turned towards home," the dean went on, "and that led us past a lot of places I never had seen before. We passed a farm where strange people barked at us, and we met a new animal with a beard and a very fine smell. The question arose as to whether we should hunt him, but he lowered his horns at us, and jumped round so quickly that the horns were always pointing the wrong way. So we decided we would not hunt him, and told him we would come and hunt him some other day, when it was not so late and we had more time; and we went on towards home. Presently we saw a window shining at us, and it did not look right. It was a small house and all shut up, and it looked as though bad people might be hiding in it. I asked Lion-hunter if we should go up to the house and bark at them; but he thought that they might be asleep, and that it was better to let bad people go on sleeping. So we went by the lighted window, but it looked very bad in the night. Then the moon came over a ridge of the downs, but not large enough to be barked at. And then we came to a wood, and it turned out to be our own wood. And we ran down the hill and came to my house and barked under the window. And Lion-hunter said that he thought he would go back to his own house now, in case our door should open and anyone come out of it angry. And I said that might be best. And the door opened, and a great one appeared. And I said that I had been hunting and that I never would hunt again, and that I had stayed out much much too late, an that the shame of my sin was so great that I could not enter the house, and would only just crawl into it. So I crawled in and had a beating, and shook myself, and it was a splendid evening. I lay down in front of the fire and enjoyed the warmth of it, and turned over the memory of our hunt slowly in my mind; and the fire and my memories and the whole of the night seemed brightened by my beating. How beautiful the fire was! Warmer than the sun, warmer than eating can make you, or running or good straw, or even beatings, it is the most mysterious and splendid of all the powers of man. For man makes fire with his own hand. There is no completer life than lying and watching the fire. Other occupations may be as complete, but with none of them do the glow, the warmth and the satisfaction that there are in a fire come to one without any effort of one's own. Before a fire these things come merely by gazing. They are placed in the fire by man, in order to warm dogs, and to replenish his own magical powers. Wherever there is a fire there is man, even out of doors. It is his greatest wonder. On the day that he gives to dogs that secret, as he one day will, dogs and men shall be equal. But that day is not yet. I stray a little, perhaps, from my reminiscences. These things are taught, and are known to be true, but they are not of course any part of my personal observations."

"Who discovered that?" said Wrather before I could stop him.

"We do not know," said the dean.

"Then how do you know it's true?" asked Wrather.

"They shall be equal one day, and on that day," said the dean.

"What day?" asked Wrather.

"Why, the day on which man tells dogs the secret of fire," I said to end the discussion.

"Exactly," said the dean.

I frowned at Wrather, for we were getting near something very strange; and though Wrather's interruption did not bring the dean back, as I feared every moment it might, we heard no more of that strange belief from him. He talked of common things, the ordinary experiences of a dog on a rug at the fireside, things that one might have guessed, nothing that it needed a spiritual traveler to come from a past age to tell us.

12

I pass over many weeks, weeks that brought no success to my investigation. A feeling that I had sometimes come very near to strange discoveries only increased my disappointment. It seemed to me that a dog had some such knowledge of the whereabouts of his home as the mariner has of the North Pole: the mariner knows by his compass: how does the dog know? And then I had gathered from the dean that a dog can detect rabies in another dog, before any signs of it appear to the eyes of men. How was that done? What a valuable discovery that might be, if only I could follow it up. But I had no more than a hint of it. And then the strange faith of which the dean had said only one or two sentences. All the rest that I had got was no more than what an observant man taking notes might have found out or guessed about dogs; but these three things beckoned to me, promising something far more, like three patches of gold on far peaks in some El Dorado of knowledge. The lure of them never left me. I had long talks with Wrather. I let him see that it was more to me than a mere matter of amusement; and he stuck to me and promised to do what he could. He and the dean and I dined together again, and Wrather and I did our utmost; but I began to see that, in spite of those lapses, induced partly by the rarity of the wine and mainly by the perseverance of deliberate efforts to lure him away from sobriety, the dean was an abstemious man. Only at the end of our dinner for three or four minutes he stepped back into that mid-Victorian age that he seemed able to enter in memory when the glare of today was dimmed for him; and the things that he said were trivial, and far from the secrets I sought. Nor were they the sort of things that one much cared to hear; there are many habits and tricks we forgive to dogs on account of their boundless affection, which somehow jar when heard from the lips of a dean.

Once more we dined together, and at that dinner the dean said nothing that would have surprised the timidest of any flock that he had ever tended. And the next day Wrather told me definitely that he could do no more with the dean.

"I won't say he's a teetotaller," said Wrather, "because I wouldn't say that lightly of any man and I know he is not; but he has a damned strong tendency that way. We have got him over it once or twice, but he'll develop it yet. I can do no more with him."

Not the way to talk; but never mind that: so much was at stake.

"What's to be done?" I said desperately.

"I'll help you all I can," said Wrather, "but it's only fair to tell you when I can do no more. He's not the right sort of fellow. He may have taken his whack once or twice like a sportsman, but it wasn't because he wanted to. It was just by accident because he didn't know the strength of the booze. There are not many people that do. You want to be an emperor of Austria to gauge the strength of Tokay to a nicety."

"Then I shall never find out what I'm after," I said in despair.

"I wouldn't say that," said Wrather. "I'm not the only sportsman in the world. You want to find someone who takes a stiffer whack than I do, and takes it in a brighter way. There are men you can't help taking a glass with."

For a moment I feared that such a quest was hopeless, till I suddenly thought of the Maharajah. It was said of him that champagne was to him what Vichy water is to some people; and, if a sportsman were needed, it was said too that even India had scarcely a score who might claim to be greater sportsmen. Moreover, he knows so much of the situation already that nothing would have to be explained to him. He was the very man.

"What about the Maharajah of Haikwar?" I said.

"He's a good sportsman," said Wrather.

"You know him?" I asked.

"No," said Wrather, "but of course I've heard of him. And he might do."

"I don't want stuff about lying in front of the fire," I said. "I want to find out how dogs can find their way home, by a new route and from a strange country. And I want to know how they can detect rabies long before we can; and one or two other things."

"You'll have to get him deeper, for all that," said Wrather, "deeper than I've been able to get him. It's all very well for a dull old dog like the dean to lay down the exact number of glasses at which one ought to stop; and he's been doing a good deal of stopping just lately; but the fact remains that when you have a real bright sportsman like the Maharajah of Haikwar taking a glass or two of wine with a man, he does follow along a bit. He'll get him further than I ever got him."

"Do you think so?" I said.

"I'm sure of it," said Wrather. "It's like horses out hunting. There's no horse living that would stand perfectly still and watch the field galloping away from him, however dull and slow he was.

"You'll see when the Maharajah comes. Ask me too and I'll do my bit, and we'll drag the dean along yet."

"Further than he's been hitherto?" I asked.

"The man's human, after all," said Wrather.

And somehow, from the way he spoke, I hoped again.

The next thing was to get the Maharajah. I called on his secretary, Captain Haram Bhaj, to ask if he and the Maharajah would come and dine with me. "The fact is," I said, "that the proof of one of the principal tenets of his religion, and yours, is at stake. A friend of mine has a memory of a former incarnation. I will get him to come to the dinner. And if we can get him to speak, we may have inestimable revelations that may be of the utmost value to all of your faith."

"Of course what His Highness is really interested in," said Captain Haram Bhaj, "is his handicap."

"His handicap," I lamely repeated.

"At polo," said Haram Bhaj.

"But surely," I said, "his religion must mean something to him."

"Oh yes," said Haram Bhaj. "Only, polo is His Highness's first interest."

And then I thought of Wrather.

"I have a friend," I said, "who used to play a good deal of polo once. It would be a great pleasure to him to meet the Maharajah sahib, if His Highness will come and dine with me."

Wrather had not actually spoken to me of polo, but I had a kind of feeling about him, which turned out to be right, that he had been a polo-player. When Captain Haram Bhaj saw that polo was likely to be the topic at dinner he said that he thought the Maharajah would come. And as it turned out, he did. I warned Wrather about the polo, and a few nights later we were all gathered at my table, the Maharajah of Haikwar, Captain Haram Bhaj, Wrather and I and the dean; the first four of these resolved to rob the fifth of a secret that might justify the hope of the East and astound Europe.

13

Dean Spanley was asking the Maharajah of Haikwar about ancient customs in India, about Indian music, Indian dress and the tribes that live in the jungle. Wrather was talking to the Maharajah upon his other side, whenever he got an opportunity, about polo. And Haram Bhaj was watching.

Wrather had contributed to our efforts with one splendid remark that he had made to the dean before the Indians arrived. "In the East they think it is a discourtesy if all the guests at a party do not drink glass for glass."

The remark created the perfect atmosphere in which the Maharajah's efforts and mine would have the best chance of thriving. The dean had drawn me aside and said: "Is this good for Mr. Wrather?" And I had said: "Yes, it is ideal for him. The Maharajah never goes one drop beyond what a man should."

So now the plot was in progress with every chance of success. A base plot, some may say. Perhaps all plots are base. But look what there was at stake: a secret to which champagne and Tokay were the only keys. And what a secret! I felt that the world was waiting expectant outside the door.

We were all drinking champagne. Tokay was to come at the end as a coup de grâce. I flatter myself that the champagne was a good vintage, and the evening progressed to a point at which the Maharajah laid bare his heart and told Wrather the ambition of his life. I do not think that with an Oriental you always get a clear sight of his innermost feelings, but I think that it was so with the Maharajah of Haikwar. His ambition was to have a handicap of eight at polo. At present he was only seven. And as yet the dean had not spoken at all of anything nearer himself than the customs of Indian villages.

There was no servant in the room; my butler had gone to bed; and we passed round the champagne among ourselves. Haram Bhaj was particularly helpful. And the dean was holding back all the time. Yet that force was present that is sometimes found at the pastime of table turning, when everybody combines to pull the same way; and though Dean Spanley set himself against this force, he gradually went with it. More and more I felt that the world was hushed and waiting. And then with the first glass of the Tokay he spoke, spoke from that other century and sojourn. The Maharajah looked interested. But as yet nothing came that was stranger than what we had already heard, nothing that is not known or could not be guessed among those that have carefully studied the ways of dogs. I passed round more Tokay, and the Maharajah and Haram Bhaj and Wrather helped me. The dean was telling a story about a dog-fight, not greatly different from the one that I have already given my reader. As in the former one he went for the ear, and succeeded in getting the grip, and brought that tale to a close with a good deal of boasting. It was without doubt a dog that was speaking to us, but a dog with nothing to tell us we did not know. I tried yet more Tokay, and everyone helped me. We got a little idyll then of a spring morning some decades back into the century that is gone, not very interesting except for the shining eyes of the dean as he told it, and not very seemly. The stock of Tokay was running low but was equal to one grand effort: we were all drinking it now in claret glasses. And suddenly I felt that the moment was hovering when what I waited for would be revealed, something that Man could not know unless told like this; and I knew that Dean Spanley's secrets were about to be laid bare.

I knew that the Maharajah cared more for his handicap than for those religious tenets that he mainly left to the Brahmins, and that the interest he had shown already was little more than the interest that he took as a sportsman in dogfights, but now that the moment was coming for which I had waited so long I held up my hand to hush them, and as a sign that the mystery of which I had spoken was going to be shown to us now. And so it was. And so it was.

Everything I had sought was laid bare with open hands. I learned the faith of the dog; I knew how they see rabies in the eyes of another long before men guess it; I knew how dogs go home. I knew more about scent than all the Masters of Hounds in England have ever guessed with all their speculations added together. I knew the wonderful secrets of transmigration. For half an hour that evening I might have spoken with Brahmins, and they would at least have listened to what I had to say without that quiet scorn lying under a faint smile, with which they listen to all else that we may say. For half an hour I knew things that they know. Of this I am sure. And now my readers will wish to hear them too. Be not too hard on me, reader. It is no easy thing to make a dean drunk. For a cause less stupendous I should not have attempted it. I attempted it for a secret unknown to Europe; and with the help of the Maharajah and the two others, drinking glass for glass, I accomplished it. All that I remember. What Dean Spanley said after his tale of the dog-fight and his little love-affair, I do not remember. I know that he held the key to some strange mysteries, and that he told us all. I remember the warm room and the lighted candles, and light shining in the champagne and in the Tokay, and people talk-ing, and the words "Never trust a teetotaller or a man who wears elastic-sided boots." Then I noticed that a window was open, and some of the candles were out and all the rest were low, and everybody seemed to have gone. I went to the window then and leaned out to refresh myself, and when I came back to my chair, I kicked against a body on the floor and found that Wrather was still there, partly under the table; the Maharajah and Haram Bhaj and the dean were gone.

And I propped up Wrather against the legs of a chair, and after a while he spoke. And he said: "For God's sake give me a whiskey and soda. No more Tokay. For God's sake a whiskey and soda."

And I gave him a whiskey and soda, and that brought him round, and I took a little myself. And his first words after that were: "Well, we got the old dog to talk."

"Yes," I said. "What did he say?"

"That's what I can't remember," he said.

And that was my trouble too.

I gave Wrather a bed, and I went to bed myself, and in the morning our memories were no clearer.

Knowing the enormous importance of what was said I went round after a light breakfast to see Haram Bhaj.

He had been to Vine Street and stayed the night there, and they had let him go in the morning; and the only clue he had to what he had heard overnight was that he had told the inspector at Vine Street that he, Haram Bhaj, was a black and gray spaniel and could get home by himself.

"Now why did I say that?" he said.

But there was not enough in that to be of any use whatever; and later in the day I called on the Maharajah.

"It was a very jolly evening," he said; and he was evidently grateful to me. But after a while I saw that I should lose his attention unless I talked of polo. Either he remembered nothing, or the secrets of transmigration, if they were secrets from him, scarcely attracted his interest and he left all such things to the Brahmins.

It only remained to try Dean Spanley again, and this I shall never do now. For very soon after that dinner the dean was promoted to bishop. He still knows me, still greets me, whenever we meet at the Club. But I shall never get his secret. One of the shrewdest observers of the last century, the lady after whom the greater part of that hundred years was named, stated in one of her letters that she had never known a man who became a bishop to be quite the same as he was before. It was so with Dean Spanley. I can remember no act or word of his that ever showed it, and yet I have sufficiently felt the change never to trouble him with invitations to dine with me any more.

Wrather and I often dined together and, I trust, will often again. We feel like travelers who once, for a short while, have seen something very strange; and neither of us can remember what it was.